Granny.

With best wishes and much
love for Christmas, 1968.

Mark and Edward

*Louise Mountbatten, Queen of Sweden*

*Portrait of Princess Louise by Philip Laszlo de Lombos painted in Darmstadt, 1907*

# LOUISE MOUNTBATTEN
# QUEEN OF SWEDEN

MARGIT FJELLMAN

LONDON
GEORGE ALLEN AND UNWIN LTD

*English edition, specially enlarged and adapted*
© *George Allen and Unwin Ltd,* 1968

SBN 04 923 044 1

*Swedish edition: Drottning Louise*
*published by Albert Bonniers Forlag, Stockholm* 1965
© *Margit Fjellman* 1965

PRINTED IN GREAT BRITAIN
*in* 12 *on* 13 *pt Fournier type*
BY UNWIN BROTHERS LTD
WOKING AND LONDON

## Publisher's Note

The material for this book was collected by the author immediately after the death of Queen Louise of Sweden in 1965. As the reader will discover, Queen Louise was an extremely colourful and sympathetic person and the seventy-six years of her life spanned a period in which the royal families of Europe experienced perhaps the greatest changes they have ever known. Many of their members were, of course, exiled or assassinated, but even those who retained their thrones had to accept a new way of life, and adapt their position to the twentieth century.

The story of Queen Louise's family will undoubtedly be of great interest to many people throughout Europe and the English-speaking world. Her parents were Prince and Princess Louis of Battenberg (later the Marquess and Marchioness of Milford Haven). Of their four children, Alice the elder daughter married Prince Andrew of Greece in 1903 and came home only on occasional visits. George, the elder brother, who died in 1938, married Countess Nada de Torby, the daughter of Grand Duke Michael of Russia, in 1916. Louise, of course, married Crown Prince Gustaf Adolf of Sweden in 1923, while Louis married Edwina Ashley, the daughter of Lord Mount Temple in 1922. The younger son and daughter were therefore exceptionally close to one another and they always visited each other or wrote each other long and intimate letters at every opportunity. For this reason, the Queen's family and her younger brother in particular inevitably figure prominently in this biography.

Although this book is published with the permission of the King of Sweden and with the concurrence of Earl Mountbatten of Burma, it was written quite independently and entirely on the initiative of the author.

Much of the book was made possible by interviews with, or information supplied by, Lord Mountbatten and his two daughters, Lady Brabourne and Lady Pamela Hicks, the Margravine Theodora of Baden, Prince Bertil of Sweden, Countess

Estelle Bernadotte, Astrid Rudebeck (the Mistress of the Robes at the Swedish Court), Admiral Stig H:son Ericson (the Grand Marshal of the Swedish Court), Kerstin Laurin (the widow of the late publisher and art collector Thorsten Laurin), Lady Zia Wernher (the sister of Nada, Marchioness of Milford Haven), Dame Beryl Oliver, the Hon. Mrs Clive Pearson, Mrs John Preston (the daughter of the Queen's close friend, the late Mrs Margaret Heywood), Count Gösta Lewenhaupt (Lord-in-Waiting at the Swedish Court and President of I.B.M. in Sweden), Stina Reuterswärd and Brita Steuch (who were Ladies-in-Waiting to Queen Louise), and Baron Carl-Fredrik Palmstierna (the Private Secretary to the King). The author would like to thank them all for their kindness and assistance.

The author would also like to thank Sigyn Reimers, the Swedish authority on international royal genealogy, and Mr Cyril Hankinson for his great care in checking dates, titles and facts for the English edition, which has been greatly enlarged and modified so as to be of special interest to English readers. Above all, she would like to thank Joan Tate, upon whose translation from the Swedish this edition is based.

Finally, the greatest debt of thanks of all is due to King Gustaf Adolf, who has authorized the publication of the letters in chapter eleven as a matter of historical interest. In the case of Lord Mountbatten's letters to Queen Louise in chapters six and eight, His Majesty obtained Lord Mountbatten's concurrence to their publication.

## Editorial Note

Although after her marriage Princess Victoria of Great Britain and Ireland should properly be referred to as Princess Louis of Battenberg (or Princess Louis for short) until she became Marchioness of Milford Haven, nevertheless for the sake of greater clarity and easier reading she is here always referred to as Princess Victoria except where her full title is given.

# QUEEN LOUISE'S DESCENT FROM QUEEN VICTORIA
(Showing Brothers' Children)

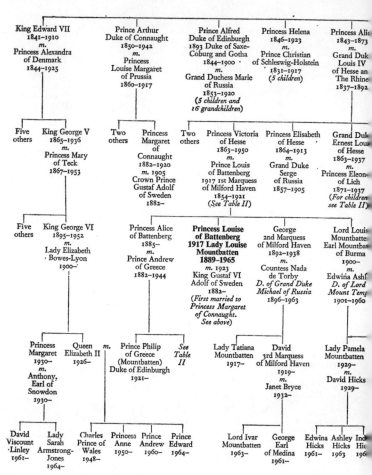

Queen Victoria
Empress of India
1819–1901

King Edward VII
1841–1910
m.
Princess Alexandra
of Denmark
1844–1925

Prince Arthur
Duke of Connaught
1850–1942
m.
Princess
Louise Margaret
of Prussia
1860–1917

Prince Alfred
Duke of Edinburgh
1893 Duke of Saxe-
Coburg and Gotha
1844–1900 ·
m.
Grand Duchess Marie
of Russia
1853–1920
(5 children and
16 grandchildren)

Princess Helena
1846–1923
m.
Prince Christian
of Schleswig-Holstein
1831–1917
(5 children)

Princess Alic
1843–1873
m.
Grand Duk
Louis IV
of Hesse an
The Rhine
1837–1892

Five
others

King George V
1865–1936
m.
Princess Mary
of Teck
1867–1953

Two
others

Princess
Margaret
of
Connaught
1882–1920
m. 1905
Crown Prince
Gustaf Adolf
of Sweden
1882–

Two
others

Princess Victoria
of Hesse
1863–1950
m.
Prince Louis
of Battenberg
1917 1st Marquess
of Milford Haven
1854–1921
(See Table II)

Princess Elisabeth
of Hesse
1864–1913
m.
Grand Duke
Serge
of Russia
1857–1905

Grand Duk
Ernest Lou
of Hesse
1863–1937
m.
Princess Eleon
of Lich
1871–1937
(For children
see Table II)

Five
others

King George VI
1895–1952
m.
Lady Elizabeth
· Bowes-Lyon
1900–

Princess Alice
of Battenberg
1885–
m.
Prince Andrew
of Greece
1882–1944

**Princess Louise
of Battenberg
1917 Lady Louise
Mountbatten
1889–1965**
m. 1923
King Gustaf VI
Adolf of Sweden
1882–
(First married to
Princess Margaret
of Connaught.
See above)

George
2nd Marquess
of Milford Haven
1892–1938
m.
Countess Nada
de Torby
D. of Grand Duke
Michael of Russia
1896–1963

Lord Loui
Mountbatte
Earl Mountba
of Burma
1900–
m.
Edwina Ashf
D. of Lord
Mount Temp
1901–1960

Princess
Margaret
1930–
m.
Anthony,
Earl of
Snowdon
1930–

Queen
Elizabeth II
1926–

m.

Prince Philip
of Greece
(Mountbatten)
Duke of Edinburgh
1921–

See
Table
II

Lady Tatiana
Mountbatten
1917–

David
3rd Marquess
of Milford Haven
1919–
m.
Janet Bryce
1932–

Lady Pamela
Mountbatten
1929–
m.
David Hicks
1929–

David
Viscount
·Linley
1961–

Lady
Sarah
Armstrong-
Jones
1964–

Charles
Prince of
Wales
1948–

Princess
Anne
1950–

Prince
Andrew
1960–

Prince
Edward
1964–

Lord Ivar
Mountbatten
1963–

George
Earl
of Medina
1961–

Edwina
Hicks
1961–

Ashley
Hicks
1963

Ind
Hic
196

Note: Children not shown in order of ages, but see dates of birth.

# TABLE I

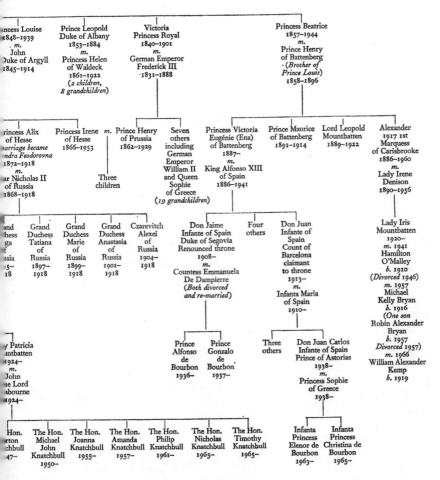

e Albert
.e-Coburg
·otha
1861

ncess Louise
1848–1939
. m.
John
Duke of Argyll
1845–1914

Prince Leopold
Duke of Albany
1853–1884
m.
Princess Helen
of Waldeck
1861–1922
(2 children,
8 grandchildren)

Victoria
Princess Royal
1840–1901
m.
German Emperor
Frederick III
·1831–1888

Princess Beatrice
1857–1944
m.
Prince Henry
of Battenberg
·(Brother of
Prince Louis)
1858–1896

rincess Alix
of Hesse
narriage became
ndra Feodorovna
1872–1918
m.
ar Nicholas II
of Russia
1868–1918

Princess Irene
of Hesse
1866–1953

m. Prince Henry
of Prussia
1862–1929

Three
children

Seven
others
including
German
Emperor
William II
and Queen
Sophie
of Greece
(19 grandchildren)

Princess Victoria
Eugénie (Ena)
of Battenberg
1887–
m.
King Alfonso XIII
of Spain
1886–1941

Prince Maurice
of Battenberg
1891–1914

Lord Leopold
Mountbatten
1889–1922

Alexander
1917 1st
Marquess
of Carisbrooke
1886–1960
m.
Lady Irene
Denison
1890–1956

and
hess
ga
%–
18

Grand
Duchess
Tatiana
of
Russia
1897–
1918

Grand
Duchess
Marie
of
Russia
1899–
1918

Grand
Duchess
Anastasia
of
Russia
1901–
1918

Czarevitch
Alexei
of
Russia
1904–
1918

Don Jaime
Infante of Spain
Duke of Segovia
Renounced throne
1908–
m.
Countess Emmanuela
De Dampierre
(Both divorced
and re-married)

Four
others

Don Juan
Infante of
Spain
Count of
Barcelona
claimant
to throne
1913–
m.
Infanta Maria
of Spain
1910–

Lady Iris
Mountbatten
1920–
m. 1941
Hamilton
O'Malley
(Divorced 1946)
m. 1957
Michael
Kelly Bryan
b. 1916
(One son
Robin Alexander
Bryan
b. 1957
Divorced 1957)
m. 1966
William Alexander
Kemp
b. 1919

y Patricia
untbatten
1924–
m.
John
e Lord
abourne
1924–

Prince
Alfonso
de
Bourbon
1936–

Prince
Gonzalo
de
Bourbon
1937–

Three
others

Don Juan Carlos
Infante of Spain
Prince of Astorias
1938–
m.
Princess Sophie
of Greece
1938–

Hon.
rton
chbull
47–

The Hon.
Michael
John
Knatchbull
1950–

The Hon.
Joanna
Knatchbull
1955–

The Hon.
Amanda
Knatchbull
1957–

The Hon.
Philip
Knatchbull
1961–

The Hon.
Nicholas
Knatchbull
1965–

The Hon.
Timothy
Knatchbull
1965–

Infanta
Princess
Elenor de
Bourbon
1963–

Infanta
Princess
Christina de
Bourbon
1965–

# QUEEN LOUISE'S DESCENT FROM LOUIS II OF HESSE (Showing Sister's Children)

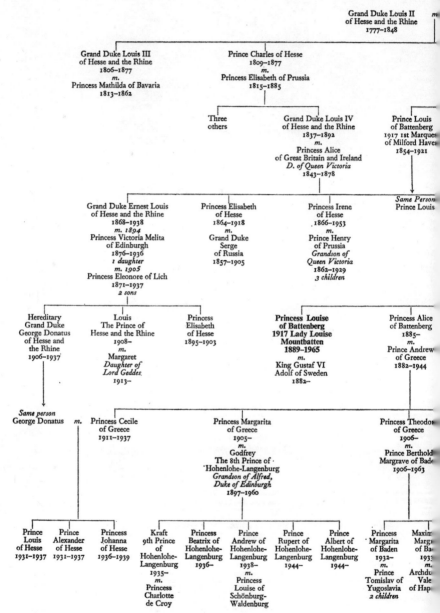

**Grand Duke Louis II**
of Hesse and the Rhine
1777–1848

**Grand Duke Louis III**
of Hesse and the Rhine
1806–1877
*m.*
Princess Mathilda of Bavaria
1813–1862

**Prince Charles of Hesse**
1809–1877
*m.*
Princess Elisabeth of Prussia
1815–1885

Three
others

**Grand Duke Louis IV**
of Hesse and the Rhine
1837–1892
*m.*
Princess Alice
of Great Britain and Ireland
*D. of Queen Victoria*
1843–1878

**Prince Louis**
of Battenberg
1917 1st Marques
of Milford Haver
1854–1921

*Same Person*
Prince Louis

**Grand Duke Ernest Louis**
of Hesse and the Rhine
1868–1938
*m. 1894*
Princess Victoria Melita
of Edinburgh
1876–1936
*1 daughter*
*m. 1905*
Princess Eleonore of Lich
1871–1937
*2 sons*

**Princess Elisabeth**
of Hesse
1864–1918
*m.*
Grand Duke
Serge
of Russia
1857–1905

**Princess Irene**
of Hesse
1866–1953
*m.*
Prince Henry
of Prussia
*Grandson of*
*Queen Victoria*
1862–1929
*3 children*

**Hereditary**
**Grand Duke**
**George Donatus**
of Hesse and
the Rhine
1906–1937

**Louis**
The Prince of
Hesse and the Rhine
1908–
*m.*
Margaret
*Daughter of*
*Lord Geddes.*
1913–

**Princess**
**Elisabeth**
of Hesse
1895–1903

**Princess Louise**
**of Battenberg**
**1917 Lady Louise**
**Mountbatten**
**1889–1965**
*m.*
King Gustaf VI
Adolf of Sweden
1882–

**Princess Alice**
of Battenberg
1885–
*m.*
Prince Andrew
of Greece
1882–1944

*Same person*
George Donatus *m.*

**Princess Cecile**
of Greece
1911–1937

**Princess Margarita**
of Greece
1905–
*m.*
Godfrey
The 8th Prince of ·
Hohenlohe-Langenburg
*Grandson of Alfred,*
*Duke of Edinburgh*
1897–1960

**Princess Theodor**
of Greece
1906–
*m.*
Prince Berthold
Margrave of Bade
1906–1963

**Prince**
**Louis**
**of Hesse**
1931–1937

**Prince**
**Alexander**
**of Hesse**
1931–1937

**Princess**
**Johanna**
**of Hesse**
1936–1939

**Kraft**
**9th Prince**
**of**
**Hohenlohe-**
**Langenburg**
1935–
*m.*
Princess
Charlotte
de Croy

**Princess**
**Beatrix of**
**Hohenlohe-**
**Langenburg**
1936–

**Prince**
**Andrew of**
**Hohenlohe-**
**Langenburg**
1938–
*m.*
Princess
Louise of
Schönburg-
Waldenburg

**Prince**
**Rupert of**
**Hohenlohe-**
**Langenburg**
1944–

**Prince**
**Albert of**
**Hohenlohe-**
**Langenburg**
1944–

**Princess**
**Margarita**
**of Baden**
1932–
*m.*
Prince
Tomislav of
Yugoslavia
*2 children*

**Maxim**
**of Ba**
193
*m.*
Archdu
Vale
of Hap

Note: Children not shown in order of ages, but see dates of birth.

# TABLE II

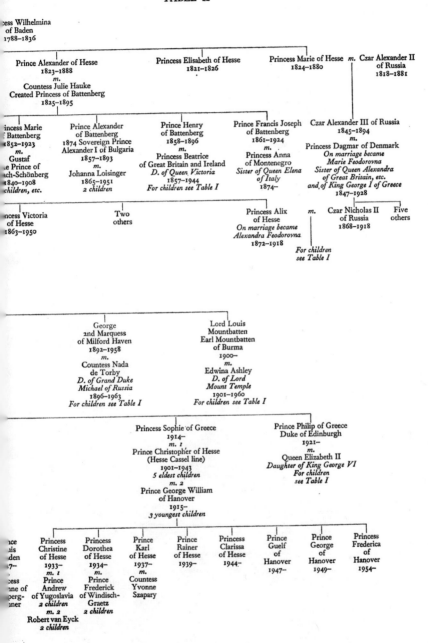

Princess Wilhelmina of Baden
1788–1836

Prince Alexander of Hesse
1823–1888
m.
Countess Julie Hauke
Created Princess of Battenberg
1825–1895

Princess Elisabeth of Hesse
1821–1826

Princess Marie of Hesse  m.  Czar Alexander II
1824–1880                     of Russia
                              1818–1881

Princess Marie of Battenberg
1852–1923
m.
Gustaf
Prince of
Erbach-Schönberg
1840–1908
children, etc.

Prince Alexander
of Battenberg
1874 Sovereign Prince
Alexander I of Bulgaria
1857–1893
m.
Johanna Loisinger
1865–1951
2 children

Prince Henry
of Battenberg
1858–1896
m.
Princess Beatrice
of Great Britain and Ireland
D. of Queen Victoria
1857–1944
For children see Table I

Prince Francis Joseph
of Battenberg
1861–1924
m.
Princess Anna
of Montenegro
Sister of Queen Elena
of Italy
1874–

Czar Alexander III of Russia
1845–1894
m.
Princess Dagmar of Denmark
On marriage became
Marie Feodorovna
Sister of Queen Alexandra
of Great Britain, etc.
and of King George I of Greece
1847–1928

Princess Victoria
of Hesse
1863–1950

Two
others

Princess Alix
of Hesse
On marriage became
Alexandra Feodorovna
1872–1918

m.  Czar Nicholas II
    of Russia
    1868–1918
    For children
    see Table I

Five
others

George
2nd Marquess
of Milford Haven
1892–1958
m.
Countess Nada
de Torby
D. of Grand Duke
Michael of Russia
1896–1963
For children see Table I

Lord Louis
Mountbatten
Earl Mountbatten
of Burma
1900–
m.
Edwina Ashley
D. of Lord
Mount Temple
1901–1960
For children see Table I

Princess Sophie of Greece
1914–
m. 1
Prince Christopher of Hesse
(Hesse Cassel line)
1901–1943
5 eldest children
m. 2
Prince George William
of Hanover
1915–
3 youngest children

Prince Philip of Greece
Duke of Edinburgh
1921–
m.
Queen Elizabeth II
Daughter of King George VI
For children
see Table I

Prince
Louis
Baden
7–

cess
ane of
perg-
ner

Princess
Christine
of Hesse
1933–
m. 1
Prince
Andrew
of Yugoslavia
2 children
m. 2
Robert van Eyck
2 children

Princess
Dorothea
of Hesse
1934–
m.
Prince
Frederick
of Windisch-
Graetz
2 children

Prince
Karl
of Hesse
1937–
m.
Countess
Yvonne
Szapary

Prince
Rainer
of Hesse
1939–

Princess
Clarissa
of Hesse
1944–

Prince
Guelf
of
Hanover
1947–

Prince
George
of
Hanover
1949–

Princess
Frederica
of
Hanover
1954–

# THE SWEDISH ROYAL FAMILY

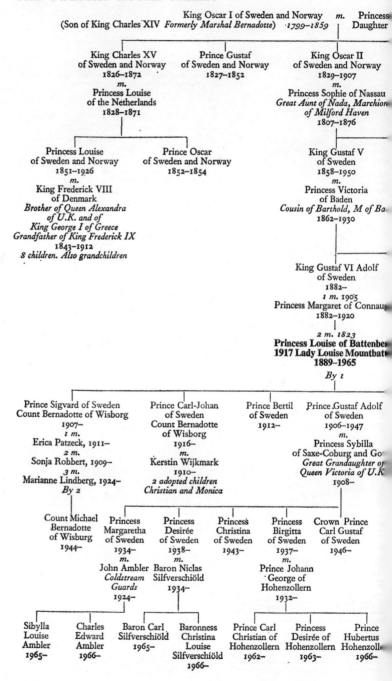

King Oscar I of Sweden and Norway  *m.*  Princess
(Son of King Charles XIV *Formerly Marshal Bernadotte*) ·1799–1859  Daughter

King Charles XV
of Sweden and Norway
1826–1872
*m.*
Princess Louise
of the Netherlands
1828–1871

Prince Gustaf
of Sweden and Norway
1827–1852

King Oscar II
of Sweden and Norway
1829–1907
*m.*
Princess Sophie of Nassau
*Great Aunt of Nada, Marchion*
*of Milford Haven*
1807–1876

Princess Louise
of Sweden and Norway
1851–1926
*m.*
King Frederick VIII
of Denmark
*Brother of Queen Alexandra*
*of U.K. and of*
*King George I of Greece*
*Grandfather of King Frederick IX*
1843–1912
*8 children. Also grandchildren*

Prince Oscar
of Sweden and Norway
1852–1854

King Gustaf V
of Sweden
1858–1950
*m.*
Princess Victoria
of Baden
*Cousin of Barthold, M of Ba*
1862–1930

King Gustaf VI Adolf
of Sweden
1882–
*1 m.* 1905
Princess Margaret of Connau
1882–1920

*2 m. 1823*
**Princess Louise of Battenbe**
**1917 Lady Louise Mountbat**
**1889–1965**

*By 1*

Prince Sigvard of Sweden
Count Bernadotte of Wisborg
1907–
*1 m.*
Erica Patzeck, 1911–
*2 m.*
Sonja Robbert, 1909–
*3 m.*
Marianne Lindberg, 1924–
*By 2*

Prince Carl-Johan
of Sweden
Count Bernadotte
of Wisborg
1916–
*m.*
Kerstin Wijkmark
1910–
*2 adopted children*
*Christian and Monica*

Prince Bertil
of Sweden
1912–

Prince Gustaf Adolf
of Sweden
1906–1947
*m.*
Princess Sybilla
of Saxe-Coburg and Go
*Great Grandaughter of*
*Queen Victoria of U.K.*
1908–

Count Michael
Bernadotte
of Wisburg
1944–

Princess
Margaretha
of Sweden
1934–
*m.*
John Ambler
*Coldstream*
*Guards*
1924–

Princess
Desirée
of Sweden
1938–
*m.*
Baron Niclas
Silfverschiöld
1934–

Princess
Christina
of Sweden
1943–

Princess
Birgitta
of Sweden
1937–
*m.*
Prince Johann
George of
Hohenzollern
1932–

Crown Prince
Carl Gustaf
of Sweden
1946–

Sibylla
Louise
Ambler
1965–

Charles
Edward
Ambler
1966–

Baron Carl
Silfverschiöld
1965–

Baronness
Christina
Louise
Silfverschiöld
1966–

Prince Carl
Christian of
Hohenzollern
1962–

Princess
Desirée of
Hohenzollern
1963–

Prince
Hubertus
Hohenzoll
1966–

# TABLE III

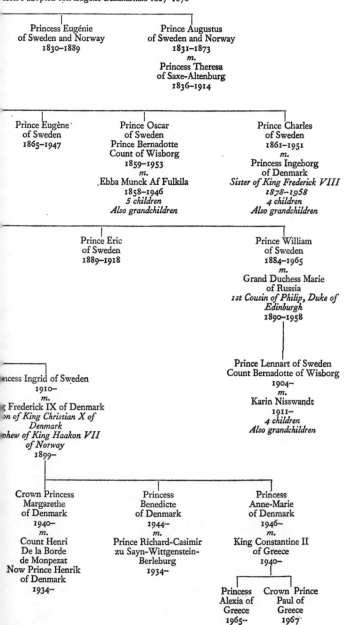

...hine of Bologna
...leon's adopted son Eugène Beauharnais 1807–1876

Princess Eugénie
of Sweden and Norway
1830–1889

Prince Augustus
of Sweden and Norway
1831–1873
*m.*
Princess Theresa
of Saxe-Altenburg
1836–1914

Prince Eugène
of Sweden
1865–1947

Prince Oscar
of Sweden
Prince Bernadotte
Count of Wisborg
1859–1953
*m.*
Ebba Munck Af Fulkila
1858–1946
*5 children*
*Also grandchildren*

Prince Charles
of Sweden
1861–1951
*m.*
Princess Ingeborg
of Denmark
*Sister of King Frederick VIII*
*1878–1958*
*4 children*
*Also grandchildren*

Prince Eric
of Sweden
1889–1918

Prince William
of Sweden
1884–1965
*m.*
Grand Duchess Marie
of Russia
*1st Cousin of Philip, Duke of*
*Edinburgh*
*1890–1958*

Prince Lennart of Sweden
Count Bernadotte of Wisborg
1904–
*m.*
Karin Nisswandt
1911–
*4 children*
*Also grandchildren*

...ncess Ingrid of Sweden
1910–
*m.*
...g Frederick IX of Denmark
...on of King Christian X of
Denmark
...phew of King Haakon VII
of Norway
1899–

Crown Princess
Margarethe
of Denmark
1940–
*m.*
Count Henri
De la Borde
de Monpezat
Now Prince Henrik
of Denmark
1934–

Princess
Benedicte
of Denmark
1944–
*m.*
Prince Richard-Casimir
zu Sayn-Wittgenstein-
Berleburg
1934–

Princess
Anne-Marie
of Denmark
1946–
*m.*
King Constantine II
of Greece
1940–

Princess
Alexia of
Greece
1965–

Crown Prince
Paul of
Greece
1967

# Contents

B

# Illustrations

Portrait of Princess Louise by Philip Lazlo
de Lombos                                       *frontispiece*

# Introduction

## The Mountbattens: Family Background

A MONG the noble families of Europe, one of the most intriguing are the Mountbattens. For among their ancestors they can claim Charlemagne and the great medieval kings of the Franks, among their relatives can be numbered almost every royal family in Europe, and among their descendants will be the future heirs to the throne of England. Although their ancestors came from Hesse, the Grand Duchy beside the river Rhine, to describe their ancestry would be to trace nearly the whole of European history and so in this Introduction the reader will simply find the remarkable story of the grandparents of Princess Louise of Battenberg, or Lady Louise Mountbatten, as she was later to be known, and the details of her immediate family. But, as Princess Louise used to say half seriously, half joking: 'Hesse is the centre of the world.' And so it will appear that the story of the Mountbattens is something much more than family history.

Princess Louise's grandfather was Prince Alexander, the fourth son of the reigning Grand Duke Louis II of Hesse and the Rhine. He was born on July 15, 1823, at Darmstadt and on September 10, 1833—at the age of ten—he was appointed Second Lieutenant in the Life Company of the First Hessian Infantry. This was rather older than was usual among his family for a first military appointment in Hesse, but he had already made up for it by being appointed a Lieutenant in the Imperial *Russian* Army on the day of his christening, thanks to his godfather, Emperor Alexander I of All the Russias, who was married to his aunt, Elizabeth-Louise of Baden. Naturally, there was a close bond between the Imperial Russian Family and their relatives in Hesse;

and as a result of it Princess Marie of Hesse (Prince Alexander's younger sister) became engaged to the Tsarevitch in May 1840 and the Emperor[1] invited Alexander to come with Marie to the Royal Court of St Petersburg, so that she might have company. So in the spring of 1841, when Alexander was only seventeen and Marie still sixteen, they set out for Russia together. At St Petersburg, the speed of Alexander's military progress was quite miraculous. Soon after their arrival, he was promoted to First Lieutenant in the Household Cavalry, then two months later to Colonel in the Chevalier Guards, in October 1843 to Major General, and two months later to Colonel-in-Chief of the 17th Borissoglebosky Lancers, which were renamed 'Prince Alexander of Hesse's Lancers' in his honour.

On April 28, 1841 Marie was married in great splendour in St Petersburg. In the meantime, however, Alexander had been courting the Tsarevitch's sister, Olga; but, unfortunately, the Emperor had more ambitious plans for his daughter's marriage[2] and so, disappointed in love, Alexander volunteered for the Caucasian Campaign against the rebel leader Shamyl. He showed great coolness and courage during the Campaign and actually picked up Shamyl's Koran, with some of his papers, which had been dropped on the battlefield. From then on, he received more and more important commands; but in 1851 he made his last appearance in Russian uniform, for much to the Emperor's despair he had fallen head over heels in love with one of his sister's Ladies-in-Waiting, Countess Julie of Hauke, and eloped with her to Breslau where they were married on October 28, 1851. For his disobedience, he was deprived of the rank of General and dismissed from the Russian Army.[3]

According to all accounts, Countess Julie was an outstandingly

[1] Nicholas I, who had succeeded his brother Alexander I as Tsar in 1825.

[2] Olga was to be engaged to Charles I (later King of Württemberg), whom she married in 1846.

[3] The Emperor had wanted Alexander to marry his niece, the Grand Duchess Catherine Michailovna, with whom Alexander was not in love. Thus, by marrying Countess Julie of Hauke, Alexander committed the double offence of marrying morganatically without the Emperor's permission and also of rejecting the Emperor's chosen bride.

beautiful woman and their daughter, Princess Marie, gives a particularly engaging description of her in her *Reminiscences*. 'My mother was not specially tall,' she wrote; 'she had quite a powerful figure, large warm-brown eyes and a lovely mouth. Her hands were the most exquisite shape. Her voice was full of charm and she had a delightful ringing laugh—so that when she laughed you saw a row of pearl white teeth.' And, although Julie occupied a relatively lowly position in the Russian Court, nevertheless, both her father and mother came from distinguished families. Her father's name was Maurice, Count Hauke and although he was of German origin he eventually became the Minister of War in the Kingdom of Poland. Maurice is described in a family chronicle as 'a handsome man with an open expression, curly hair and brown, expressive eyes'; he was a cadet in the School of Engineers and Artillery, when war broke out between Poland and Russia, and as he was still too young to become an officer (being only seventeen at the time), he enrolled as a non-commissioned officer in the Polish Army. In his very first taste of war, he showed signs of great courage and in future the whole of his military career was to be marked by feats of heroism. At the Battle of Terracina, for example, when he was fighting in one of the Polish Free Corps, against Austrian troops in Italy, his right arm was hit by a bullet early in the battle and after the wound had been bandaged, he advanced against the enemy at the head of his men brandishing his sabre in his left hand. Although he was bleeding heavily, Maurice managed to keep his men together and it was only six hours later, after the battle had been won, that finally he fainted. During the battle, infection had already begun to set in but thanks to his comrades' admiration and affection, enough money was collected to transfer him to hospital in Rome where the best treatment was available. Restored to health, in 1807 he married Sophie de Lafontaine, the daughter of Leopold de Lafontaine, who was one of the most famous surgeons of his time and was then Court Doctor to the last King of Poland. They had an extremely happy marriage and Julie was born to them at Warsaw on November 12, 1825. Unfortunately, five years later, the Polish Revolution broke out and as Minister of War, her father was responsible for keeping law and order. On the evening when the Revolution began, the Hauke family were playing whist with a few friends at home. Suddenly the door burst open and Colonel Menciszewski rushed in with the news that shots were being exchanged in the streets. General Hauke had been keeping a horse ready saddled day and night in case of unrest and although his wife clung to the stirrup, pleading with him not to go, he at once went out to try to restore calm. At the Royal Palace he met an angry crowd. He tried to persuade them to return home but they opened fire and he was shot dead. Several months later his wife died too and the Emperor of Russia ordered that their two small daughters, Emilie and Julie, should be brought to St Petersburg, where they were cared for by the Tsarina, and educated at the Tsar's expense. When they grew up they both became Ladies-in-Waiting at the Russian Court and it was there that Julie met and married Prince Alexander of Hesse.

As we have seen, when Prince Alexander and Countess Julie were married, they aroused the Tsar's displeasure. Also, their marriage posed a problem of title. Since Julie was not *ebenbürtig* (equal in rank) their marriage was morganatic and she could not take the title of Princess Alexander of Hesse. A week after the wedding Alexander's brother, the Grand Duke Louis III of Hesse and the Rhine, created Julie Countess of Battenberg, a small town in the north of Hesse where Prince Alexander's family possessed large properties and a castle. Later (on September 26, 1858) she was made Princess Julie of Battenberg and their children were given the title of Prince or Princess. After their marriage, Alexander joined the Austrian Army in which he became a General, and amongst other acts of bravery, saved a rout at the Battle of Solferino, by seizing one of the regimental colours and rallying his men to counter-attack. By now, he was beginning to long for a more regular life, and so in 1862 he retired from active service and until his death in 1886 made his home in Hesse, where during the summer his family lived in Heiligenberg Castle (which he had inherited from his mother), while the winter was spent at the Alexander Palace in Darmstadt.

It was Alexander and Julie's eldest son, Prince Louis of Battenberg (born at Graz on May 24, 1854) who was the father of Louise Mountbatten. It was because of his passion for the sea that he came to settle in Britain and it was because of the hostility to Germany roused by World War I, that he and his family changed their names from Battenberg to Mountbatten.

As anti-German feeling was running high, in 1917 Lloyd George suggested to King George V that the three branches of the British Royal Family who bore German names and titles should change them for English ones. Accordingly, King George changed his family's name from Wettin to Windsor and the name of his dynasty from the House of Saxe-Coburg and Gotha (Prince Albert's title) to the House of Windsor. Also Queen Mary's relatives changed their names from Teck to Cambridge, the Duke of Teck becoming the Marquess of Cambridge and Queen Mary's younger brother, Prince Alexander George of Teck, becoming the Earl of Athlone. Similarly, the Battenbergs had to change their name and title. It was decided, therefore, to translate their name literally from German into English and this was particularly suitable seeing that Prince Louis of Battenberg had had a distinguished career in the British Navy and Mount Batten (itself Crown property) was right in the heart of Plymouth Sound. Prince Louis was given the title of Marquess of Milford Haven. His eldest son, Prince George of Battenberg took the courtesy title of the Earl of Medina and his two youngest children, Prince Louis and Princess Louise, became Lord Louis and Lady Louise Mountbatten. As his eldest daughter, Princess Alice, was already married to Prince Andrew of Greece, the change of title did not affect her. Prince Louis was sad at losing his family name but, nevertheless, he had a strong sense of humour. On July 17th, when the change of name was announced, he was staying at his eldest son's house near Rossyth. On July

15th he entered in the visitor's book 'arrived Prince Jekyll' and on July 20th, when he signed out, he put 'departed Lord Hyde'.

\*     \*     \*

Now, a few details about the other members of Princess Louise's family. First, the aunts and uncles on her father's side. Of these, the eldest was Prince Louis' sister, Princess Marie of Battenberg (born at Geneva on July 15, 1852) who married Gustavus (later Prince) Count of Erbach-Schönberg in 1870. They had three sons and a daughter, six grandchildren and eight great-grandchildren, and Princess Marie died at Schönberg Castle in 1923, leaving a number of family pictures to the collection now at Broadlands.

Prince Louis' three brothers were all colourful characters. Alexander (Sandro) of Battenberg, born at Verona on April 5, 1857, served in the Hessian, Prussian and Russian Armies rising to the rank of Colonel-in-Chief. On April 29, 1879 when he was barely twenty-two, he was elected Sovereign Prince by the National Assembly of Bulgaria, which had recently obtained its freedom from Turkey, though the Sultan of Turkey still claimed suzerainty and the country was largely under the control of the Russians. He landed in Bulgaria at Varna in June and the following February went to St Petersburg where he unwittingly saved the life of the Emperor Alexander II of Russia. As he had to wait for his father's train to arrive, he caused the family dinner which had been planned for the evening of their arrival to start late. While the family were waiting for him, a time bomb exploded in the dining-room, killing or wounding some hundred of the Finnish guard—and, if it had not been for his lateness, the whole family would already have been seated at table.

Alexander II had a great affection for Prince Alexander, whom he always regarded as one of his favourite nephews. But unfortunately his successor, the Emperor Alexander III, who was crowned in 1882, quarrelled with Prince Alexander and eventually the two cousins became inveterate enemies. While Prince

Alexander was away in Russia for the Emperor's coronation, two Russian generals who had been trusted with the Regency during his absence, acted disloyally and naturally Prince Alexander was obliged to dismiss them from office. This, of course, enraged the Emperor but made Alexander very popular in Bulgaria. After further disputes between Alexander and the Emperor, on November 14, 1885 King Milan of Serbia declared war on Bulgaria, believing that the Bulgarian Army was completely disorganized, since all its Russian commanders and staff officers had been recalled. Prince Alexander was forced to fill all posts of the rank of Captain and above with young and inexperienced Bulgarian officers; but nevertheless he took over supreme command of the Army himself, and supported by his brother, Francis Joseph, inflicted an overwhelming defeat on the Serbians at Slivnitza, as is mentioned in George Bernard Shaw's play *Arms and the Man*.

Alexander's victory, together with a successful *rapprochement* with Turkey only deepened the feud with Russia and, as a result, the Russians now organized a secret plot against Alexander. They persuaded a group of disaffected Bulgarian officers to induce Alexander to send his best troops to the frontier, in the belief that Serbia was mobilizing against him. Loyal officers tried to warn Alexander in vain and on August 21, 1886 Bulgarian troops who had been won over by the Russians, stormed the Royal palace in Sofia. Alexander and his brother Francis Joseph were taken prisoner and driven off in a carriage, under escort, to the royal yacht at Rachovo. The Russians forced the crew of the yacht to take them to the Russian port of Reni where the two princes were allowed to leave for Lemberg by train. Meanwhile, as soon as the Bulgarian people and the rest of the Army had heard the news of Alexander's capture a counter-revolution broke out. The Prince's bodyguard, the Alexander Regiment, recaptured the palace and the government buildings, and a telegram was sent to Prince Alexander of Hesse asking him to urge his son to return to the throne. On August 28th the three brothers, Prince Alexander of

Bulgaria, Prince Louis and Prince Francis Joseph of Battenberg, met at Lemberg and the next day Prince Alexander landed in Bulgaria again, accompanied by Prince Louis.

The Tsar of Russia, however, now made it clear that Bulgaria would only be saved from the permanent enmity of Russia if Prince Alexander resigned the throne. Despite the protests of his people, Alexander felt that it was his duty to sacrifice himself for his country and a week after his triumphant return he abdicated and left Bulgaria. Earlier, he had wanted to marry Princess Victoria, the daughter of Crown Prince Frederick and Princess Victoria of Prussia, but Bismarck managed to stop the marriage on political grounds because of Alexander's feud with Russia, remarking that 'to give the Bulgarian a Prussian princess would be like throwing a marshal's baton over the walls of a besieged fortress'. Now, he decided to marry one of the stars of the opera in Darmstadt, Johanna Loisinger, whose family were Austrians, and so he entered the Austrian army as a second Colonel and he died at Graz on November 17, 1893, aged only thirty-six. During his brief life, he had made a great name for himself not only as ruler of Bulgaria but also by the unassuming way in which he went back to second in command of a regiment, after being a sovereign with considerable power. On his marriage he had been granted the title of Count Hartenau by the Grand Duke of Hesse, and his widow, Johanna Hartenau, survived him by fifty-eight years, dying on July 20, 1951, in Vienna.

Prince Louis' second brother was Prince Henry (Liko) of Battenberg, who was born in Milan on October 5, 1858. Until he was twenty-seven, he served in the army and then in July 1885 he married Queen Victoria's youngest daughter, Princess Beatrice of Great Britain and Ireland, at Whippingham Church near Osborne. He now became a British subject and was granted the title of Royal Highness, but he was bound by a tiresome undertaking that he and his wife should live with Queen Victoria, as she refused to be parted from her last unmarried daughter. He was also made a Privy Councillor, Governor and Captain of the

Isle of Wight, and Governor of Carisbrooke Castle, in the Isle of Wight. When the military expedition was being organized to Ashanti on the Gold Coast (now Ghana), he pleaded hard with Queen Victoria to be allowed to see active service again and eventually the Queen gave in. During the campaign he contracted malaria and was sent home on board H.M.S. *Blonde*, but he died at sea on January 20, 1896 at the age of thirty-eight. Like his elder brother, he was long survived by his widow, and Princess Beatrice only died forty-eight years later, at Brandridge Park, Sussex, in October 1944. Of their children, Prince Alexander (Drino) of Battenberg married Lady Irene Denison, daughter of the second Earl of Londesborough. He too changed his name to Mountbatten, when the British Royal Family changed their German name in 1917, and at the same time he became Marquess of Carisbrooke, Earl of Berkhamsted and Viscount Launceston. His sister, Princess Victoria Eugénie (Ena) of Battenberg married King Alfonso XIII of Spain in 1906 (a bomb was thrown at their coach during their wedding procession but they were able to continue in a spare coach although spattered with blood), but Alfonso was deposed during the Spanish Revolution of 1931. Of his two younger brothers, Prince Leopold (Leo) of Battenberg, who became Lord Leopold Mountbatten in 1917, with great courage volunteered for the Army on the outbreak of World War I, despite haemophilia, but died in London in April 1922. The remaining brother, Prince Maurice of Battenberg, was a cadet at Sandhurst, but was killed in action during World War I.

Finally, there was Prince Francis Joseph (Franzjos) of Battenberg, born at Padua on September 24, 1861. He served in the Prussian Footguards, went to Bulgaria with his elder brother Alexander and fought with him at the Battle of Slivnitza (as has been mentioned above) and on his marriage in 1897 to Princess Anna Petrovitch-Niegosh of Montenegro (sister of the late Queen of Italy) became a Colonel in the Montenegrin Army. He was, however, never a professional soldier at heart and his real interest lay in philosophy and literature. In 1891 he earned a doctor of philosophy degree at the University of Leipzig and he died in Switzerland in 1924. His widow, Princess Anna, is still living today.

*     *     *

Now, we come to the aunts and uncles on the other side of Princess Louise's family. Her mother was Princess Victoria, the daughter of Grand Duke Louis IV of Hesse and the Rhine and Queen Victoria of England's second daughter, Princess Alice. Princess Victoria had four sisters and two brothers, all younger than herself and all having the title Prince or Princess of Hesse and the Rhine. The eldest, Elisabeth (Ella), born at Bessungen, on November 1, 1864, married the Grand Duke Serge Alexandrovitch, the fourth son of the Emperor Alexander II and Princess Marie of Hesse and the Rhine, but more will be said of her later in this book.[1]

Another of Princess Victoria's sisters, Alix (born at Darmstadt on June 6, 1872), also married into the Russian royal family. On April 20, 1894, her engagement was announced to Nicholas, the Tsarevitch of Russia. Then, at the end of October, when Nicholas' father, the Emperor Alexander III, was dying in the Crimea, Nicholas telegraphed Alix asking her to come to Russia at once. On the first day of November, Nicholas—at the age of twenty-four—succeeded his father as Tsar.

On the advice of their uncle, the Prince of Wales (later Edward VII) they were married quietly in St Petersburg later that month and Alix was received into the Orthodox Church, taking the name Alexandra Feodorovna. They had four daughters (Olga, Tatiana, Marie and Anastasia) and finally a son and heir, Alexei, who unfortunately suffered from haemophilia. The children were very friendly with Princess Louise and some of their letters to her are reproduced in this book.[2] The fate of the Russian Imperial family is well known. At the beginning of the Russian Revolution (on March 15, 1917) Nicholas abdicated. He, Alix and their children

---

[1] See Chapters 1 and 5 especially.          [2] See Appendix.

were kept under arrest and the following year were moved first to Tobolsk and then to Ekaterinburg, where they were imprisoned in the villa Ipatiev. On the night of July 16, 1918, they were assassinated by shooting, but Anastasia survived the fusilade and, according to the most reliable account, she was killed with eighteen bayonet thrusts, while screaming for help.

Of Princess Victoria's other brothers and sisters Irène (born at Darmstadt on July 11, 1866) married Prince Henry of Prussia (brother of Kaiser William II of Germany), who was a professional naval officer and rose to the rank of Grand Admiral in the German Imperial Navy, with the honorary rank of Admiral of the Fleet in the British Royal Navy.

The eldest brother, Ernest Louis (born at Darmstadt, on November 25, 1868) was the last reigning Grand Duke of Hesse. After studying at the universities of Leipzig and Giessen, he had an active military career up to his succession as Grand Duke in 1892. He was then only twenty-three; his youngest sister, Alix, not yet twenty. And on the day of his succession their grandmother, Queen Victoria of England, wrote in her journal: 'Poor darling Ernie, how he is to be pitied with his great youth burdened now with responsibilities, and poor sweet Alicky, without a parent, and I the only one left of the grandparents.' Ernest Louis introduced an extremely progressive programme of social and health legislation, and he was also an outstanding patron of science and the arts. In his youth, he was greatly influenced by Ruskin and William Morris, and, following their ideas, he handed over one of his parks in Darmstadt to promising architects and artists, where they were given complete freedom to design and build first their own houses, and then small modern houses for other families on the estate. This became known as the Darmstadt Artists' Colony (*Künstler kolonie*) and after the first famous exhibition there in 1901 the Colony became an important centre for art exhibitions, which were made possible not only because of the Grand Duke's financial support, but also his initiative and enthusiasm. The last of these exhibitions was the Great Century

C

Exhibition of German Art held in 1914 and they only ended when the Grand Duke was deposed. He also built up the reputation of the Court theatre and orchestra, and was one of the few men of influence who opposed the Kaiser in earnest at the start of World War I. It was at the end of the war that Ernest Louis lost his throne. Hesse, in common with all other German Kingdoms and Grand Duchies declared for the 'Free German Socialist Republic' in November 1918. The Grand Duke refused to abdicate on principle and, although he could not avoid being deposed by the revolutionaries, they treated him with respect and consideration since he had been a popular ruler. Details of his two marriages can be found in the family tree at the start of this book. He died at Wolfsgarten on October 9, 1937, and his widow, Grand Duchess Eleanore, was killed in the air crash at Ostend on November 16th, some five weeks later.

Princess Victoria's other brother and sister both died in infancy. On the morning of May 29, 1873 Prince Frederick (Fritzie) was playing hide and seek with his brother; in the excitement, he rushed out of a second floor window and was killed on the stone terrace beneath. A year and a half later, on November 16, 1878, the youngest sister, Marie (May), died of diphtheria.

*          *          *

Princess Louise's own sister and brothers will, of course, appear often in these pages. The eldest was Princess Alice, who was four years older and was born at Windsor Castle on February 15, 1885. She was named after their grandmother (Princess Alice, the second daughter of Queen Victoria of England), and she was born in the same bed where her mother had been born twenty-two years before. Queen Victoria sat beside Princess Victoria's bed from seven o'clock in the morning until the baby was born at five o'clock in the afternoon, and she found it 'strange and affecting' to think that she had been present at the birth of both mother and child. At the age of eighteen, Princess Alice became engaged to Prince Andrew of Greece, the son of King George I of the Hellenes. King George had been born Prince William of Denmark and he was the brother of Queen Alexandra, the wife of King Edward VII of the United Kingdom, and of the Empress Marie Feodorovna, the wife of Emperor Alexander III of Russia, who was originally Princess Dagmar of Denmark. On June 6, 1863 he had been chosen by the great powers to fill the vacant throne of Greece—only five months before his father became King Christian IX of Denmark.

Princess Alice and Prince Andrew were married in Darmstadt. Many of the guests described the wedding as one of the loveliest they could remember but sadly it proved to be the last occasion on which all the members of the Battenberg and Hessian families were together.

Because of the political events in Greece, Princess Alice and Prince Andrew's life was rather an unstable one. Prince Andrew served in the Greek Army and fought in the Balkan Wars of 1912 and 1913. Then, on March 18, 1913, his father (King George I) was assassinated in Salonica and he was succeeded by his eldest son, Constantine. Only four years later, in June 1917, the Allies turned out Constantine and replaced him with his second son, Alexander, who was then twenty-four years old. As a result, the Prime Minister Venizelos dismissed three thousand officers loyal to Constantine, among them Prince Andrew. Then, in October 1920, King Alexander died from a monkey bite. In June, Venizelos had launched the disastrous campaign against the Turks in Asia Minor and now, a month after Alexander's death, elections were held which resulted in the fall of Venizelos and the return of King Constantine. The other members of the Greek royal family, including Prince Andrew and Princess Alice, landed at Phaleron Bay and, after being pulled out of their car, were carried by the excited crowds shoulder high all the way to Athens.

It was now that the great opportunity of Prince Andrew's military career occurred. The following year he was given command of the 12th Division of the Greek Army and he was in command during the great victory at Eski Shehr in July 1921. For his part in the battle, he was promptly promoted to Lieutenant-General and given the command of the Second Army Corps, but during September—in order to show his dissatisfaction with the way in which the Army was being run—he twice asked to be relieved of his command. The Commander-in-Chief, General Papulas, refused: but eventually Prince Andrew succeeded in obtaining a transfer to the command of the 5th Army Corps of Epirus and the Ionian Islands. He had constantly warned that the Greek Army was heading for disaster and eventually, in 1922, the Army suffered a humiliating defeat in Asia Minor and King Constantine was forced to abdicate. His eldest son, King George II (Prince Andrew's nephew), succeeded him on September 27th for eighteen uneasy months, then he too was exiled and on March 25, 1924 Greece was declared a Republic.

Meanwhile, Prince Andrew had resigned from the Army and was told that he and his family could remain at their lovely home, *Mon Repos*, in Corfu. A month later he was arrested, brought to Athens where he was kept prisoner for seven weeks, and on December 2nd, tried by a court in the Chamber of Deputies, who had already decided to shoot him. However, his first cousin King George V of England intervened in the nick of time and ordered H.M.S. *Calypso* to head for Phaleron Bay, on the eve of the trial, while Captain Talbot was sent ahead overland to plead with the dictator Pangalos. Prince Andrew's trial finished at midnight and Captain Talbot's pleas went unheeded—until the following morning when the Court heard that the cruiser had arrived and ordered Prince Andrew's release. Later in the day, Pangalos himself drove Prince Andrew and Princess Alice to Phaleron Bay, from where the *Calypso* set sail for Corfu, to pick up their five young children and from there the royal refugees made their way to London and on to Paris.

In France, the Prince and Princess settled down on an estate at St Cloud near Paris, not far away from Prince Andrew's brother Nicholas and his family, of whom the youngest, Marina, was later to become the Duchess of Kent. Of Prince Andrew and Princess Alice's children, the eldest Margarita married Godfrey, Hereditary Prince of Hohenlohe-Langenburg. The second daughter, Theodora (Dolla) married Berthold, Margrave of Baden. Their third daughter, Princess Cecile married George Donatus (Don) Hereditary Grand Duke of Hesse and the Rhine. Their fourth daughter, Sophie, married Prince Christopher of Hesse, and after Prince Christopher had been killed while flying for the German Air Force in World War II, she then married Prince George William of Hanover.

Prince Andrew and Princess Alice's son was, of course, Prince Philip of Greece, who is now the Duke of Edinburgh and the husband of Queen Elizabeth II of England whom he married on November 20, 1947. Prince Philip was born in Corfu, on June 10, 1921 and was only one year old when Prince Andrew and Princess Alice left Greece for good. He first attended a day school at St Cloud, then went to Cheam Preparatory School for three years. After Cheam, he spent three terms at the School run by Kurt Hahn in Salem Castle, which was owned by his brother-in-law, Berthold, Margrave of Baden.[1] In September 1934, he transferred to Gordonstoun, which was a sister school founded by Doctor Hahn in Scotland, after he had been forced to flee from Germany because of Nazi persecution. Gordonstoun was followed by the Royal Naval College, Dartmouth and then on January 1, 1940 Prince Philip became a midshipman. He served on board the battleship H.M.S. *Ramillies*, the cruisers *Kent* and *Shropshire*, and finally on the battleship *Valiant*—and it was while on board H.M.S. *Valiant*, that he earned a mention in dispatches for the way in which he carried out his duties as Searchlight Control Officer during the Battle of Matapan. In February 1944 he was appointed First Lieutenant of a destroyer and after the war, he was one of the instructors who created the new Petty Officers' School at Corsham, H.M.S. *Royal Arthur*, and in 1948 he served

[1] See page 209.

for three months in the Operations Division of the Admiralty, then did the Naval Staff Course at Greenwich.

When the Greek Monarchy was restored in 1935, and King George II resumed the throne, Prince Andrew did not go back to Greece as he feared that his return would only result in a third period of exile. And sure enough, his fear proved justified—for six years later King George was exiled from Greece again, this time by the Germans in 1941. Princess Alice, however, and her sister-in-law, Princess Helen, decided to return to Greece and during the war they worked there for the Swedish and Swiss Red Cross. Both of them were treated quite courteously by the Germans—because by this time Princess Louise had become Queen of Sweden and so the Nazis were anxious not to antagonize a neutral country by maltreating the Queen's sister—but both refused to accept any special favours and, like many other members of European royal families, they were faced with the tragedy of finding their children living in countries that were at war. Princess Alice's three surviving daughters had all married Germans, while her son was serving in the British Navy. Similarly, two of Princess Helen's daughters had married into German families (Olga was married to Paul, the Prince Regent of Yugoslavia, and Elizabeth was the wife of a Bavarian Count), while her third daughter, Marina, had become the Duchess of Kent. Prince Andrew, who had been living in Monaco, died there in 1944, and so Princess Alice stayed on in Athens where she was active in charity and welfare work, until the summer of 1967 when she moved to England for medical treatment. Sadly, however, Princess Alice's four original sons-in-law (the brothers-in-law of Prince Philip) are all now dead.

Like Prince Philip, and like their father, Princess Louise's two brothers both loved the sea. The elder of them, George, was born at Darmstadt on November 6, 1892. Of all the Battenbergs, he was the most mechanically minded—and he gave early evidence of this! At the age of five, he took to pieces one of his father's clocks to see how it worked and when threatened with punishment succeeded in putting it back together. For, knowing that this was likely to happen, he had stuck pins all over a large sheet of cardboard and arranged each little piece of the clock in order on the pins, as he took it out. As a result, he was able to put the clock together again without difficulty, and this proved to be only the first of a long series of mechanical experiments which revealed him to be a born engineer. At the Royal Naval College, Osborne, Sir James Watt, the second master, remarked that Prince George was the cleverest and, at the same time, the laziest cadet he had ever known; and once Prince George had joined the Navy, examples of his mechanical ingenuity were always to be found in his cabin, whenever he was at sea. In 1913 he air-conditioned his cabin with a thermostat which switched on a fan if the cabin became too hot, and a radiator if it became too cold. In the days before there was running water in cabins, he laid on his own supply of hot and cold, using little electric lathe-motors to pump the water. And he actually invented a device controlled by an alarm clock to wake him up with early morning tea, years before such a contrivance appeared on the market in England.

While he was still a midshipman and only nineteen years old, Prince George was invited by King George V to accompany him to the Durbar in Delhi. As he was a member of the royal party, Prince George rode in a place of honour in the procession. Unfortunately, unlike most of his family, he was never a really first-class horseman and his mount proved rather temperamental. The horse backed through three or four ranks of senior officers—until one of the generals, riding in the procession, offered to exchange mounts. Prince George rode on perfectly happily; but a little later he looked back and saw the general backing through a Guard of Honour!

In 1913, he visited New Zealand (as a sub-lieutenant aboard H.M.S. *New Zealand*, the battle cruiser which had been given to the Royal Navy by that country), where he was exceedingly popular and was given a small plot of land by the Maoris so that he could be said to own a small part of New Zealand. By the outbreak of the war, he was a Lieutenant and he continued to serve aboard the *New Zealand*, commanding a 12-inch gun turret during the Battles of Heligoland Bight, Dogger Bank and Jutland. His own gun turret fired more heavy shells at the enemy throughout the war than any other and accordingly he was decorated with the Russian Cross of St George for Valour. He did not, however, receive a British decoration—as it was very rare for a member of the royal family to be given a decoration for gallantry—and another officer aboard the *New Zealand* who was awarded a D.S.O. wrote to Princess Victoria telling her how distressed he was that her son had not received any decoration.

In November 1916 Prince George married the Countess Nadejda (Nada) de Torby, daughter of Grand Duke Michael of Russia, at the Chapel Royal, St James. In 1917 when the rest of the royal family changed their names he became the Earl of Medina, and on Prince Louis' death in 1921 he became the second Marquess of Milford Haven.

Two months after his father's death, just after his brother (who had now become Lord Louis Mountbatten) sailed with the Prince of Wales for India aboard the *Renown*, King George V sent for the new Lord Milford Haven and told him that fifty per cent of the officers in Lord Louis' year were compulsorily to be retired under the 'Geddes axe'. Officers with private means were to be the first to go and so, since Lord Louis was absent, the King asked Lord Milford Haven to give his consent to his brother's retirement. George knew what the Royal Navy meant to his brother and that his whole interest in life was wrapped up in the Service, and so, thinking quickly, he asked the King whether he thought Dickie (as Lord Mountbatten was called in the family) ought to look for proper work if he was axed. The King replied that every young man should do a proper job—and so George retaliated by pleading that to do a proper job in civil life Dickie would have to displace some other man and, seeing that Dickie had no experience outside the Navy, he would be a poor substitute, while if he remained in the service he would probably be an outstanding success. As a result the King spoke to the First Lord of the Admiralty and Dickie was not axed.

Ten years later Milford Haven left the Navy himself. Although he had done very well, being appointed to the experimental department of the Gunnery School and being promoted to Commander, nevertheless his private means had been greatly reduced by the war, and so he retired from the Navy in order to join the Sperry Gyroscope Company. Within a few years, he became chairman and managing director of the British Sperry Company and under his management, the Company expanded rapidly.

Then, in February 1938, Lord Milford Haven fell and broke his hip. He was taken to hospital where they discovered that he was suffering from cancer of the bone and on April 8th he died, at the age of forty-six. His death was a great sadness to the family and Princess Louise, who had always been specially fond of her brother, was very deeply shaken. Lord Milford Haven and his wife had two children, Lady Tatiana Mountbatten, born in Edinburgh on November 16, 1917, and David, eighteen months younger, who succeeded as Marquess of Milford Haven on his father's death.

The youngest of Princess Louise's brothers was, of course, Prince Louis of Battenberg, who later became Earl Mountbatten of Burma. Prince Louis was born at Windsor on June 25, 1900 and was the last of Queen Victoria's great-grandchildren to be born during her lifetime. He was, in fact, held by Queen Victoria at his christening and, much to her surprise, succeeded in knocking off her glasses with a sudden movement of his arm. The details of Lord Mountbatten's life are so well known, that only a brief outline will be given here. After Locker's Park Preparatory School, he entered the Royal Navy as a cadet and attended the Royal Naval Colleges at Osborne, Dartmouth and Keyham. He joined Admiral Beatty's famous flagship the battle cruiser *Lion* as a Midshipman in 1916, transferred to the battleship *Queen*

*Elizabeth* in 1917, served for two months in H.M. Submarine *K6*, and when barely eighteen years old became the first lieutenant and second-in-command of the escort ship *P.31*. After the war he was sent with other naval 'war babies' for two terms to Christ's College, Cambridge, and then accompanied his cousin, the Prince of Wales, on his tour to Australasia in 1920 and to India and the Far East the following year. He specialized in Signals and Wireless, captained the Royal Navy Polo team, and wrote text books on wireless and polo which are still in use today. He was promoted to Commander in 1932, to Captain in 1937 and in the Second World War, of course, he was given first the command of H.M.S. *Kelly* and the Fifth Destroyer Flotilla and then the air-craft carrier *Illustrious*. Finally, he became Chief of Combined Operations in 1941 and Supreme Allied Commander, South East Asia in 1943. It was for these wartime services that he was created Viscount Mountbatten of Burma in 1946.

The following year the Prime Minister invited Lord Mount-batten to become Viceroy of India, and asked him to supervise India's passage to independence. Mountbatten at first refused, as he wanted to continue his career in the Navy. But when King George VI urged him to accept and the Admiralty promised to safeguard his future, he eventually agreed. After the transfer of power—which was far from easy—the Indian Constituent Assembly asked Mountbatten to become the first Governor General, but in June 1948 he returned to the Navy—with the remark to a friend, 'Thank God I have finished with politics'. In 1947, he had been created Earl Mountbatten of Burma and he now went back to naval service with the rank of Rear Admiral and he took up the command of the First Cruiser Squadron. In 1952, Mountbatten became Commander in Chief, Mediterranean; in 1955, First Sea Lord; in 1956, Admiral of the Fleet; from 1959 to 1965, when his active service came to an end, he was Chief of the Defence Staff, and his last achievement as such was to propose the amalgamation of the Admiralty, War Office and Air Ministry into a unified Ministry of Defence, which was carried out in 1964.

In 1922, Lord Mountbatten had become engaged to Edwina Ashley, while he was on a tour in India as A.D.C. to the Prince of Wales. Edwina—whom Lord Mountbatten had met for the first time at a ball given at Claridge's by Mrs Cornelius Vander-bilt two or three months before he sailed for India—was the daughter of Colonel Wilfrid Ashley (who was to become Minister of Transport in February 1924 and was later to be created Lord Mount Temple) and Maud Ashley, who was the only daughter of Sir Ernest Cassel. The wedding took place at St Margaret's, Westminster, with the Prince of Wales as best man and almost every member of the royal family was there. In 1911 when Edwina's mother had died, she had inherited a part of her grandfather's fortune. As a result, the newly-weds were able to live extremely comfortably and to lead a gay social life for the first years after their marriage. Edwina was a great traveller—she visited Siberia, the deserts of the Middle East and the Andes—but, despite her wealth, Edwina travelled very simply nor was she afraid of discomfort and once, when she went to the South Seas, she spent four months aboard a schooner. She also did a tremendous amount of charity work and it was during a tour of the Far East for the St John Ambulance Brigade, of which she was Superintendent-in-Chief, that Lady Mountbatten died in 1960.

Finally, of course, there are Lord Mountbatten's daughters. The relationship between Princess Louise and her nieces was exceptionally close and she was especially fond of Patricia and Pamela Mountbatten. Patricia was born on February 14, 1924, and married John, seventh Lord Brabourne, whom she met at her father's headquarters in Singapore. Patricia had joined the W.R.N.S. in 1943, and both she and Lord Brabourne were serving on her father's staff. Lord Mountbatten's younger daughter, Pamela, was born at Barcelona an April 19, 1929. She accompanied Queen Elizabeth II on her trip round the world in 1953–1954 as Senior Lady-in-Waiting and is married to David Hicks, the interior decorator. As Lord Mountbatten has no sons he was granted the very unusual privilege of succession 'by special remainder'. This means that, on his death, Lady Brabourne will become the Countess Mountbatten of Burma in her own right, and that, should Lady Brabourne's male line become extinct (which it is not likely to do since she has five sons), the title would then revert to Lady Pamela Hicks and her male descendants.

~~~~~~

# CHAPTER I

# *Flight from Russia*

In the late summer of 1914, not many weeks before the outbreak of the First World War, Tsar Nicholas II of Russia lent the royal river yacht to some relatives for a grand cruise on the River Volga. Among the guests were his two sisters-in-law Grand Duchess Elisabeth (Ella) of Russia and Princess Victoria of Battenberg, together with her daughter Princess Louise and her Lady-in-Waiting, Nona Kerr.[1] Also invited were Princess Victoria's husband, Prince Louis of Battenberg, and their son Louis. Because of Prince Louis' duties as First Sea Lord, however, they had said that they would not be able to join the party until the end of July. The royal yacht had been built for the celebration of the tercentenary of the House of Romanov in 1913, which from the standpoint of extravagant splendour has probably had no match in the whole of European history. Originally the yacht had been designed to take the Tsar's family for trips on the Volga, and now, a year after the tercentenary celebrations, once again it was put to the same use.

On board there was a feeling of uneasy calm. The guests were extremely worried about Rasputin's influence over the Tsar's family; but even quicker than they had anticipated, the general political situation came to a head and the party were forced to disperse. During the first ten days of the cruise (until July 25, 1914) Princess Louise kept a short diary which gives a vivid account of their journey and which is reproduced below, together with a continuation which she wrote from memory,

---

[1] Nona Kerr was the grand-daughter of the Marquess of Lothian. She later married Colonel Richard Crichton.

piecing together some of the names and dates from her photograph album and from her mother's own recollections.[1]

## Diary from the Volga

### July 15th

'Mama, Nona and I with our maids, Clayden and Edith Pye and our butler Valentin Schmidt left London in the evening, crossed by Flushing and went by train to Berlin.

### July 16th

'We arrived at Berlin in the afternoon and went to the Central Hotel for a bath and dinner and went out and did a little shopping. We left again. We took care not to inform William (the Kaiser) of our passage through Berlin as we had no special desire to see him.

### July 17th

'We got to Kalisch in the morning and here a comfortable, special Russian railway carriage had been sent to await us, with the usual railway staff, inspectors and A.D.Cs. We stopped for a couple of hours in Warsaw where the Governor came and met us and entertained us.

### July 18th

'We arrived at Moscow at 3.45 p.m. and went at once to Aunt Ella (the Grand Duchess Elisabeth of Russia, widow of the Grand Duke Serge) and went across to Aunt Ella's Martha and Mary Convent. This was the Nursing Order she founded after her husband, the Grand Duke Serge, had been assassinated by the Nihilists. The building was lovely and simple with a new church standing in its own grounds, alongside the Convent home, part of which was situated in old buildings which had been

---

[1] The whole diary was written in a kind of compressed 'telegraphese'. The entries have been slightly expanded with the occasional word of explanation added, so as to be intelligible to the reader.

renovated. We left in the evening with Aunt Ella and her former lady, Madame Gordeiev, who had now also become a nun in the Order of Martha and Mary, Monsieur Karnilov and Monsieur Sourov.[1]

### *July 19th*

'We arrived at Nijni Novgorod at 9 a.m. Aunt Ella went to a church service but we drove straight on down to the famous river steamer yacht which had been reconstructed and redecorated last year for Uncle Nicky and the Russian family, for the Romanov Tercentenary celebration during which they toured the whole country and, of course, went up country on the Volga. The steamer was perfectly charming, such very nice cabins, lots of bathrooms and excellently decorated in the most luxurious style.

'Nona and I sat together on deck chairs most of the afternoon. One passed masses of steamers of all sorts, barges and large rafts, and the scenes on the banks were fascinating. Particularly when we passed Makaresh where the annual big fair used to be held.

### *July 20th*

'We stopped at Tcheboksar for Aunt Ella to go to church again in the morning, for as she has now taken Holy Orders she naturally can hardly pass a town with a church without thinking she should go to a service, and indeed the local population always planned this as the high spot of her visit. So Nona and I went ashore, and went for a short walk. We walked through the town and found it had a great number of churches, and then we re-embarked and the steamer went on to the next stop, at Sviajsk, where Aunt Ella visited the local convent. While she did so, Mama, Nona and I walked about in the countryside, through the fields and picked lots of lovely blue thistles. The Abbess Barbara of Kazan joined us, when we got to Kazan at 6.30 p.m.

'Here, the Governor and all the important local dignitaries

---

[1] Arcadi Petrovitch Karnilov was Marshal of the Court of the Grand Duchess Serge (Aunt Ella) and Alexander Alexandrovitch Sourov was Marshal of the Household.

were awaiting to receive Aunt Ella formally as a member of the imperial family. Mama, Nona and I and Sourov drove with the Governor and his wife round the town sight-seeing. It was big but unfortunately rather ugly. Some seven kilometres from the river in the summer, though of course when the river is high it is much nearer. The Governor gave us tea with his wife in the Palace of the Old Kremlin which has a very fine Tartar tower. Aunt Ella and, of course, Madame Gordeiev who was always with her, spent the night together at the Convent, but we went back on board to sleep.

## July 21st

'At 11 a.m. we motored over to the Convent to join Aunt Ella, this was the Convent of Kazan—Abbess Barbara showed us all round and took us down to the underground chapel where there is a copy in an old frame of the famous Kazan image.[1] They gave us a sort of high-tea lunch, with lots of sweet things of which the Russians are so fond. The Governor and his wife and the other officials, the Bishop and all the priests were there and we had to make conversation to them. At 2 p.m. we left again and at 7 p.m. the yacht entered the Kama river which is very broad like the Volga. After dinner, we walked about on deck and it was really lovely.

## July 22nd

'Today was a hot day, even the wind was hot. It blew up to a storm in the afternoon and after that it got cooler. We stopped at Tchistopol for Aunt Ella once more to go to church. Of course this trip is largely a question of her visiting all the churches and convents. It is fascinating to see lots of Tartars about with their distinctive appearance and dress. Mama, Nona and I and Karnilov walked in a small wood consisting almost entirely of attractive lime

---

[1] 'The famous Kazan image' was an image of the Black Virgin, which was said to work miracles. The Convent of Kazan was built for its reception in 1579—but the image was removed to Moscow in 1612 and then to St Petersburg in 1710, only a copy of the image being kept in Kazan.

trees. When we got back on board, we all helped to do up the various presents which were to be given to school children, each tied up in a separate, typically Russian handkerchief.

## July 23rd

'It was a warm day, but the wind was cold. We spent the day at Nicolo-Bereozov, where of course Aunt Ella naturally went to church again while Mama, Nona and I went for a walk in the countryside and through a lovely big wood. We lunched with the Bishop, Prince Outramsky, Abbess Marie, the Vice-Governor Tolstoy, two Maréchals de la Noblesse and various other officials. In the afternoon, we went to the convent to help Aunt Ella give the prizes to the school children and also the gifts which we had been preparing for teachers and nuns. We had a large tea there and then after an open air service we all three went back on board.

## July 25th

'We arrived at Perm. Here, we left the steamer. Aunt Ella and Madame Gordeiev and Monsieur Sourov went off on a tour to visit the various convents and monasteries in the neighbourhood. Escorted by Karnilov, we and our three servants left by train, for a tour in the Urals. Again, we had a special carriage and lived in great luxury and were wonderfully looked after. The first place we visited was the town of Kishtym. No member of the Imperial family had visited the town since Alexander I. So great was the excitement that Mama, the sister of the present Empress, had come in person. Great crowds collected and everywhere on the tour we were given presents of the most varied kinds. Often carved Russian wooden figures and books and shawls, and *kakoshniks*[1] and so forth. All of those we had eventually to leave behind in Russia except for some nuggets from a platinum

---

[1] *Kakoshniks* were a form of Russian peasant headdress made from stiff cardboard covered with material. They were adopted (usually with the addition of a diamond tiara in front of the *kakoshnik*) as part of the official Court dress worn by the Imperial family and their ladies-in-waiting.

D

mine in which my father had shares. These nuggets we felt we were entitled to keep and we took them with us and a small collection of precious and semi-precious stones which we found in the Urals.

'At Kungur, we visited a grotto of ice which is on the shore of the lake, deep in the hillside. There was a tiny tent in which we could put on warm coats and overshoes; and then in front of a large crowd, who were fascinated to see members of the imperial family on their hands and knees, we crawled into the cave. It was very lovely with the ice shining bright blue and great icicles formed from the ceiling. The contrast between the great heat outside and the cave was tremendous as it was below freezing point inside the cave. It was a wonderful experience. Nijni Tagil was one of the places we visited; and I believe it was here that a sect of Old Believers, in their lovely old costumes of great historic interest, received us and presented us with the traditional bread and salt on fine carved wooden platters. Of course, everywhere there were large official lunches or official dinners with masses and masses of food, usually preceded by the *sakuska*,[1] so one would have already eaten one's fill before all the courses were served. These dinners were sometimes given by the owners of the local mines, sometimes by local officials and government representatives. Exhibitions of local products were organzied specially for us, so we could see what was being done locally in colleges and in home industry.

'I must confess that I found the Ural mountains a bit disappointing, as I thought there would be great masses of mountains at least as high as the Alps; but, of course, the Urals are perched on a high plateau, so that the actual peaks that come out of the plateau do not seem proportionately very high. There are lakes and rivers, the trees are mostly pine trees and spruce, but curiously there are no very big trees here. We visited various mines and saw platinum dredging. The platinum is found like diamonds in alluvial deposits and has to be got out in much the same way.

[1] *Sakuska* is a sumptuous form of *hors d'oeuvres* popular in Russia.

We slept most of the time in our very comfortable train. One night, we slept in the big old palace of Meller Zakomsky which was flanked by two fine towers which were very picturesque. Twice we stopped at Ekaterinburg—sleeping on the train—in retrospect, it is sad to think that we passed the tragic house where Uncle Nicky and Aunt Alix, and the four girls and Alexei were to be murdered within four years.[1] We were shown a craft exhibition in a school for arts and crafts, got up specially for us. It was really striking how gifted all these young peasants were and what artistic and fine products they made.

'The second time we were at Ekaterinburg we were given lunch on the outskirts of the town looking over a lake or river— where they told us that there was a very nasty infectious throat-germ going about. Unfortunately, we caught it. It broke out when we left Perm. Mama and Aunt Ella escaped it, but Nona and I and the maids got it badly. The last place we visited was Kusoma, a mining centre—in those days there was an iron-ore hill called Blagodat and open cast mining was under way and much of the hill had already been cut away. Here, we were given a fine luncheon by the Governor of the place. I remember us sitting out on the verandah and our feelings when the Governor suddenly announced to us that he had just received a telegram that Germany had declared war on Russia. Thank God, awful as it was, we did not then know the tragic and ghastly results of the war for Russia.[1]

'From there we went back to Perm where Aunt Ella joined us. We had to spend two nights there in the train, the day in the imperial waiting-room as we had to wait for our steamer to return with all our heavy luggage on board. We were originally planning to join our steamer at Samara, but now all our plans were changed and most of us felt pretty rotten with our bad throats. Twice, at stations, we had to get a doctor to come in to see us. At every big station we stopped at we saw masses of

[1] These afterthoughts were added to the diary when Princess Louise was re-editing it after World War I.

soldiers, still in their civilian clothes, who had been called up and were on their way to join their military depots. Often, of course, they were going in the opposite direction to the Austrian frontier, as they had to concentrate at the depots first before moving on to the front. This in a way made it easier for our train to get through.

'Finally, we arrived at St Petersburg on the fourth day, the very day that England declared war on Germany. We were lodged at the Winter Palace in rooms hurriedly got ready for us —as all of us, except Mama and Aunt Ella, were really quite ill with bad throats and high temperatures. Doctors came to see us and treated our sore throats with all sorts of strong medicines, which on the whole proved quite successful—except for Valentin Schmidt (the butler) who got it so badly that he had to be sent to a German hospital with an abscess of the throat and had to be left behind there, and that was the last we saw of him. Alas, being ill, I was not able to see Uncle Nicky[1] and the cousins, though of course Mama spent all her time with them. Nona and I could only see Aunt Alix[2] at the door of our rooms, where she waved to us and talked to us and gave us presents and the most useful thick warm coats, as of course, we only had summer coats with us and had to go back via Sweden.

'My mother and I left all our jewels we had brought with us for the official parties which we were expecting to attend later on in Moscow and St Petersburg with Aunt Alix. All Mama's heirlooms—tiaras, big necklaces and bracelets—were left there in the great jewel box which we had brought with us, and we had no idea that we should never see them again, and presumably the Bolshevik government will one day sell them.

*August 7th*

'We left by special train for the Swedish frontier, which Uncle Nicky advised was the best way of getting us home. The British Embassy kindly attached a Foreign Office courier, Mr Wilton, to

[1] The Tsar.                                                    [2] The Tsarina.

us to help our party, which now only consisted of five women—Mama, Nona, myself and our two maids. Mr Wilton was a great help at Haparanda[1] and on the way to Stockholm, as he used to dash out at the various stations to try and get some sort of food for us. On one occasion he only just managed to climb back into our saloon carriage at the very last moment, as the train was going out, Nona holding on to him as he climbed in.

'Uncle Nicky very thoughtfully had arranged to draw a large number of gold sovereigns for us at the bank in St Petersburg before we left. We divided them into small bags which were under our skirts. We passed another special train coming from Finland in which was Aunty Minnie[2] who had been in Denmark with their family, coming back to Russia. We weren't able to speak to her although the trains slowed down, so we were able to wave to each other and shout good wishes as we passed. At Haparanda, with the help of Mr Wilton, we were able to hire another saloon carriage, which was, in fact, the special saloon carriage which had brought Aunt Minnie to the frontier. This was a great piece of luck, as every place had been taken in the train, by people who were leaving Russia, the Austrian Embassy staff and their families.

*August 11th*

'We arrived in the morning at Stockholm, to our great relief, and here Gustaf[3] met us and took us all on to Drottningholm, where he and Daisy[4] and the children were temporarily living. It was wonderful being with them and even more wonderful to be able

[1] The first Swedish town across the frontier from Finland (then part of Russia).

[2] Widow of Tsar Alexander III. Born Princess Dagmar of Denmark, she was the sister of King George I of the Hellenes and of Queen Alexandra of Great Britain (wife of King Edward VII). When she married her name became Marie Feodorovna and she was sometimes referred to as the Empress Marie-Dagmar. To the children of the Tsar's family, however, she was simply 'Amama'.

[3] Crown Prince Gustaf Adolf of Sweden.

[4] Crown Princess Margaret of Sweden. The Crown Prince's first wife was born Princess Margaret of Connaught. She was the daughter of Arthur, Duke of Connaught (the son of Queen Victoria). She was born in 1882 and died in 1920, and was always known in the family as 'Daisy'.

to have a bath at last. We just longed to creep into the lovely warm-looking beds but in fact, after a happy day, chatting together and gossiping, we finally had to set off on the night train to Oslo.

'Here, Charles and Maud[1] met us and then took us out to Bygdö Kongsgaard for the day; but, by the greatest piece of luck, a steamer was due to sail from Bergen the very next day, so we were packed off in the night train again and got to Bergen on the 13th. Here we embarked in the steamer, which was over-crowded with people going home. We three luckily got a cabin together, but it was a very bad crossing and it was hardly pleasant for those like me who were not sea-sick, to have meals in the dining-room where people had spent the night. We landed at Newcastle and arrived back in London on August 17th, thankful we were safely home.

'We found Papa absorbed in his work, which occupied him at night as well as by day, and he told me how very worried he had been and I am glad he didn't know what steamer we were crossing by, as he would have felt very tempted to try and give us a special escort, which would have been wrong. The risk was mainly interception—especially just outside territorial waters at the beginning of the trip, but even this was not so great.'

*       *       *

So it was that during this flight from Russia, Princess Louise had an opportunity to really meet Crown Prince Gustaf Adolf for the first time. Because of their kinship, they had met fleetingly once or twice before in London, but this was the first time they were able to meet as individuals and Princess Louise's first opportunity to talk to her future husband at length.

Finally, Princess Louise's niece Dolla (the Margravine of Baden) adds an epilogue to the story. When Princess Victoria and Princess Louise returned to London from Russia, Louise gave

[1] King Haakon and Queen Maud of Norway.

Dolla and her sister the gold and platinum nuggets with which they had been presented during their trip. 'Later,' the Margravine says, 'we sold them and received so much for them that we were able to buy a little car!'

The Margravine also points out that, as Princess Louise and her mother were the last two non-Russian relatives to see the Tsar's family alive, they were therefore probably the last to see Anastasia. She says that, for two reasons especially, they were quite convinced that the woman who was saved from a suicide attempt in the Landwehr Canal in Berlin in 1921 was not Anastasia. Firstly, Baroness Isa Buxhoevden, who went with the Tsar's family to Ekaterinburg, and who had for years been their Lady-in-Waiting, was one of the first people to meet the self-aclaimed Anastasia at the mental hospital where she was taken after her rescue from the canal. 'I can remember,' says Dolla, 'her exact words when she told me about this meeting: *I stared at a completely strange woman and the strange woman stared back at me with total lack of recognition in her eyes.*'

Secondly, there was the question of Anastasia's hands. Relatives of the Russian royal family read with some scepticism newspaper articles about how the Grand Duchess Anastasia, with a royal gesture, had held out her hand for it to be kissed. 'Anastasia,' Dolla explains, 'would *never* have made such a gesture—anyhow not in that way. She had such a complex about her hands, which she thought were ugly—and they were, too!—that she always preferred to hold them behind her back. And Anastasia also had what we called the Hessian ears—the upper bit of the ear was as if squared off and the woman who purported to be the youngest daughter of the Tsar did not have them.'

# CHAPTER 2

# Prince Louis and Princess Victoria

U P to this time, and indeed until her marriage to King Gustaf VI Adolf in 1923, the centre of Princess Louise's life had been England and the great figure who undoubtedly stood out during her childhood was her father, Prince Louis of Battenberg. Prince Louis was a fine looking man with a handsome, open face and—although the Battenbergs had always been renowned for their courage, both as soldiers and statesmen—it was Prince Louis' great love of the sea that turned the name Battenberg into a naval legend. At the age of fourteen, isolated from the sea by the forests of Hesse, he had dreamed of becoming a naval officer. At that time, however, his dreams were scarcely realistic as in those days a German Navy as such did not exist. According to his diaries, Prince Louis first raised the question of going to sea in 1868. And when his parents asked him how he was going to make a career for himself at sea, he answered unhesitatingly that he wanted to join the British Navy.

This was, of course, a great source of worry to Prince Louis' parents, for they realized that if he joined the British Navy it would mean a complete break with his native country and a change of nationality. Prince Louis himself tells of the ensuing family battle in *Bachelor Recollections 1854–1884*, which he wrote specially for his children.

'My desires were discussed in the family,' he wrote, 'and met with great opposition, especially on the part of my mother. Your grandmother, Alice,[1] with whom I discussed my plans, encouraged me very much, for it was always understood that it was

[1] Second daughter of Queen Victoria and wife of Grand Duke Louis IV of Hesse (and thus also Prince Louis' first cousin by marriage).

the British Navy I was to enter. There was no German Empire at that time and the few Prussian ships which existed had been merged into a North German Confederation Navy.

'At last my father suggested as a compromise that I should enter the Austrian Navy, he himself being an Austrian General. But I stuck to my idea, saying that if I had to go into foreign service, I might as well enter the largest and most powerful navy, that of England. Very reluctantly my father finally gave in some time in the summer of 1868 and correspondence ensued with the British authorities through Cousin Alice[1] and her mother.'

In as much that the matter had been taken up at this level, the question was settled. Prince Louis' career will not be discussed in detail here but it is interesting to note some of the episodes and some of the testimonies from people who knew him.

'On October 14th, Dr Burney took me to a Notary Public at Gosport where I took the oath of allegiance to the Queen and was made to kiss a very dirty Bible. I then signed a paper making me a British subject. . . . On December 14th, I passed my examination at the Naval College and found it quite easy. . . . And now a change in my future plans. The Prince and Princess of Wales (Uncle Bertie and Aunt Alix) were going to start in January on a cruise round the Mediterranean in the frigate *Ariadne*, which was being specially fitted out for them. Your grandmama, Alice, his favourite sister, having asked the Prince of Wales to be kind to me, he promptly asked the Admiralty to appoint me to the *Ariadne* instead of the *Bristol*. I thus came in for a delightful cruise. . . .'[2]

Indeed it was a delightful cruise. Even Prince Louis' factual account of the royal party's life on board the *Ariadne* and the journey up the Nile has a flavour of the Arabian Nights about it and there is no doubt that its lavishness belongs to an era now wholly extinct, as the following passage from his memoirs shows.

---

[1] See footnote on preceding page.　　　　　　[2] From *Bachelor Recollections*.

'After two days' sightseeing in Cairo, we embarked for our journey up the Nile on February 6th. We had quite a flotilla: first came a large paddle steamer towing a barge or houseboat, on which a roomy deckhouse had been built containing cabins for Their Royal Highnesses and General Grey,[1] and his Swedish wife. The rest of the party had sleeping cabins in the steamer, where also all meals took place in the large deckhouse. This was followed by the kitchen steamer and the provision steamer carrying, *inter alia*, 1,000 bottles Champagne, 2,000 of Claret, 10,000 of Beer, 20,000 of Soda water etc. The last-named steamer towed a floating stable with Arabs for us to ride, and a splendid white donkey for the Princess.'

But all was indeed not royalty and brilliance. Louis of Battenberg made a thorough acquaintance with the hard life of a seaman:

'During the latter part of the cruise, when I was kept with the other Midshipmen with nose to the grindstone, I began to dislike the life on board and all its surroundings: hard work night and day in all weathers, horrid and insufficient food, rough handling in the Gun Room at all times and desperate home-sickness.'

But Prince Louis did not give up, and in examinations and in different kinds of service his talents, his good judgement and his whole personality began more and more to be noticed. During a significant part of his career Prince Louis acted as Chief Secretary to the joint Naval and Military Committee of Defence, and of this period Admiral Mark Kerr, in his biography of Prince Louis of Battenberg, wrote:

'At this time there was a great deal of friction between the Admiralty, and the War Office, and in this Prince Louis' extraordinary broadmindedness and tact were invaluable. . . . Colonel Sir Matthew Nathan, who was with Prince Louis on the joint

---

[1] This is almost certainly the General Grey who was Private Secretary to Prince Albert, the Prince Consort. After Prince Albert's death, he was taken on by Queen Victoria and thus became the first Private Secretary ever appointed to a British Sovereign.

Naval and Military Committee for the Defence of the United Kingdom, writes, with regard to their work, that he was struck by Prince Louis' attractive personality, his high intelligence, sound sense, and affection for the British Navy.'

At every new step in his career, similar judgements were reiterated and a captain who was one of Prince Louis' Assistant Directors summed up his opinion as follows:

'The personal charm and outstanding ability of Prince Louis earned for him as Director of Naval Intelligence at the Admiralty (as it always had done during his service afloat), the devotion and admiration of all those who had the privilege of serving under him. Directly after he had arrived his influence of revered leader was established.'

A characteristic which was especially notable in Prince Louis was that he never lost his temper and never showed anger. It was said within the family that he had only been angry twice in his life, and then it affected him so badly that both times he had to retire to bed.

To complete the picture we have a description of Prince Louis which appeared in an Australian newspaper, when as a young naval lieutenant in 1882 he took part in a British naval visit to Australia:

'Tall, well-made, with a carriage of the head which denotes high physical training and perfect "set-up", a well-moulded face, keenly intelligent, and a firm mouth.'

Prince Louis' career was constantly followed by success and in the spring of 1884 he married one of Queen Victoria's granddaughters, Princess Victoria of Hesse and the Rhine. Her father was Grand Duke Louis IV of Hesse and her mother was the same Princess Alice who had so strongly backed Prince Louis when he decided on a future in the British Navy, but more will be said about their courtship and marriage during the course of the chapter.

Prince Louis and Princess Victoria were extremely happy together; it is enough here to give an extract from a letter which Prince Louis wrote to a close friend, Commander the Hon. Francis Spring Rice (later Lord Monteagle of Brandon) on June 23, 1885:

'Now that I am married, I positively hate going to a ball alone, as I could not dance with the only woman I would care to. I should so much like you to make my wife's acquaintance. She is really more English than German, and we invariably speak English together, which may seem strange at first sight. She is a regular sailor's wife, and takes an immense interest in all naval matters. She knows all my naval chums and all about them, including yourself, of course. Now that I have got such a splendid lift through the yacht, *Victoria and Albert*, I am more keen than ever about serving on, and she is ready to go anywhere with me. We are not blessed much with earthly goods, and have to live in a small way, though we are happier for it, I believe.'

\*       \*       \*

Louise's mother (Princess Victoria of Hesse and the Rhine) was a colourful diarist with remarkable powers of observation and her *Recollections 1863–1914* give such an unusual picture of royal life at that time that the remainder of this chapter will consist of extracts from it.

'I was born,' she wrote, 'in the same room at Windsor Castle in which my (eldest) daughter Alice[1] was to be born, on Easter Sunday April 5th 1863. The day is supposed to be a very lucky one and those born on it are said to be able to see fairies and find hidden treasure—neither of which I have ever done.

'The bedroom I was born in was alongside the "Tapestry" Room—looking straight on to the Long Walk. I remember my grandmother sitting with me in the latter after Alice's birth and

[1] Princess Alice, the wife of Prince Andrew of Greece.

saying: "I detest this room". She told me that in it she had been terribly scolded by her mother who had accused her of making up to King William IV at the dinner he had given for her birthday, when he had drunk her health and insulted the Duchess of Kent.

'I had a heap of godparents; I was given the names of Victoria, Alberta (after the Prince Consort), Elizabeth (after my German grandmother), Matilda (in memory of the old Grand Duchess of Hesse), and Marie—one of my god-mothers being Queen Marie Amalie, widow of Louis Philippe, King of the French, who died a short time after my birth in 1866. She gave me a locket (which the Bolsheviks have)—a little round one with a *pavé* of pearls, separated by little brilliants, which contained a lock of her hair.

'I have heard from Princess Françoise, wife of Prince Christopher of Greece, that the little locket originally belonged to Marie Antoinette. I do not remember who my god-fathers were—one of them was Uncle Bertie, Prince of Wales.'

But she does remember that the whole of her father's cavalry brigade stood godfather to her!

Princess Victoria gives a series of tableaux of life in Darmstadt. There was her grandparents' old house, where she spent the first three years of her life, with its tiny hidden staircases which left such a strong impression on her infant mind that she said she used to dream of them for the rest of her life; and there was the New Palace, where the family moved in 1866.

In the summer of 1869 she remembers visiting her Prussian relatives and seeing Kaiser William II (then aged eleven) in a guards regiment parade, dressed in the complete uniform of a lieutenant—but being so short that 'his hand was held by a tall sergeant during the march past, to keep in pace with the men'. A highlight of their stay at the Prussian court was the visit to Berlin of the Khedive of Egypt and his son. Princess Victoria and William's nine year old sister Charlotte attended a ball in their honour.

'The Khedive's son was dressed in a little frock coat,' she wrote, 'with a Grand Cross and Star, and wore a fez on his head. He was about nine. He sat between Charlotte and me. As we could not talk to him (he only spoke his own language) to show our good will, we took turns in kissing his little yellow cheeks. He looked solemn and greatly bored.'

Another childhood memory was of being photographed.

'This was then a very lengthy proceeding. An iron support was put behind your head and one behind your waist to keep you quiet while the photographer counted up to ten, very slowly, for the exposure of the plate. As there were four of us and after a group each had to be done separately besides, the whole forenoon was spent on the operation. I read a little book most of the time which had lain on the photographer's table, of which I only remember there was a picnic party during which pancakes were made. So vivid was my recollection of that scene, that many years afterwards, when as a grown up woman I read Theodore Storm's *Immensée* I found the scene and knew it to be the book I had read!'

She remembers too, 'a little black servant girl my mother had in the sixties who wore a fez, a blue embroidered Zouave jacket and wide trousers. She served at table and sat on the seat behind my mother's in the pony carriage when she drove herself.'

A figure who stood out very clearly in her memory was Grand Duke Louis III of Hesse.

'He was immensely tall,' she says, 'and stooped very much when I knew him. He had two little stiff curls over his ears. Uncle Louis and my grandfather were most severely brought up. When, as children, they refused spinach and it was not all eaten up for dinner it was served for supper cold, and if some remained it reappeared at breakfast the next day. To go to their rooms at night they had to walk unaccompanied down a long unlit passage

and suffered agonies of terror from a tame raven which sometimes popped out on them.

'Uncle Louis still used the old fashioned mode of address to
the lower orders in the third person, "*Er*". An amusing incident
was told me in connection with this custom which occurred to
the Grand Duke of Saxe Weimar, the son of Goethe's patron.
He was driving from one of his castles to another and on coming
to crossroads, his coachman did not know which was the right
turning. The Grand Duke, seeing a man standing by, addressed
him: "Which is the way to Eisenbach?" "You must take the
turning to the right and drive straight ahead." "Must! Must!" the
old prince fumed. "He thinks he is the Grand Duke. He is stupid
enough for it."

'Grand Duke Louis' personal attendants were three brothers
Fleck who ran him and his household. One was his Major-domo,
one his valet and the third his coiffeur, and without them he never
went anywhere. He visited Marie Erbach, my sister-in-law soon
after her marriage at Schönberg, his carriage having been preceded by another containing his three Flecks. At lunch, unfortunately, he wanted to use his handkerchief—had not got one—
and in spite of the offer of a handkerchief on the part of his host,
he continued sniffling until his valet, who was walking in the
garden, came and produced one of the Grand Duke's own, the
size of a small tablecloth.

'He was a great collector of pipes and watches, which were
daily wound up. He made them into heirlooms in his will. His
valet smoked the meerschaums for him till they were the right
colour. He had the great merit of having put all the family's
country houses which he had found in great disrepair, into a
proper state again. In all these houses,[1] Uncle Louis arranged a
little apartment for himself, which he never allowed anyone else
to occupy, the bedrooms of which were identical in every house
—dark green wallpaper, mahogany furniture upholstered in green
rep. In each apartment there was a small collection of novels and

---

[1] Altogether the family owned some thirty castles, palaces and country houses in Hesse.

memoirs bound in black, as well as a musical stand for cigars, and a packet of payrus—stale tobacco wrapped in rice paper. By the time I took to smoking as a girl, and tried them, they tasted as if made of dust. All these places were visited by the Grand Duke in turn, usually for one night, and in the summer he gave Sunday family dinners in those that were not too far distant from Darmstadt. These dinners my mother was greatly bored by. They took place at 4.30 p.m. and spoilt the Sunday, when my father was free of his military duties, and we of our lessons. We often had to appear at the end of them, beautifully got up, and were presented with finger biscuits by the old gentleman, my mother having protested against the free distribution of sweets. We were amused, but also rather terrified by a series of grimaces our great Uncle produced for our benefit.

'In his latter years he married his housemaid, who was kept discreetly out of sight. She was an unassuming, kindly body and my mother befriended her after his death.'

Another intriguing figure was her grandfather Prince Charles of Hesse and the Rhine.

'He was a gentle person, lived a retired life and was very old-fashioned in his habits. He was a good looking man with a clean-shaven face, framed by side whiskers. He wore high cravats, like stocks, and fancy waistcoats and generally a frock coat. Out of doors, in winter, he always wore a black silk "respirator" over his mouth. He had a passion for collecting all kinds of odds and ends. He had a cabinet in his dressing room which was filled with all sorts of collections: in one drawer were seals cut off from envelopes. When enough seals were collected, they were melted down for a new stick of sealing wax. In another drawer, were used postage stamps and I was told the missionaries employed them in China—the Chinese were supposed to paper the walls with them. In a further drawer were old capsules from wine bottles and silver paper off chocolates. From this, lead spoons for orphanages were cast. He had also a number of small *bon-bonnières* which contained rolled breadcrumbs with which he fed the gold fish in his garden pond. When in his little house in Rosenhöhe he used to walk down a certain avenue after lunch, sucking a caramel, the coloured paper wrapper was always thrust into the same hole in an old tree. He was devoted to birds and had several cages with exotic birds in his room. In the winter evenings, he and my grandmother sat at a round table under the Holbein Madonna. He cut out pictures for scrapbooks. It was a great honour when one was allowed to assist him—and my grandmother knitted or read aloud. He was very kind to us little girls and we were fond of him. My grandfather died only three months before his brother—Grand Duke Louis III—so my father succeeded the latter as Grand Duke.'

Princess Victoria's grandmother (who was Princess Elisabeth of Prussia before she married Prince Charles) was also a sympathetic, if awesome, person. She was exceedingly shy and deeply religious. But, although old-fashioned in her views, she was still tolerant of young people's ideas and Princess Victoria can remember her listening with an amused smile as, at the age of sixteen, she lectured her grandmother on Home Rule for Ireland and the advantages of Socialism. Her grandmother often used to talk to her about her youth and recalled that she had been born on the day of the Battle of Waterloo; that Field Marshal Blücher and the Duke of Wellington were her god-fathers; and that her father, Prince William of Prussia, had lived for a year in Paris as a hostage to Napoleon. When Princess Victoria was confirmed, her grandmother gave her a special cross, with a gilded case inscribed with a verse from the Bible and in the centre of which was set an emerald. When the outer case was opened, a smaller enamel cross was revealed inside, which had been given to Princess Victoria for her baptism and which was embossed with jewels. The smaller cross was ornamented with a medal commemorating the Battle of Waterloo, and on the back of it, under

E

a little cover, was later placed a fragment of the wedding dress worn in 1221 by St Elisabeth,[1] who was the common ancestress of both Princess Victoria and Prince Louis.

To revert to the 1870s, Princess Victoria gives a delightful portrait of her parents. Her mother was passionately interested in music and was a great friend of the head of the music publishing house of Schott in Mayence, whom Princess Victoria describes as 'an old lady much painted and bewigged'. When Schott wanted to introduce new blood into the business she asked Princess Alice if she knew of anyone who would make a good partner. Princess Alice recommended Louis Strecker, who did so well that all Wagner's later operas were published by the House of Schott.

Princess Victoria describes her mother as 'interested in every kind of movement in her time' and she also knew many of their leaders. Professor David Strauss dedicated his *Life of Voltaire* to her and Princess Victoria remembers him coming to read the Voltaire manuscript to her mother in 1870, 'a very thin, dried up looking man'.

Like both her daughter and grand-daughter, Princess Alice was interested in the emancipation of women. Of a women's conference at Darmstadt in 1872, Princess Victoria wrote:

'I remember a Mrs Carpenter who was one of the guests at our house for the occasion, one of the initiators of the movement for

---

[1] Saint Elisabeth, the daughter of King Andrew of Hungary, was born in 1207 and at fourteen married the Landgrave Louis IV of Thuringia. She was one of the first followers of St Francis of Assisi and was famed for her kindness to her husband's harshly-treated subjects. According to legend, her husband forbade her to practise charity and when one day he surprised her leaving the castle with her apron full of bread, he demanded to know what she was carrying. 'Only roses,' she replied, and being challenged with 'a likely tale in mid-winter, show me,' she let her apron fall and found the bread had been turned into roses. St Elisabeth lived in the famous Wartburg Castle in Thuringia, the scene of the singers' contest in Wagner's opera *Tannhäuser*. In 1231 she died, only twenty-six years old, worn out by the austerity of her existence, and her tomb in Marburg in Hesse became a celebrated place of pilgrimage. Three centuries later her direct descendant, Landgrave Philip the Magnanimous of Hesse, secretly had her body removed and cremated, since he was the leader of the League of Protestant Princes, who supported Martin Luther, and believed it to be his duty 'to put an end to the idolatrous worship of saints'.

the education of women in India. I fancy it was also there I saw Miss Octavia Hill, whose educational work among the poor is well known. Women's welfare associations had already been started in Germany but in 1867 my mother founded the *Alice Frauenverein* (Women's Institute or Association) for Hesse, the chief branch of which was the training of Red Cross nurses. She consulted Florence Nightingale about the work and the first matron of their centre the Alice Hospital was trained in London under Miss Nightingale.

'Another branch took over the supervision of destitute orphans, provided for from the town rates, who by my mother's advice were given homes in respectable working men's families instead of being assembled in orphanages. When my mother married there was no provision in the country for lunatics and it was she who persuaded the state to take over a lunatic asylum she had started with the money collected by means of bazaars. She founded a shop called "Alice" Bazaar where poor ladies could be given work, which they sold. She further created a school where girls were given training as clerks and teachers of handicraft and needlework. This school has been taken over by the town and has now become a technical school for women workers.'

In their household in Darmstadt there were

'. . . certain fixed rules for our life, which my mother had adopted from those used in her youth. We rose early; when I was about thirteen, I remember my sister Ella and I getting up in the winter by candlelight, starting lessons at seven. We breakfasted with our parents at nine o'clock, and had an hour's exercise out of doors, after which we had what we called "little lunch" consisting of milk, fruit and biscuits at eleven, and at two o'clock we lunched with our parents. I would mention here that my mother adhered to the diet Queen Victoria and the Prince Consort had instituted for their children. We were never given spiced or rich food, simple dishes being served up for us. We never objected to anything given us at home, but the awful bread and butter puddings without a raisin in them or the stodgy tapioca pudding full of lumps we got in Queen Victoria's houses I still remember with a shudder of disgust. On the rarest of occasions were we given a sweet or a bon-bon, but we were always allowed a lump of sugar if we wanted something sweet, and to this simple fare I attribute my excellent digestion in after life. After lunch, we again went out for one and a half hours in all weathers and had schoolroom tea at five. This over, we went down to my mother's room, where we played with the younger children. We went to bed at six-thirty, later on at seven.'

The summer months were often spent at Kranichstein or else at Seeheim. At Kranichstein the young princesses used to go for long walks in the woods, each of them leading a Shetland pony and with Princess Alice's bull terrier, which had a mania for chasing wild boar. During one of these summers, 'Cousin Mary of Cambridge' (later Queen Mary of England) paid a visit and 'on leaving, presented my father with a light English boat for the lake instead of the clumsy old thing hitherto in use on it. In later years, I often rowed myself about in it and, if there was a breeze, employed a large Japanese parasol as a sail.'

Princess Victoria's father was a great lover of animals. They had a small roe-deer when they were children, and later dwarf sheep and dwarf goats in the garden. From time to time they would take in baby wild boar as pets, but they never got tame and they always had to be freed when they grew bigger. There was a fox that lived in the New Palace garden for many years and 'smelt abominably'. Also a lamb, 'which grew to be a big sheep, which we used to lead about by the collar and which did not always want to go in the direction we intended, coughing shockingly when it was half strangled in the tussle'. One day, it occurred to Princess Victoria that it would be better to tie the string to the sheep's leg instead, as its throat seemed to be becoming more and more sensitive. 'To our surprise and great amusement, when the dissension about the direction to be taken arose between it and us, the sheep immediately produced its usual strangled cough!' The royal children also kept countless white rabbits and guinea pigs in a small artificial warren in the palace garden, not to mention Turkish ducks 'that had bald necks and snapped at us'.

These days of joy came to an end suddenly. Early in November 1878 Princess Victoria fell ill with diphtheria.

'Well do I remember,' she wrote, 'the Saturday half holiday when, in spite of a very sore throat, I read aloud out of *Alice in Wonderland* to the little ones. That night I had high fever and, the illness being recognized, Ella[1] was moved downstairs to Irène's[1] room. When the latter, in her turn, developed the disease, Ella, still not showing signs of it, was sent to my grandmother and remained free of it. All the other children and my father went down with it in turn. My father was very ill and so was Ernie, and my poor little sister May died of it on November 16th. The disease was very virulent that year, and of course no serum existed at that time. Slowly the others all recovered, and rooms had already been taken for us at the big hotel above the old Schloss at Heidelberg to convalesce. Then my mother fell ill too, and we children were all moved to the Schloss in Darmstadt, only my father remaining at the New Palace with her. She had no strength left to resist the disease, thoroughly worn out as she was by nursing us all, and died on 14th December, the anniversary of the death of her beloved father.

'My mother's death was an irreparable loss to us all and left a great gap in our lives. She had, indeed, been the mistress of the house, a wise and loving wife and mother, whom we respected as much as we loved. My childhood ended with her death for I became the eldest and most responsible of her orphaned children.'

At the time of her mother's death, Princess Victoria was only fifteen years old. It was six years later, when she was twenty-one, that Princess Victoria married Prince Louis, who was her father's first cousin, the wedding taking place at Darmstadt in the spring.

[1] Princess Victoria's sisters.

Princess Victoria had, of course, known him for some time, but they first became close friends during the winter of 1882 when Prince Louis stayed with his parents at Darmstadt, after completing his world tour aboard H.M.S. *Inconstant*.

'We considered him our "English cousin", Princess Victoria wrote, 'and I have never forgotten how kind he was to Ella and me years before when we were schoolgirls and he was a young sub-lieutenant studying at Greenwich and lodging at Marlborough House, where he had a room every time when he came up to London. He was a very smart man about town yet found time to call on his two young cousins at Buckingham Palace. Our great ambition had been to go in a boat on the Buckingham Palace lake, but our governess would not allow it, if we had not an experienced person to take charge of us. Louis' visit was not an opportunity to be missed, and though he was in his best town clothes he good naturedly agreed to take us out for a row.'

Their wedding was somewhat dramatic. First, the bride's uncle Prince Leopold, Duke of Albany, had died suddenly at Cannes in March and the wedding had to be postponed. The postponement could not be for long, however, as it was considered imperative that the young couple should be married before May, since Queen Victoria had a strong superstition about the ill luck of May marriages. Secondly, on the evening of the wedding day, Princess Victoria's father was secretly married in a room in the Schloss to Alexandrine, daughter of Count Adam of Hutten-Chapsky, the divorced wife of M. de Kolemine, who was the Russian chargé d'affaires in Darmstadt.

'Influenced, I fancy, by Madame de Kolemine's dread of opposition to the marriage, nobody had been told of it, except his children and prospective sons-in-law,' Princess Victoria recalled, 'though Louis and Serge were in despair about it, they gave their promise to keep it a secret. We others quite liked the lady, who was full of attentions towards us, and I hoped my father would feel less lonely when married to a woman he was much in love with.

'On the next day, the secret came out. The Prussian family by order from above, left immediately. My grandmother and Uncle Bertie persuaded my father to have his marriage annulled, as they convinced him that the lady's past and reputation was such as to make it impossible for his young unmarried daughters, Irène and Alix,[1] to grow up in her care. The annulment took place almost immediately, she retaining the title of Græfin Romrod and receiving a large yearly allowance until her death, many years later—though, in the meanwhile, she had got married to a Russian diplomat, M. de Bacheracht. The episode was a nine days scandal in the whole of Europe, and a painful one for my father, alas.'

Such then were the exciting circumstances in which Princess Louise's parents met and were married, and the background against which her early life was lived.

[1] Princess Victoria's sisters.

# CHAPTER 3

## Early Life

PRINCESS LOUISE was born on July 13, 1889 at Heiligenberg Castle in Hesse, where Princess Victoria—since her husband was at that time serving in the Mediterranean Fleet—was staying with her mother-in-law Princess Julie of Battenberg. The baby arrived a fortnight before it was expected and Princess Victoria attributed Louise's early appearance 'to a drive along a rather rough road the day before she was born'. In her diary, Princess Victoria wrote: 'Unlike Alice, who was a fine sturdy baby, Louise was rather a miserable little object, and the nickname "Shrimp" which Louis then gave her, remained attached to her during her childhood.' On August 9th, Louise was christened at the Castle—her godparents being her father, her uncle Alexander (Sandro) formerly Prince of Bulgaria, her great-aunt Marie Duchess of Edinburgh, and her aunt Irène (Princess Henry of Prussia)—and she received the names of Louise Alexandra Marie Irène.

Louise's childhood was an extremely happy one, although her family seem to have been in a perpetual state of motion. Prince Louis was often away for long spells at sea and the family then usually stayed with relatives in palaces in different parts of Europe. Queen Victoria, who loved to assemble children, grandchildren and great-grandchildren round her, always received them with open arms at Osborne in the Isle of Wight. In the Queen's letters, collected and published in 1907,[1] visits by 'Victoria B. and her children' are often mentioned and Louise always remembered how Queen Victoria used to give the children a shilling for the collection at church on Sundays. 'But,' Louise once told a

---

[1] *Letters of H.M. Queen Victoria 1831-1861*, published on the authority of King Edward VII and edited by Arthur Christopher Benson and Viscount Esher. John Murray, 1907.

friend, 'it was with some hesitation that I put the shilling in. For, as children, we were brought up with very little money of our own.' The family was just as welcome at the homes of Princess Victoria's three sisters, and in a diary of the places where she lived from 1889 to 1923, Louise shows that her family scarcely ever remained in the same house both for summer and winter, especially up to the outbreak of the First World War. They alternated between Heiligenberg, Malta, Darmstadt and a variety of houses in England.

In those days it was of course unthinkable for a princess to go to an ordinary school and Louise's early education was undertaken by her mother. Princess Victoria was an astonishingly intelligent woman and from her Louise inherited a great deal of knowledge, as well as her fanatical interest in books. In fact, her mother took reading so seriously that she kept little notebooks in which she jotted down which books she had read each month and made little comments about them. All the family developed the habit of reading in several languages and Louise certainly read in four languages, while her brother Louis still consistently reads in three. Indeed, the whole atmosphere of their home was conducive to learning. Princess Victoria has been described as 'the most progressive woman of her era in any royal family' and Prince Louis was not only kind, thoughtful and an ideal father, but was also a man of great culture, being a fine artist and a fine musician, and it was one of his great delights to conduct his own orchestra or to play piano duets.

'Life at home,' Lord Mountbatten recalls, 'was absolutely delightful not only because we had extremely intelligent and high class parents but also because the whole family were devoted to each other. There is no doubt that my elder sister Alice and my elder brother George took more after their father—being extremely quiet, deep thinking and not very talkative, whereas my sister Louise and I took after my mother, and babbled endlessly. We talked the whole time. I wouldn't quite say we were extroverts but we did both talk a very great deal. All the same, my sister Alice and my mother were both very shy; also, they took no interest in clothes and disliked dressing up! And Princess Victoria's maid used to say that before a great function, such as a ball, when Prince Louis would have to wear full dress and Princess Victoria a train, tiara, jewels and decorations, the staff used to assemble in the hall to wait to see them depart; Prince Louis would come out nice and early, and walk up and down preening himself and smiling at the staff, and then at the last moment, the door would open and the Princess would rush out with her head lowered and race to the car!

'Louise and I were extremely close to one another, both when we were young and in later life. This may have been because her elder sister Alice married in 1903, our brother George in 1916 and she and I were married within a year of each other in 1923 and 1922 respectively, so we were the ones who were always at home together. But it was more than this, we thought the same, we spoke alike, we were deeply devoted to each other and we constantly corresponded with each other. And later, when we were married, we often visited each other, either I and my wife going to Sweden or she and her husband coming to Malta or to England.'

Eventually, during the part of the year when they were in Darmstadt, Princess Louise was sent to a form of day school, run for a select number of English girls by Fraulein Anna Textor, a distant relation of Goethe, and when they were in England there was a daily governess who taught Louise German and English.

The early part of Princess Louise's life was, of course, largely punctuated by family events. During the winter of 1890–1891, Prince Louis was in command of a small torpedo gun boat, H.M.S. *Scout* and so Louise was transported with her elder sister Alice and her mother to Malta. In April 1894, the family took Elm Grove, a house at Walton on Thames and there the Tsarevitch (who became Tsar Nicholas II in December of that year), stayed with them, so that he could see something of Louise's Aunt Alix, whom he married seven months later. After his visit, the family moved back to Heiligenberg Castle, from where the three children were sent for a month to Bad Kreuznach, for Louise to take the baths so as to strengthen her weak constitution. Louise seems always to have been 'taking the waters' that year (though she was only five) and in June, Aunt Alix wrote to her friend Polly Radcliff from Harrogate:

> Harrogate
> up on the Marlow Moors
> in a bath chair
> June 14, 1894

*'Darling Pollie,*

'I am staying up here and hasten to use the occasion to send you a few lines of love and tender thanks for your dear birthday letter which touched me deeply and gave me much pleasure. It is really the first warm day again though a strong wind is blowing up here. The view is lovely. A blue haze over the distant hills and a delicious breeze. Little Louise Battenberg is with me. I had begged Victoria to spare her for eight days and really she looks better since she is here and is taking one of the waters. It makes such a difference having a child in the room.

'The twins which turned up the day before we arrived were christened yesterday and I was Godmother to both Nicholas and Alix. Of course there was a crowd when we went to church though we tried to keep it secret.

'The people are a nuisance staring at one so. One feels such a fool. I bathe daily and take my water.

'What a disappointment you cannot come to England this year. It would have been such fun if we had met. I am leaving on the 19th or 20th for Walton when you can guess who is coming. After about three days we go then again to Windsor probably till the Queen goes to Osborne. A loving kiss

*Ever your devoted friend*
*Alix.'*

The year 1897, when Louise was eight years old, was one of great excitement, as it was Queen Victoria's Diamond Jubilee. The Battenbergs stayed at Kensington Palace for the celebrations and then spent part of the summer at Heiligenberg Castle and part at the new summer residence at Kiel called Hemmelmark, which had just been built by her Uncle Harry and Aunt Irène. Louise also retained vivid memories of the year 1899, when her father was appointed Assistant Director of Naval Intelligence at the Admiralty and they lived at 40 Grosvenor Gardens, near Victoria Station, where Louise often used to watch the troops marching off to the South African War—a scene that was re-called years later when she saw Noel Coward's play *Cavalcade*. The winter of 1900 was spent at 4 Hans Crescent, London so as to be near Prince Louis, who was working at the Admiralty. Christmas of that year was a quiet one, as Queen Victoria was ill and on January 22, 1901 she died. All the family went to the funeral, including Louise, who had always been extremely fond of the old Queen.

Towards the end of 1901, Prince Louis decided that the time had come to acquire a house of his own in Malta, since he so often served in the Mediterranean Fleet, and so he bought the Palazzo Scaglia at 52 Strada Mezzodi (now re-named South Street) next door to Admiralty House, the Commander-in-Chief's residence in Valletta. The family's only permanent home had always been and really remained Heiligenberg Castle, which Prince Louis inherited from his father in 1888, though they invariably rented houses in England when Prince Louis was serv-ing at the Admiralty or on the home station. Prince Louis had always kept up the Heiligenberg estate and spent as much of his leave there as possible. It was also at the Heiligenberg estate that the family kept their large possessions, furniture, pictures etc. and they regarded it as their central base.

The whole family loved Heiligenberg, which Princess Louise's Aunt Marie described in her *Memoirs* as 'scenery of the Rhine valley, smiling, beautiful, rolling countryside, forest-clad hills, a

romantic landscape which binds its inhaibtants with strong ties.'
But they also became extremely fond of Malta. At Malta they
loved the sea, the enchanting Mediterranean climate, and the
lively garrison life. As a matter of fact Lord Mountbatten's first
clear memory of his sister comes from Malta, from the days when
their father was Second-in-Command of the Mediterranean Fleet.
Lord Mountbatten was then aged seven—and already developing
a passion for the sea—and Louise was eighteen. 'I remember her
dancing and flirting with the officers from the British naval station,'
he says, 'she was very beautiful at that time, before ill health had
made her so thin.' Because of Lord Mountbatten's naval career,
Louise often went back to Malta and it was there, in October 1952,
that she and Lord Mountbatten narrowly escaped death. Lord
Mountbatten had become a great aqualung enthusiast and had
spent the day spear fishing off the island of Comino (the same
place where he successfully speared a 230 lb. sting ray on another
occasion). Louise had spent the day on his barge, and in the
evening they landed at Marfa and drove back in two cars. Lord
Mountbatten was driving ahead in his small Riley, with his sister
beside him and her Mistress of the Robes, Astrid Rudebeck, in
the back seat; and behind them, in the official Rolls Royce, came
King Gustaf Adolf, Lord Mountbatten's wife, Edwina, and Nils
Rudebeck, the Lord Chamberlain at the Swedish Court. Lord
Mountbatten had been diving up to depths of one hundred feet
and was quite exhausted. As they drove along, he felt himself
becoming drowsy, his foot must have slipped off the accelerator,
the car slowed down, gradually ran into a stone wall near St Paul's
Bay and turned over completely on its side. Louise fell on top of
her brother, bruising her knee on the steering column, and
Astrid Rudebeck's back was bruised, but otherwise there were no
injuries. One can imagine the shock to the King and Lady
Mountbatten as they drove into sight and saw the car lying over-
turned in the road. They of course ran over to the car, wrenched
the door open and pulled the occupants out, and at that moment
a lorry with twenty Royal Marine commandos in it, appeared

round the bend. Lord Mountbatten stopped them, instructed them to gather round and lift up his car, and they were able to set it back on its wheels at once. He then asked them not to tell anyone of the incident, so as to avoid unfortunate publicity in the press. And the Royal Marines proved so loyal that not one of them leaked a word to the newspapers and the world was robbed of the headline 'Commander-in-Chief overturns the Queen of Sweden in his car'.

To revert to Louise's early life, the family only lived in Malta while Prince Louis was Captain of the *Implacable*, from 1901 to 1902, and while he was Second-in-Command of the Mediterranean Fleet, from 1907 to 1908. But when, to his surprise, Prince Louis was appointed Commander-in-Chief of the Atlantic Fleet, they then sold the house. During the summer of 1903 they had borrowed a delightful country house at Sopwell, near St Albans, which belonged to the Earl of Verulam, but at this time they had no real permanent home in England, although they once actually bought a plot of land and a farmhouse intending to convert it, but it never proved more than a dream and the family continued to move from one residence to the next.

In the summer of 1906 Louise had her first taste of flying. While staying at Heiligenberg she was taken up in a blimp airship of the Parsifal type—with her young brother Dickie (Earl Mountbatten of Burma) hoisted aboard in lieu of ballast. As the heat of the sun had expanded the gas in the airship, the captain wanted to wait for some more sandbags. The next moment, the Grand Duke of Hesse picked up Dickie by the scruff of the neck and shouting 'This will do for ballast!' swung him into the gondola. The Battenberg family were all keen flying enthusiasts and in 1909 they went to the international flying exhibition, at Frankfurt on Main, where among other of the great pioneers they saw Bleriot. Many of the machines never got off the ground at all and when any of them did succeed in taking off there was always a great shout of triumph and the aircraft often proved remarkably manœuvrable, flying under stretched ropes and accomplishing wonderful feats of aerobatics. In June 1911 Princess Louise had her first opportunity to fly in a heavier-than-air craft. It was a 'Stringbag' biplane, built by Short. Air Chief Marshal Sir Arthur Longmore (then a lieutenant in the Navy) took up Louise and Dickie from the Naval Air Station at East-church in the Isle of Sheppey—and Louise, who must have been one of the first women ever to fly, had to sit on the petrol tank behind the pilot's shoulders, holding on to a couple of struts.

In November 1909 the Battenberg family stayed at Windsor for a couple of nights for the visit of King Manuel of Portugal. While they were there a fishbone stuck in Louise's throat and she had to be taken to hospital. 'We went to St George's,' Princess Victoria relates, 'thinking that it could be quietly pulled out in the Outpatients Department. Unfortunately, when they heard our names, we were taken round to the big hospital and ushered into a special room where the "extraction" took place. By ill luck a reporter was in the hospital, enquiring after some accident case, and so the story of Louise's treatment was in the papers next day, causing a lot of unnecessary enquiries.' Later that year King Manuel of Portugal asked for Louise's hand in marriage. He was very much in love with her and Edward VII was delighted. As ruler of the British Empire, it suited him admirably that yet another member of the English Royal Family should grace a foreign throne. But both kings were doomed to disappointment. Neither King Manuel's attempts to gain her affections nor Edward VII's powers of persuasion were enough to induce Louise to accept. King Edward sent for her and told her it was her duty to agree to the young Portuguese monarch's proposal, but Louise replied that she found the prospect of becoming a Queen quite frightening and, in any event, the most important thing was lacking—she was not in love with Manuel. So it was, that even before the First World War, a Queen's crown hovered over Princess Louise's head, but it was just as well for Louise that she refused—for in October of the next year revolution broke out in Portugal and the entire Portuguese royal family were driven from the country.

About the same time Louise began to take a real interest in charitable work. The next winter she and Nona Kerr became very busy with 'Happy Evenings'. These were arranged by Lady Dallas in Bermondsey and their aim was to provide entertainment and to supervise games for small boys. The evenings were extremely popular with the children and were held in a local school until the Council said they could not see their way to lend it for the purpose any longer. Also, Louise and Nona became interested in a young Cockney couple called Hiscock. They had several small children, but the husband could not find work and they were almost starving. Eventually, arrangements were made for the Hiscocks to emigrate to Newfoundland where Mr Hiscock found a steady job and their children were able to grow up in better conditions. Louise was very attached to the family and continued to keep in touch with Mrs Hiscock until her death.

In December 1912 Prince Louis became First Sea Lord and so the family moved to his official residence at Mall House in the northern Wing of Admiralty Arch. This was the peak of Prince Louis' career and in some ways the peak of happiness for his family, for although he had reached the highest position in the British Navy and had proved himself to be the man most fitted to handle the Supreme Command, within less than two years he had toppled from power. During the early stages of World War I Britain was swept by a wave of hatred for all things German. German governesses were insulted; dachshunds were kicked in the streets; no band would dare play *Tannhauser* or *The Ring* because Wagner was German; shop-keepers who had been in England for generations but who had German-sounding names had their shops broken into and looted; even Lord Haldane, who had been responsible for the modernization of the Army and its readiness for war, was attacked because he had attended a German university; and in the hysteria of the moment, despite the skill and foresight he had shown as First Sea Lord, Prince Louis could hardly hope to escape suspicion. Gradually, rumours and agitation began to mount against him; slogans appeared more and more frequently in the newspapers, repeating vehemently that 'a Prince of German origin may not lead England's Navy into war' and that 'Louis Battenberg must go'. Then, steadily, the press whipped up a frenzied campaign which reached its climax on October 28th (not long after Princess Louise returned from her journey to Russia described in Chapter I). A newspaper published on one page a glowing tribute to Prince Maurice of Battenberg, who had been killed during the Retreat from Mons and was the first member of the royal family to give his life for his country, and on another page in the same issue featured a libellous attack on the loyalty of Prince Louis. This was the last straw. Prince Louis felt that such an attack could undermine public confidence in the Navy and so, on the following day, tendered his resignation to the First Lord.

The same evening the King wrote in his diary:

'Have spent a very tiring and strenuous day. At 11.30 I received Winston Churchill who informed me that Louis of Battenberg had tendered his resignation as First Sea Lord. The Press and the public have expressed so many apprehensions as to his German origins and maintained that he should not hold the highest Command of the Navy. Finally, he had no choice. I feel deeply with him: there is no more loyal man in this country.'

The events of the days preceding the outbreak of World War I have been woven into a narrative by Earl Mountbatten of Burma and Queen Louise, in which they describe how Prince Louis virtually took upon his own shoulders the whole responsibility for the test mobilization of the British Fleet. This document, which is given on the next page, was drawn up less than a year before Queen Louise's death.

F

STANDING THE FLEET FAST IN 1914

*The part played by the First Sea Lord, Admiral Prince Louis of Battenberg (later Admiral of the Fleet, the 1st Marquess of Milford Haven).*

*Lord Mountbatten's statement*

'I remember discussing events which occurred during my father's time at the Admiralty with him, after I myself joined the Royal Navy as a Cadet in May 1913, at various times up to his death in September 1921 when I was a Lieutenant, R.N. The events during the last week of July were frequently gone over with the family, and they became graven on our memories.

'I remember his explaining to me his responsibilities when he was Director of Naval Intelligence from 1903 to 1905 and being greatly struck that his staff was in fact the only "Naval Staff" as we now understand it. Under him, among other divisions was one that dealt solely with the Mobilization of the Fleets for War.

'I know that he attached great importance to the Mobilization division, and my father was always rather worried whether the vast and elaborate organization set up on paper to recall all the reservists and arrange for them to man the ships of the Reserve Fleet and get them to sea and worked up would in fact work smoothly in practice.

'When he became 2nd Sea Lord, in charge of Naval Personnel, in December 1911 he began to think of having a "Test Mobilization", but he did not wish to rush matters and had not yet his scheme up in writing, when in December 1912 he became the 1st Sea Lord. Other pressing matters engaged his attention, but he had not forgotten his great scheme for a Test Mobilization and during 1913, with the agreement of the new 2nd Sea Lord, Vice-Admiral Sir John Jellicoe, he raised the matter with the First Lord, Mr Winston Churchill. After the latter had given the matter further thought he himself wrote the memorandum suggesting that a Test Mobilization of the Third Fleet should be held.

'To mobilize could be construed as a provocative act by powers who feared Great Britain, and so the Foreign Office was asked to clear with all interested powers, the staging of a Test Mobilization in July 1914 by the Royal Navy; and an announcement was made in Parliament in the Spring of 1914.

'During the holidays my father, who often discussed naval matters with my brother and myself, told us of this pet scheme of his. He explained that the Midshipmen for the Reserve Fleet would be found by the Naval Cadets from the Training Cruiser and the Royal Naval College, Dartmouth. Cadets at the Royal Naval College, Osborne (where Cadets spent their first two years before going on to Dartmouth) would not be required to man the Reserve Fleet.

'Naturally I, who would have completed my fourth term at Osborne, was indignant at being left out. My father, however, set my mind at rest by saying that the Osborne Cadets would be divided among the Capital Ships and Cruisers of the Active Fleet, to witness the Mobilization and the visit of the King to the Fleet at Spithead. He said we would be allowed to stay for the "Steam Past" the King and the Tactical Exercises (known by the Fleet Signal Book Group "PZ") but that we would be disembarked before the Fleet moved to Portland and Weymouth Bay for their main exercises.

'And so it was. My father thoughtfully arranged that I should be "mobilized" on board my brother's ship, the Battle Cruiser *New Zealand*, whilst he and the First Lord, Mr Winston Churchill shared the Admiralty yacht, *Enchantress*.

'For the late summer of 1914, the Emperor Nicholas II of Russia had lent his Imperial River Yacht, (specially constructed on the Volga for the celebrations of the Tercentenary of the House of Romanov the year before) to his sister-in-law, the Grand Duchess Sergius (my Aunt Ella) who had invited my mother (her elder sister) and my sister Louise to join her on the Volga in mid-July. It had been arranged that my father and I should go out to join them at the end of July.

'The officially advertised dates for the Test Mobilization were from Wednesday 15th to Monday, July 27th. The combined Home Fleets were to concentrate at Spithead for the review by King George V from the 17th to the 18th July. Some 20,000 men were to man ships of the Reserve Fleet who were put into commission and joined the Active Fleet. So far as I can remember ships of the Active Fleet had their complements brought up to full war strength and the exercises and manoeuvres which took place ensured that virtually the whole of the Royal Navy was at a strength and pitch of training never before achieved in history.

'The cadets from R.N.C. Osborne went direct from Cowes and joined the Fleet on the morning of Saturday, July 18th. After the "Steam Past" and "PZ" we were disembarked off Cowes on the afternoon on Monday, July, 20th after which the vast Fleet sailed for exercises based on Portland.

'We had to complete our examinations at Osborne and broke up some ten days later. I went to London to stay with my father in the First Sea Lord's official residence in the Admiralty Arch, known as "Mall House" and stayed there alone with him. We had all our meals together, nearly always alone, and as I was in the Navy (albeit very junior) he talked with complete candour of the problems with which he was dealing. In particular I remember his discussing with some emotion the critical week-end he had passed alone, just before I arrived.

'I distinctly remember his remarking to me that politicians were incorrigible, for with a real world crisis blowing up the First Lord of the Admiralty had gone to Cromer for the week-end leaving him in sole charge. He explained that the constitution of the Board of Admiralty was different to other ministries as it was not one of the other Admiralty Ministers who took over the responsibility for the Navy, but the First Sea Lord, who was an officer and not a Minister. On top of this, he said, that the vital cabinet Ministers, such as the Prime Minister and Foreign Secretary had all gone away for the week-end, leaving him very much alone in charge of the Navy at the moment of the country's greatest peril.

'My father told me the situation looked so bad that he had telegraphed to my mother to say we could not leave on July 31st, as arranged, to join them in Russia and urged her to return. My mother, her Lady-in-waiting, Nona Kerr, and my sister Louise had great difficulties in getting back via Sweden and Norway, arriving home in mid-August.

'My father told me that at breakfast time on Sunday 26th Mr Churchill rang him up from Cromer for news. My father made it clear that the situation was deteriorating. At lunch time another telephone conversation took place and my father warned him that war looked more and more likely, and that a decision was required that very day whether to let the Test Mobilization end the following morning, when the Fleet were due to disperse, or whether the Fleets were to be ordered to "stand fast".

'It appears that Mr Churchill reminded my father that in his absence the First Sea Lord was in sole charge and would have to make the decision himself. He reminded him of the political implications of not ending the Mobilization on the advertised date.

'When it became quite clear to my father that he was not going to get any advice he realized that he had no alternative but to stand the fleet fast himself. So he went ahead and on his own authority cancelled the Demobilization Orders so as to hold the fleet in readiness for war and informed the Foreign Office and the King of his decision.

'As the Admiralty was, as usual, deserted on the Sunday afternoon my father and the resident clerk had to write out all the telegrams and send them off themselves and see to the consequential actions.

'My father explained to me that he considered he had no choice. Had he allowed the Fleets to be demobilized, disperse to home ports and give general leave on July 27th it would have been an extremely difficult and lengthy task to collect men together again had war broken out during the next few days. Most reservists had planned to join their families direct at their holiday resorts and holiday addresses were not recorded in the Admiralty.

'Either the Combined British Fleets could be in a state of unparalleled readiness for war or dispersed, disbanded and becoming every day less ready than at any other time to meet the possible immediate threat of the High Seas Fleet and U Boats. But the great risk my father took knowingly was that had war not broken out and the Austrians or Germans had lodged complaints about our continuing our mobilization he would have been held responsible for this provocative act. He realized that in the circumstances it was he who would become the scape goat, but he also felt that this unapproved act might not be unwelcome to the Cabinet since their hand would be strengthened in the negotiations with Germany and Austria.

'In fact when the First Lord and other Ministers returned to London on Sunday night they fully approved the action my father had taken, without Ministerial instructions or advice.

'In his letter of October 29th, 1914 accepting my father's resignation as First Sea Lord Mr Churchill generously gives him the credit for the action he took for he wrote:

> "The first step which secured the timely concentration of the Fleet was taken by you." '

*(signed) Mountbatten of Burma*
*Admiral of the Fleet*
May 18th, 1964

*Queen Louise's statement*

'Although I was away from England from mid-July to mid-August for the reason given in my brother's statement, the events of that month; and more particularly of the fateful last week in July were the subject of several family discussions after my mother and I returned.

'I cannot of course confirm all the naval details my brother gives in his statement, but I well remember hearing from my father of the events, in particular of the weekend of July 25th and of his telephone conversations with Mr Churchill. Neither I, nor anyone really close to my father at that time can be in the least doubt that he made the decision to stand fast the Fleets on July 26th alone and unaided and took the full responsibility.'

*(signed) Louise*
*Queen of Sweden*
May 19th, 1964

Both Louis and Louise were deeply affected by the news of their father's resignation and, as Alden Hatch wrote in *The Mountbattens—The Last Royal Success Story*, on the day that the news reached the cadet school at Osborne in the Isle of Wight where Dickie was training, another cadet Stephen Fry happened to go out into the great hall where a mast had been erected, rigged as on a ship. Beside the mast stood a small cadet who evidently thought he was alone. He was standing staring out into the October rain, making no attempt to hide the tears which were pouring down his cheeks. It was Dickie. All his friends knew how proud he had always been of his father's brilliant success. 'Fry was old enough to realize that he was witnessing a moment of genuine tragedy, but of course he did not know that he was seeing the psychological birth of Earl Mountbatten of Burma.'[1]

Lord Mountbatten's memory of the events leading up to his father's resignation is still extremely vivid.

'The Coming of the First World War,' he says, 'was a most appalling shock to the family, because they were completely British, every one of them, even my father who only became naturalized in 1868. They thought of themselves as completely British, and yet had homes and friends and relations in Germany. So now, they were fighting the Germans who were behaving outrageously and deeply offending all the susceptibilities of the family. On the other hand, relations in Russia were allies and fighting on our side, and so were the Italians, and it must be remembered that the Queen of Italy was the sister of Princess Anna, who married Prince Francis Joseph of Battenberg—our father's youngest brother. So it was a terrible matter for the family, adjusting themselves to this. And yet, their heart was so completely in the British war effort that it was sadness at Germany's behaviour which upset them most.

'Our father's resignation cut up Louise very, very much. She knew what the Navy meant to her father, she knew that from 1868–1914, almost half a century, he had given up his entire life to the Navy. It was his one passion and his one joy, his one pride. Few had done more than he to bring the Navy really to perfection—it was his idea to have the test mobilization, he personally took the responsibility of standing the Fleet fast—as he himself put it—he presented England with a drawn sword in her hand against Germany.'

So, as Princess Alice recalls, 'when the rumours started and the troubles, Louise and all the rest of us felt it very much'.

\*　　　\*　　　\*

Fortunately, the considerable will-power with which both

[1] Alden Hatch, *The Mountbattens—The Last Royal Success Story*. London: W. H. Allen, 1966.

Prince Louis and his wife were blessed was inherited by their children, for the sequence of events which led up to 1914 was a test of their courage in more ways than one. As has been seen, the campaign which caused their father's resignation was a terrible blow for the family, and against the background of the developing war the presence of this personal tragedy cast a sense of unreality over their lives.

August began with suffocating heat and war. Young men crowded to the recruiting offices and were rapidly trained then sent to the trenches, in many cases to death; and the young women of the family also did what they could for the country. Louise and her friend Alicia Knatchbull-Hugessen (later Mrs Clive Pearson) went to work for the Soldiers and Sailors Families Association and then after that for an organization which Lady Denman started in her London house, 4 Buckingham Gate, called Smokes for Soldiers and Sailors, which sent cigarettes and tobacco to soldiers in the trenches and to crews of ships. They used to go to 4 Buckingham Gate, every morning, and would stay there all day. Alicia was among Louise's closest friends and, although Princess Louise was not by nature a games player, in the days before World War I the two of them used to love to go roller-skating or ice-skating together. Curiously, Alicia was the daughter of the first Lord Brabourne and today Louise's niece, Patricia Mountbatten, is married to the seventh Lord Brabourne. When they were children, Princess Louise gave her the nickname 'Ali' because of the popular paper *Ally Sloper's Half Holiday*, then it was changed to 'Sloper' and as 'Sloper' she was known ever after.

After the New Year, however, Louise decided that the work she was doing was not enough. She felt that her place was in a military hospital and that her knowledge of French and German would be an advantage nearer the Front. She therefore turned to Mrs Beryl Oliver (later Dame Beryl Oliver) of the Red Cross, who was head of a detachment of 23,000 women volunteers trained in first-aid and in nursing, known as the V.A.D. or

Voluntary Aid Detachments. So, as soon as Louise had completed the necessary training, Mrs Oliver arranged for her to go to a French Military hospital at Nevers on the River Loire and she clearly remembers the report which was later sent in by the doctor under whom Princess Louise worked: his name was Dr Haden Guest (later Lord Haden Guest) and he commended the young princess for the splendid work she had done.

As Beryl Oliver points out, Princess Louise must have worked under particularly difficult circumstances. World War I was a much more 'unpleasant war' then the Second World War. There were the dank trenches where the soldiers had to stand, up to their waists in muddy water, day and night during the heavy autumn rain. There was the lack of proper equipment for treating severe wounds, and one has to remember that penicillin had not been discovered, that blood transfusions were rarely given and that, when they were, patient and donor had to lie so close to each other that there was often a risk of infection and very often the donor died from blood poisoning. In World War I it is estimated that 702,410 British soldiers were killed; while during World War II the number is said to have been only about 264,443.

The hospital to which Princess Louise was sent in Nevers was situated in the administration building of a railway repair yard and with two of the nurses, Miss Ida Wheatley and Miss Eardley-Wilmot, Princess Louise formed life-long friendships.

I met Miss Wheatley at her little house with its garden of lavender and roses, which was part of a farm outside Kenilworth in Warwickshire. She told me that after Louise became Queen she still corresponded with her regularly, and that whenever Louise visited England she always went to see her. In fact, the day that Queen Louise died Miss Wheatley received a letter from her in which Louise wrote that she felt very depressed and thought she would never get well again.

In Nevers—Miss Wheatley recalled—the railway workshops where the hospital was situated had originally been designed to serve the Paris–Lyons railway. The Administration Block was converted into a hospital by Mrs Robert Woods-Bliss whose husband was the American Minister in Stockholm for a few years during the 1920s, and as a result Princess Louise and Mrs Woods-Bliss became firm friends. The railway lines ran practically up to the building, so the wagons could discharge their loads of wounded directly into the hospital. After a major engagement such as Verdun, the railway wagons would arrive during the evening and then the nurses would often have to work for as much as thirty-six hours at a stretch.

Princess Louise, Miss Wheatley says, did not have a strong constitution but she did possess stamina. She worked extremely hard, did her share of heavy chores, just like any other nurse, never took a rest from her duties and, on the one occasion when she was forced by mumps to rest, Miss Wheatley looked after her herself. Miss Wheatley also dispelled the myth which has from time to time been printed in Swedish newspapers, that the Queen used to sit holding the hands of dying men. 'We never had time for that sort of thing. But part of our duties was, of course, helping the most severely wounded men to write home to their families. One got used to watching young men dying, for then they didn't have to suffer any more. But what we never got used to, was the tragedy of those who had had half their faces shot away. We never knew what to say to them and we had to be careful to keep mirrors away from them.'

At Christmas, the staff tried to arrange some type of entertainment for the wounded. Eardley-Wilmot (they always used surnames) wrote a play and Wheatley played the part of a *poilu* in uniform, with her hair stuffed inside an army cap and a pipe hanging out of the side of her mouth. But 'we'd never have got Princess Louise to do such a thing. She hated performing. You might get her to play a little part perhaps, but she was a very bad actress.'

Once, in the summer of 1916, Princess Victoria obtained permission to visit her daughter and was allowed to stay for twelve hours. That same day a large offensive took place and the hospital staff received orders to send on all patients who could be moved. Every able bodied person was needed to help, so Princess Victoria offered her services. She knew nothing of nursing, she said, but could always scrub. Instead, however, she received a most un-royal job and spent the night escorting wounded men to and from the latrines.

The hospital in Nevers was not the only one in which Princess Louise served. In 1917, she moved on to the Princess Club Hospital in Bermondsey for a year and in the Spring of 1919 spent three months working in a French hospital for bone T.B. at Palaves, near Montpelier. As a result of her hospital work Princess Louise was awarded the War Medal of Great Britain 1914–18 and the British Red Cross Medal as well as the Medaille de la Reconnaissance Fran‚aise and the Italian Red Cross Medal. For a long time afterwards grateful patients continued to write to her and the letters nearly always began *Chère Sisteur*—a wonderful mixture of English and French.

The Battenberg family must have looked back on the period of World War I as the hardest years of their lives. Not only had they been shaken by Prince Louis' resignation, but also by the fate of many of their relatives abroad. In 1917, the Russian Revolution had broken out and the next year the entire Imperial family were murdered, among them two of Princess Victoria's sisters—Ella, who had married the Grand Duke Sergius Alexandrovitch, and Alix, who was the wife of the Tsar. Then in 1918 many of their German relations lost their thrones, including Princess Louis' brother, the Grend Duke Ernest Louis of Hesse, while another of Princess Victoria's sisters, Princess Irène of Prussia, had to flee from the naval mutineers in Kiel. And on top of all this there had been great political unrest in Greece, which led to the assassination of King George I and the exile of other members of the Royal family including Louise's brother-in-law and sister, Prince Andrew and Princess Alice.[1]

---

[1] See Introduction, pages 35-37.

In these years, the Battenbergs suffered financially too. The family had never been either very rich or very poor, but they did possess the splendid castle of Heiligenberg with its estates and farm lands, and the castle was kept up permanently with a resident staff. In the Court Guide of the Grand Duchy of Hesse, you will find Lady-in-Waiting, Chamberlain, Private Secretary, Butler, Valet, Footman and domestic staff permanently employed, quite apart from the staff in England who were either engaged locally or taken there from Heiligenberg. In addition to that Prince Louis had quite a large sum invested in platinum mines in Russia through his brother-in-law, the Tsar, which brought in a good dividend, and Princess Victoria also had a certain amount of money of her own. The Russian revolution, however, destroyed their income from the platinum mines and resulted in the confiscation of Princess Victoria's jewels. Then, after the war, they sold the castle in Germany for three quarter of a million marks—but just after the sale, the mark crashed and so they only got a fraction of its value. Nevertheless, both Prince Louis and Princess Victoria still had some money invested in England and the family were never conscious of being pressed for money. In 1902 or 1903 Prince Louis had acquired one of the first Wolseleys (he was the first member of a royal family ever to own a motor car, even before King Edward VII) and from then on they always had a motor car and, in addition to the normal staff, always kept a chauffeur.

However, the family were forced to make some economies. After Prince Louis' resignation as First Sea Lord they of course had to leave Mall House and they found refuge in Kent House on the Isle of Wight.[1] Now, they found that Kent House was too big and so they were delighted when Colonel Richard Crichton—who had recently married Nona Kerr—offered to make available to them his charming little house near Netley in Hampshire, which

---

[1] Kent House had once belonged to Queen Victoria's mother, the Duchess of Kent. She left it to her grand-daughter, Princess Louise, Duchess of Argyll. She, in turn, now gave it to Princess Victoria and so Kent House became the Battenbergs' first real home in England.

was called Fishponds. Besides gaining the benefit of a more manageable house, they were also glad to be saved the inconvenience of having to cross to and fro to the Isle of Wight by steamer.

By now, as a result of the announcement of July 1917, the family's name had, of course, been changed from Battenberg to Mountbatten.[1] Prince Louis was now the Marquess of Milford Haven: Princess Victoria, the Marchioness of Milford Haven. 'Dickie' became Lord Louis Mountbatten and Princess Louise, Lady Louise Mountbatten.

Life after the First World War was for Louise particularly forlorn. As she told her niece, Dolla (Margravine Theodora of Baden), some years later, she found herself 'figuratively and almost literally in a no-man's-land'. All the young men she and her contemporaries had danced with in the palaces of Europe, with whom they had gone on picnics and with whom they had fallen in love, were now dead. So thoroughly had death done its work on the battlefield, that they felt the most terrible loneliness. And so, finding herself in a new and crueller world, Louise now tried to help those who were less well off than herself. She had already begun to take an interest in social work during the years just before the war, particularly in the Battersea district, where she had done a good deal of children's welfare work; and now her sense of social responsibility which according to her friends Louise possessed at an early age, had been increased by her nursing experience during the war.

Before, during their period in Malta, Louise had led a very gay life. She went to fancy dress parties, to balls and picnics, and followed the usual social round of a lady of her position. As a debutante, of course, she was carefully chaperoned, when she went to parties or for country house weekends, but she managed to meet plenty of people and was gay and enjoyed herself immensely. Then later, her dealings with boys' clubs and her charity work suddenly brought her up against hardship and when she was a nurse in France, the conditions were far worse than in any

---

[1] See page 27.

hospital for British troops. Consequently, after the war, she had no desire to resume the gay life. The war had matured her and brought her face to face with suffering and, being politically conscious, she was distressed to discover how much poverty and misery there was in the world.

Her post-war life was not all sadness, however. Louise managed to do quite a lot of travelling immediately after the war, including a visit to relations in Switzerland and to her uncle, the Grand Duke of Hesse at Schloss Tarasp, at Vulpera, one of the most famous and dramatic castles in the world She also managed to stay with her sister Alice on Corfu, which made a pleasant break after the war and also a visit to Rome with her parents. Then, in August 1921, there came the event which brought great gladness to the family and softened the bitterness of Prince Louis' resignation, when as a form of somewhat tardy amends Prince Louis (now the Marquess of Milford Haven) was appointed to the rank of Admiral of the Fleet on the Retired List. The First Lord of the Admiralty, Lord Lee of Fareham, wrote to the Marquess on August 10, 1921:

'Nothing has ever given me greater satisfaction than to be able, after waiting seven years for the opportunity, to do the only thing that now is possible to right a great wrong, and to give effect to what, I am convinced, would be the unanimous desire of the whole Naval Service.'

Although the reparation came a little late, for the Marquess was now sixty-seven years old, nevertheless it was accentuated by an extra pleasure which meant a great deal to him; for he was invited to join in Scottish waters the hyper-modern battle cruiser *Repulse*, on which 'Dickie' was serving as a lieutenant. Father and son were deeply attached to one another and those days on board the *Repulse*, days of salt winds and the music of a ship at sea, the last they experienced together, were happy ones. The Marquess arrived back in London on September 10th (1921) and took a room at the Naval and Military Club overnight, with the intention of going on to visit his eldest son, George, who was, at this time, the gunnery-lieutenant, on board H.M.S. *Cardiff* which was then at Constantinople. When Louise and her mother, who were staying at a hotel near the Club, came to visit him, the Marquess complained that he was not feeling well. They went out to fetch some medicine which had been prescribed for the Marquess; on their return, they were met by the agitated housekeeper who had gone up to the Marquess' room to take away a tray and (to quote Admiral Mark Kerr, the Marquess' biographer and life-long friend) had found him lying dead in bed 'with a quiet dignity that was part of his noble character'.[1]

[1] Admiral Mark Kerr, *The Life of Prince Louis of Battenberg*, Longmans, 1934.

*a* Photograph taken at Ulriksdal Palace, not long after Louise's wedding
*Left to right:* the Crown Prince, Lady Louis Mountbatten, Louise and Lord Louis Mountbatten

*b From left to right:* Dolla (Margravine of Baden), Princess Sophia of Hanover, Princess Margarita of Hohenlohe-Langenburg and Margrave Berthold of Baden
(*Photo taken in 1950 at Salem by Count Lennart Bernadotte*)

*a* Louis and Louise Mountbatten at Sofiero in 1946
*(Reproduced by permission of Text Bilder, Stockholm)*

*b* Family gathering at Sofiero for Queen Louise's seventieth birthday
*From left to right:* Prince Bertil, the Margravine of Baden, Queen Louise and King Gustaf Adolf, Princess Benedicte of Denmark with her mother Queen Ingrid of Denmark and sister Princess Anne-Marie, Count Sigvard Bernadotte, Princess Sybilla with her children—Princess Margaretha, Princess Désirée, Princess Birgitta and Prince Carl Gustaf (the Crown Prince of Sweden)
*(Reproduced by permission of Iwallius-Bild, Hälsingborg, Sweden)*

15

*a* Louise in Palestine during the
tour of the East, 1934–1935

*b* Landing at Hawaii. *From left to right:* Captain Gösta Asbrink, Astrid Rudebeck, the
Crown Princess, the Crown Prince and Nils Rudebeck (Marshal of the Court)

*a* Louise during Worl
War II, at the time c
the *Winter Light* cam
paign

*b* Louise with Finnish
children from the refu-
gee home at Rådan.
One of her favourites,
Tuula, is sitting on her
knee

17
Crown Princess Louise in State robes, 1938

*a* Dressing up at Christmas
   to amuse the children at
   Drottningholm
   (*Photograph taken by the
   Princess of Wied*)

*b* Queen Louise shared most of her husband's interests. Here, she is salmon fishing during a holiday at Lake Tärna in Lapland
(*Photograph by the late Major Knut Stiernswärd*)

19

a The Crown Prince and Princess in the gardens at Sofiero, in 1936
  *(Reproduced by permission of Text & Bilder, Stockholm)*

b Queen Louise with her Pekinese, Eisei, at Drottningholm
  *(Photograph by the Princess of Wied)*

*a* King Gustaf Adolf and Queen Louise with President de Gaulle, a a Banquet in the Elysé Palace during their State Visit to France
(*Photograph by Chris Kindahl*)

*b* Queen Louise followed by two pages on her way to the Opening of Parliament, January 11, 1955
(*Reproduced by permission of Svenskt Pressfoto, Stockholm*)

King Gustaf Adolf and Queen Louise together with Eisei at Sofiero
(*Photograph by the Princess of Wied*)

22

a Queen Louise with the Duke [of]
Edinburgh during the State V[isit]
to Sweden, 1956
(*Reproduced by permission of Sver[ige]
Pressfoto, Stockholm*)

b The sovereigns of England [and]
Sweden on the balcony of [the]
Palace in Stockholm, ackn[ow]
ledging the cheers of the cro[wd]
(*Reproduced by permission of Kam[era]
bild, Stockholm*)

**23**

*a* At the christening of Lady Brabourne's third child, Joanna, at
Mersham Parish Church in April, 1955
*From left to right:* Queen Louise, King Gustaf holding Norton's
shoulder, Lady Brabourne holding her third child, Commander
Heywood-Lonsdale behind Michael John, the Marchioness of Sligo
and (*far right*) Lord Brabourne
(*Reproduced by permission of Keystone Press Ltd*)

*b* Newly-christened Ashley Hicks in Lady Pamela's arms, with his
sister Edwina looking on, while her godmother, Queen Louise, leans
towards her
(*Reproduced by permission of Dorothy Wilding, London*)

24
The photograph of Queen Louise which was taken in the spring of 1963 to give to her friends and relatives (*Photograph by H. Bergne, Court photographer*)

# CHAPTER 4

# Change of Country

AFTER the death of the Marquess of Milford Haven the King offered Louise and her mother apartments in Kensington Palace, where Lady Milford Haven's aunts, the Duchess of Argyll and Princess Beatrice of Battenberg were already living. They moved early in 1922 and now, after their long sequence of trials, the summer of 1923 was to mark a new phase of happiness in Louise's life, for it was in this summer that she became engaged to Crown Prince Gustaf Adolf of Sweden. Though it turned out that neither Prince Gustaf Adolf nor Louise were to be spared sorrow in the future, their meeting in 1923 plunged them into immediate happiness and the brilliance of that summer lingered throughout their lives.

In June the Crown Prince had arrived in England by boat, accompanied by his two elder sons, Prince Gustaf Adolf and Prince Sigvard, and also by the late Major Tage Lundberg. The Crown Prince had three years of loneliness behind him, for it was on May 1, 1920 that his first wife, Crown Princess Margaret (the daughter of the Duke of Connaught), had died leaving him with five children, of whom the eldest, Prince Gustaf Adolf, was fourteen and the youngest, Prince Carl Johan, only three and a half. On their arrival the party split up and the Crown Prince stayed in London for the season, while Major Lundberg took the two young princes to visit the Lake District and some factories which it was considered valuable for them to see. At first, one or two columnists noticed that Crown Prince Gustaf Adolf had appeared at Ascot with Lady Louise Mountbatten. Then, the rumours began to spread and certainly the family were no slower than the newspapers to notice was was happening. Crown Prince Gustaf Adolf was often invited down to weekend parties at a

G

country house in Southsea, belonging to Louise's elder brother George, who was now Marquess of Milford Haven and had married the Countess Nadejda (Nada) de Torby, daughter of Grand Duke Michael of Russia and a great-niece of Emperor Alexander II. As the Crown Prince was closely related to the English royal family it was quite natural for him to be invited to these weekend parties but it was also noticed how much he enjoyed Louise's company.

Dolla (the Margravine of Baden), told me, when I visited Salem, that she remembers Louise's reactions very well. Louise was clearly attracted to Prince Gustaf Adolf from the beginning, but at the same time she was frightened of the consequences. When King Manuel of Portugal had proposed to her before the war, she had confided in Dolla that she would never 'marry a king or a widower'. Suddenly it seemed as if her remark had been made with foresight and in addition Louise was also worried because she knew that if their attraction became serious, she would have to grow used to life in another country, despite her love of England and the feeling that England was her home. Slightly panic-stricken, she told Dolla and her sister, Margarita, never to leave them alone. 'Naturally,' said the Margravine, 'we did exactly the opposite and Uncle Gustaf was extremely grateful to us for doing so. I can remember exactly what he said to us: 'You are bricks!'

During this state of panic, Louise asked Lady Milford Haven and Lady Zia Wernher[1] what they thought she ought to do. Both of them urged her not to hesitate. To which Louise replied, 'It's all very well for you, sitting there comfortably anchored in your London homes. Think about me, faced with leaving England, and settling down in a strange country!'

Soon, however, all doubts were overcome, and in her own

---

[1] Lady Zia Wernher was Countess Nada de Torby's sister. Her original title was Countess Anastasia de Torby, but on her marriage to Major General Sir Harold Wernher, the third baronet, in 1917, she was given the title of Lady Zia Wernher by King George V.

shy yet joyful way Louise told the family that she had decided to marry Prince Gustaf Adolf.

'There was nothing of the blushing bride about Aunt Louise, when she told us she was going to get married,' the Margravine of Baden recalls. 'She seemed embarrassed, almost annoyed with herself, and with her typical inclination to understatement, especially on her own account, she explained that she thought she was much too old and thin to be a bride. And what was her bridal gown to be like? She was certainly not going to wear white!'

\*     \*     \*

In Sweden, the reactions to their engagement were rather confused. The Swedish Government were not sure whether Louise Mountbatten was of royal blood or not—and, since the heir to the Swedish throne is debarred from succession if he marries a commoner, they were more than a little worried. Accordingly, the Swedish Prime Minister wrote to Stanley Baldwin asking whether he could confirm that Lady Louise Mountbatten was, in fact, a member of the British royal family. Baldwin's answer was to send the Swedish Prime Minister the official printed list of precedence at Court of the members of the royal family. The Battenbergs had of course appeared on the list when they were princes and princesses—and by special direction of King George V their names had remained on the list when they received their new names and title. Once a copy of the list was produced, the Swedish authorities were quite satisfied that Louise was in fact a member of the royal family; but if any doubts had remained, she could not have married the Crown Prince.

The news of the betrothal came as a complete surprise to the people of Sweden and at first popular reaction too was a trifle confused. Little was known about Lady Louise Mountbatten in Sweden. Nevertheless, they were pleased that the Crown Prince had found a new wife after his years of loneliness and also that, from a practical point of view, Sweden would again have a Crown

Princess. Before the engagement was officially announced, the Crown Prince's sons had been told that they were to have a step-mother. Both the Crown Prince and Louise were anxious to know how they would react. At first the young Prince Gustaf Adolf proved silent and watchful. But after a day of seeing his father together with Louise, he flung his arms round her and said: 'I am so glad. I can see you're going to make my father happy'.

It was not until August, at the spa of Arcachon, in France, that Princess Ingrid and Prince Bertil had an opportunity to meet their future step-mother. Prince Andrew and Princess Alice and their family had rented a villa there and so Crown Prince Gustaf Adolf and Louise decided to join them, together with Princess Victoria and Nils Rudebeck, who was then Marshal of the Swedish Court. During the first two days nobody could get a word out of Prince Bertil (then eleven years old). The only sound he emitted was a strange humming noise and it was not until the third day that he deigned to explain that he had been a bus! Prince Bertil still remembers what the children felt:

'Naturally, it seemed strange for my sister and me. Our own mother had gone. But with great relief we saw that Aunt Louise was kind—we realized that at once. And we thought it was nice that she spoke English, which we were used to.'

Arcachon was also memorable for another reason. There was a wonderful confectioner's shop—a dreamland of pastries, and at mid-day, every day, the children used to be taken there by the Crown Prince (who was also fond of sweet things) and Prince Andrew. And either because of the atmosphere before the wedding or as a bribe to keep them happy, the children were allowed to feast on pastries to their hearts' content.

\*       \*       \*

As King George V had said he would like to give the wedding, it was decided that it should take place on November 3rd in the

Chapel Royal at St James's Palace. During the weeks before the wedding, the gifts poured in. Among the most magnificent were a jewelled diadem and brooch from the Swedish King and Queen, which had once belonged to Queen Josephine of Sweden, the daughter of Napoleon's stepson and brother-in-arms Eugène de Beauharnais. Young Prince Gustaf Adolf (the Crown Prince's son) brought it over from Sweden and the Margravine of Baden describes the Prince's arrival with the jewels:

'I can see him now, as he came marching up with the diadem in his hands. We all admired it. On the spur of the moment Prince Gustaf Adolf suddenly put it on his own curly head. He really did look like a prince out of a children's book of fairy tales. Aunt Louise was amused by what he had done and noticed that the diadem sat considerably more firmly on her step-son's thick curly hair than on her own head.'

On the day before the wedding, a brilliant array of guests assembled for dinner at Buckingham Palace. Two reigning kings were present, four queens and six princesses. The male guests wore knee-breeches and decorations; the ladies, their sashes and tiaras. And in honour of the wedding, a squadron of Swedish warships came over to England.

The wedding day was one of dripping mist. The splendour of the ceremony in the Chapel Royal must have seemed colourful to those who had travelled through the grey day. The whole of the chapel was bright with candles as for a Christmas service, the chancel was banked with flowers and the royal guests in robes and uniforms filled the church with colour.

Immediately before the ceremony began the bridegroom entered wearing Swedish general's uniform and the Order of the Bath, and with him came the best man, his brother, Prince William. Louise had been worried about the material for her wedding dress and had eventually decided upon a length of Indian silk sari-material, which Uncle Ernie (the Grand Duke Ernest

Louis of Hesse) had offered her. The sari-material hung beautifully and was of a dazzling silver-white. For her bouquet, Louise
had chosen her favourite flowers, lilies-of-the-valley, and she
looked charming as she walked slowly down the aisle. Louise was
given away by her eldest brother George, Marquess of Milford
Haven, who was now head of the family; and his children, the
little Earl of Medina and Lady Tatiana Mountbatten, acted as page
and bridesmaid, while the other bridesmaids, Louise's four nieces,
were dressed in apricot chiffon with their hair tied with gold
ribbons. The Archbishop of Canterbury conducted the
ceremony and the couple before the altar looked serious
throughout.

For the reception King George and Queen Mary provided a
magnificent setting. They had chosen the splendour of what is
perhaps historically the most famous state room in England, the
Round Room in Kensington Palace, where in June 1837 Princess
Victoria received the news that she had become Queen of
England.

For Louise, the wedding day marked the end of her home in
Britain. Their honeymoon was in Italy, then they returned to
England and crossed the North Sea to Sweden. At the beginning
of the crossing the sea was calm and the December weather so
mild that on the first night there was dancing on deck. The
passengers felt as if they were part of the wedding party and the
atmosphere was of unfettered gaiety. During the night, however,
a storm broke out with the sea running high, and so many of the
passengers fell victim to sea-sickness that the rest of the journey
was less festive. Louise had never had great physical resources,
and after the strain of the journey she must have felt in particularly bad shape when at about eleven o'clock in the morning on
December 10th, she stepped on land at Gothenburg to face the
strenuous programme of her first day in Sweden.

First there was the formal reception on the quayside, with the
presentation of the Governor of the Province of Gothenburg and
Bohuslän, Oscar von Sydow, and other notables of the city. This

was followed by a speech from the Governor, a presentation of bouquets, a parade by a Guard of Honour and ovations from the huge crowds and the Scouts who lined the quay. Then, there was the journey to the Governor's residence where lunch had been arranged, then a visit to Bishop Rodhe, to Gothenburg Children's Hospital, and to the Rohsska Museum. Then a celebration concert of Swedish music in Gothenburg Concert Hall, with pieces by Rangström, Aulin, Alfvén and Stenhammar. After the concert, there was a banquet at the Stock Exchange. Directly from the Stock Exchange, they went to the station and at last, after a torchlight display and yet another presentation of bouquets, at 11.15 p.m., twelve hours after the royal couple had arrived in Sweden, amid deafening cheers, their train slid out of the station, bound for Stockholm. For Louise, such a programme of welcome must have been completely overwhelming, no matter how well it was meant.

In Stockholm, the first day was somewhat more sparing. Queen Victoria, the Queen of Sweden, who had been prevented from attending the wedding by illness, travelled to Huddinge a few stations away from Stockholm and there joined the royal couple aboard the special train. She was thrilled at her son's remarriage and from the first moment took a liking to her new daughter-in-law. When the royal party came out on to the stone steps in front of the Central Station in Stockholm, students in the crowd burst into song. This must have cheered the Crown Princess a little, for before her all she could see of her new capital was veiled by dripping December mist and packed tight with crowds. And the Stockholmers' first glimpse of their new Princess was of a frail, thin lady wrapped up against the cold in a musquash fur coat with a large miniver collar.

Later that day, they had an opportunity to see more of Princess Louise. The newly-weds drove through the city along a route decorated with banks of lights and flags; and at the crossroads between King Street and Queen Street hung a huge illuminated crown which lit up the December grey. Finally, the climax of the capital's welcome was a *Te Deum* sung in the Palace Chapel and then later a salute from Skeppsholmen.

One can only guess Louise's thoughts that night as she wearily closed her eyes in the royal palace which, from now on would be her main home. Perhaps she was moved by the warm welcome which she had been given by the Swedish people, or was frightened by the first taste of what royal duties were like. Maybe, however, her thoughts were of her dead father and she felt that her triumphant arrival in Sweden in some way made amends for the sadness of her father's resignation and that her own honour was a form of compensation.

\*     \*     \*

Soon after their arrival in Sweden, the Crown Prince took Princess Louise to see Ulriksdal Palace, a short distance from Stockholm, which was to be their home during the spring and also for a part of the autumn each year. It was an overcast winter's day with patches of snow on the grass, and it must have been difficult for Louise to imagine what it was like in the early spring out in the park, where she always used to go to find the first blue anemones pushing through among the leaves left over from the autumn. Louise now found that she was the mistress of four households. First there was their winter home, the north-west wing of the Royal Palace in the capital; then, outside Stockholm, there was Drottningholm, the home of the Crown Prince's parents where the whole family traditionally spent Christmas. Then there was Ulriksdal, their spring and autumn home, and finally Sofiero down by the Sound. They loved Sofiero and as their diary became more and more burdened with public appearances, they came to regard it as a haven where they could relax and rest. At Sofiero, more than anything, they loved the gardens. Both of them were fond of gardening and one of the things they always looked forward to was when, at the end of April, they went down to plan the gardens and park at Sofiero for the year.

They used to walk through the ravine lined with beech trees, with their leaves in bud and anxiously inspect the rhododendrons and azaleas to see how well they had stood up to the winter. They would then stroll through the garden on the lakeside, breathing in the smell of newly turned flower beds, until they came to the orchard and the rose garden, of which they took special care and which often used to be the goal of walks during the summer. The Crown Prince was particularly fond of roses and there were seventy-eight varieties at Sofiero, including *Herzogin von Calabrien, Gruss an Tepliz, Mrs Wemyss Quin, Goldilocks, General MacArthur, Mrs G. A. van Rossem and Etoile de Holland,* to name but a few.

Again, they loved Sofiero because they were able to invite friends and relatives there undisturbed. When they had company they generally preferred to stay in the peace and quiet of the grounds, but they occasionally went on outings and liked to take their guests to see the international productions of *Hamlet* at the Kronberg Castle on the other side of the Sound. They also liked to take guests on picnics and to visit *The Lundgren Girls* coffee shop at *Skäret* ('The Skerry') or *Kullen* ('The Mound') from which there is a magnificent view. Louise took great care of her guests and would always make sure personally that the rooms were in perfect order and place fresh flowers on the bedside table together with a few books which she thought the guests might enjoy.

Princess Louise had arrived in Sweden twelve days before Christmas and, as a result, her first impressions included the colourful festivities traditional in Scandinavia between St Lucia's Day and Twelfth Night. In a letter she wrote to Dolla she describes the gaiety of her first Christmas at Drottningholm and reveals indirectly the joy her arrival brought the widowed Crown Prince and his children—something not generally acknowledged at the time. In fact, on the contrary, there was gossip in Stockholm that she did not bother about the children and complaints that she did not look very motherly.

Drottningholm, 30th December 1923

*'Darling Dolla,*

'Who would have thought last Xmas that I would be spending the next one in a strange country with a husband and a ready-made family. After you five, I think they are the nicest children I know.

'We have spent a very happy Christmas and they have enjoyed themselves enormously. This is a marvellous house for children, such heaps of rooms. We play badminton in the ballroom and the golf game in the billiard room, as it is huge and has a carpet. Then Johnnie[1] has his train and rails in the long gallery. In another room is the "listening in" apparatus[2] and also the gramophone. We always have tea in the Xmas room and sometimes I play "Mah-Jong" with the children after tea. They are all badly smitten with it; even Ingrid and Bertie play.

'This is such a lovely old Palace; you must see it one day. The situation on a big lake is so pretty. We have had the most gorgeous weather, brilliant sunshine practically the whole time. Just two days it has snowed but we have been out all the same.

'I think going on skis is fun. I do it every day and can manage to get down small slopes without falling now each time. Today we went for a long tour of an hour all round the park and outside. I got so hot keeping up with the others that I had to have a bath when I came home. Edmund[3] is awfully good on skis and of course Uncle Gustaf is. Sigvard is not allowed to ski. He usually skates with some of the others.

'Edmund has been out shooting several days with his grandfather. He is most annoyed and irritated that he has to have his tonsils out on Monday, spoiling some of his holiday.

'We all go back to town on Monday alas, with this real winter weather. I would so much rather be in the country. I believe it is not often they have snow here for Xmas.

---

[1] Prince Carl Johan is called Johnnie in the family.
[2] The wireless was at that time a new invention and was often called a 'listening-in apparatus'.          [3] Edmund—Prince Gustaf Adolf, Princess Louise eldest's stepson.

'William[1] has been laid up since two days with bronchitis; got it in the old and drafty theatre rehearsing his play.

'Lennart[2] is as tall as Edmund nearly; he is a nice boy.

'I ski in my woolly costume every day; it is just right. I wear my leather waistcoat underneath or a Shetland jersey if it is not so cold. I got a pair of ready-made skiing boots and terribly thick stockings to the knee which I wear over others. I luckily found that the grey woolly cap I got at Darmstadt two years ago goes with the costume. The waterproof breeches I wear over others to be warmer. I am such a bundle of clothes that it is most exhausting getting myself up when I fall down.

'Gustaf's parents are giving me court dress and train as an Xmas present. I got heaps of presents from them. The King gave me a sweet little tiny black cigarette holder with a little band of diamonds round it, which is just what I needed for the evening to go in my bag. He also gave me three ash trays and a bead bag and a safety-pin brooch with red, white and blue stones.

'You must both be feeling so depressed over all that is going on in Greece. I do feel for you so; it is just hateful to have to wonder and worry as to what is going to be the result of it all. I see that Venizelos has returned. He might do anything good or bad, it is difficult to tell.

'Well, I must stop now and go to tea. I miss you both very much and long to have you with me to talk about everything.

'Heaps of love and many good wishes for a very happy new year from

*Your very loving*

*Aunt Louise'*

Another letter to Dolla and her sister two years later gives a similar picture of Louise's happiness in Sweden.

---

[1] Prince Wilhelm was known as William whenever he was referred to in English.
[2] Lennart—the only son of Prince Wilhelm.

Ulriksdal,
January 14th, 1925

'*Darling Margarita and Dolla,*

'I fear that this has to be a joint letter which I am sure you will hate, but I have not time to write to both of you without keeping one waiting. There is not much object in writing separately to you both on one day, for the news would be exactly the same. I am very ashamed of my laziness in writing but it is not all laziness. I have had so many letters to write and one does want to do other things as well as write.

'I am glad to hear that the riding habits are a success. How marvellous your first hunt must have been, and how thrilling getting the mask and brush. I can well imagine what you felt like after all those hours on horseback. You are lucky creatures, the good time you manage to have wherever you go. I have told of your progresses to Rudebeck[1] and the "riding master", who were very impressed.

'I wrote to your Mama about Xmas at Drottningholm so she, I hope, told you. I like living there. The only thing that nearly kills me is the heat in my parents-in-law's rooms. I have never felt anything like it. We managed to keep our rooms cool by turning off what heating we could.

'One of the nicest presents I got was from my parents-in-law, a pair of pearl earrings, family ones my mother-in-law does not wear. It has always been my wish to have pearl earrings, so observant of my father-in-law to see I had not got any.

'We are still having quite mild weather and luckily lots of bright sunshine. The children's hopes are continually being raised by frost one day and squashed by it being quite warm the next. It has gone on like that for ten days.

'We had a dance here a few days ago. No grown-ups, only the boys' friends—just ten couples. Dinner first at seven o'clock to which Johnnie was allowed to come and was terribly proud. The dance lasted till about 12.30 with a very short interval for supper.

[1] Nils Rudebeck, the Marshal of the Court.

They danced in the dining-room and supper was at little tables in the hall. A very good house for a party. One could easily give a large dance. We four grown-ups played Mah-Jong part of the time as we could not sit about doing nothing. The children so strongly hinted that they did not want any grown-ups like last year, so we did not invite any. Bertie[1] had a lovely time first helping in the kitchen all day and then either watching the dancing or rushing about helping the servants as a waiter and eating.

'School starts this week but we stay here till the end of the month. Two days ago was the opening of Parliament. Edmund had to give his oath of allegiance, being of age. He did it very nicely and spoke so clearly and well and looked awfully nice in his uniform. I have had myself photographed in court dress and if good will send you one in return for the promised one of you in your habits.

'Uncle Eugen[2] has got a big exhibition of his pictures. I wish you could see it; so good. I do like his painting.

'This week we start going out to dinners, not many so far. My parents-in-law are giving soon two or three large dinners. I have just ordered two very smart dresses which I think will be nice. Have to be chosen and arranged with care. I am getting rather broad and will soon be like Aunt Beatrice.[3] . . .

'Well, it is lunch time, so I must stop. It will be nice if you can come here again this summer. I wish I could have Cécile[4] and Tiny[5] also.

'Heaps of love to you both. You are dears to write to me so often. I just love getting your letters.

*Your loving*

*Auntie Louise.'*

---

[1] Prince Bertil.

[2] Brother of King Gustaf V. He was well-known in Sweden as an artist.

[3] Princess Beatrice, the youngest daughter of Queen Victoria of England and widow of Prince Henry of Battenberg.

[4] Cécile—Princess Cecilia of Greece, Princess Louise's niece, at that time fourteen years old.      [5] Tiny—Princess Sophia of Greece, at that time eleven years old.

During the first year, public duties do not seem to have been too heavy and Louise was given an opportunity to get used to her new position. Naturally, she was much in demand as a patron of societies and institutions, but she always took a lively interest in any organization which she adopted, giving much more than mere patronage. She once told a friend, 'I find it difficult to be only a patron, as I've been used to practical work of my own, like an ordinary person, before I married.' And among other causes, she actively supported the Sophia Hospital, the Swedish Red Cross, Crown Princess Louise's Hospital for Children and the Eugenia Home for children disabled, crippled or incurably ill.

One of the first assignments which she had to face was the arrangement of a charity concert in the large hall of the Concert House in Stockholm. Harald Lettström, a bank director who was Chairman of the Queen's Central Committee, had agreed to help and Princess Louise devoted herself to the task with great enthusiasm but not without a touch of nerves. Eventually, she confessed to Harald Lettström that she had been so worried that she dreamed they went into the royal box together on the night of the concert and looked out over an empty hall, not a ticket sold.

*          *          *

In her second year in Sweden (1925), Princess Louise was thrilled to find that she was expecting a baby. She loved children —'especially,' as she wrote in a letter to Dolla, 'tiny ones'—and she was unusually good with them. But it was typical of Louise that she talked without a trace of sentimentality about the news, which undoubtedly gave her tremendous joy; and in the letter to Dolla quoted earlier in this chapter, the only reference to her condition is 'I am getting rather broad and will soon be like Aunt Beatrice'.

At the Swedish Court at that time, even the birth of a child was surrounded with formalities—which were laid out under the heading '*Measures in connection with a birth within the royal family*' in the *Regulations, Instructions and Ceremonial to be Observed at the Swedish Court* published in 1911, and these must have seemed antediluvian to Princess Louise. According to the regulations, only married women were allowed to attend the royal lady at the time of the birth and there were strict instructions for the procedure to be followed as soon as the baby was born:

'As witnesses, the following should be called: the Prime Minister, the Minister of Foreign Affairs, and the Earl Marshal, the Queen's Mistress-of-the-Robes and the married woman who at the time is serving the Royal Mother (Lady-in-Waiting or especially appointed lady).

'The married woman on duty at the time, as soon as the birth has taken place, is to tell the witnesses to present themselves immediately.

'Dress for witnesses: gentlemen in uniform; ladies in black court dress without train.'

Similar formalities existed among other royal families in Europe at this time and a rather delightful story is told by the Margravine of Baden about the baptism some years later of Princess Christina, the eldest daughter of her sister Princess Sophie ('Tiny' as she was called in the family) and Prince Christopher of Hesse. At the baptism, the priest—a gentle old man with a wavering voice—spoke of how 'the angels had brought this little child to the trembling mother. . . .' After the baptism, Princess Sophie (who was only nineteen when Princess Christina was born) turned to her mother and said: 'Well, I may be young, but I *do* at least know how *this child* came into the world'.

After all the preparations, however, Princess Louise's hopes were to end in bitter disappointment. On the day before Whit Sunday, 1925 (May 30th) she was delivered prematurely of a stillborn girl. Louise bore the news bravely, but she had longed to have a child. The loss of her child was the greatest tragedy of her life and although she deeply loved her step-children and step-grandchildren, there was always an ache in her heart for a child of her own.

In contrast to this time of sadness, the next year brought happiness and enjoyment, as a goodwill tour had been arranged to America and the Far East. When Oscar I of Sweden (the present King's great-grandfather) complained of the burdens of kingship to Bishop Thomander, the Bishop is said to have replied: 'Well, your Majesty, you must admit the profession has some pleasing features'. And to Princess Louise and Prince Gustaf Adolf travelling was one of the chief pleasures and compensations of being royal. Their tour took them right across the United States (with them went Nils Rudebeck, who at that time was Marshall of the Swedish Court, and his wife Astrid, the Mistress of the Robes) and, although details of the tour can be found in *U.S.A. and the Crown Prince and Princess* by the late Eric Swenne, a journalist who accompanied them from New York to San Francisco, here however only a few incidents will be given in an attempt to transmit some of the excitement and colour of the tour. In Rochester they were entertained to breakfast at the home of the Secretary of State, Frank B. Kellogg and his wife; and their maids were said to have been so over-awed by royal guests that they served no one else. At a garden party at the home of a millionaire, the Crown Prince and Princess were obliged to decline to sit on chairs raised on a platform in imitation of thrones. In the mountain town of Billings in Montana they were greeted by the ninety year old Chieftain of the Crow Indians, dressed from head to foot in white feathers, who invoked the blessings of the Mighty Spirit upon them and they were given a giant basket of strawberries by Billings' Ladies Club. And on July 13th they celebrated Princess Louise's birthday by picnicking by the edge of the Grand Canyon and listening, seated round a log fire, to legends of the Canyon.

An amusing picture of the tour (rather characteristic of

American journalism of the time) is given in the following article by Miss Kathleen Harms, which appeared in the *Salt Lake Tribune*, and describes their visit to Salt Lake City.

'The Crown Princess of Sweden let her gloved hand rest on her husband's arm, when at 8.15 yesterday morning, she carefully stepped down from the Union Pacific special train and set foot on Salt Lake soil. With a gracious smile she accepted a large bouquet of blue orchids and yellow roses which was presented by the reception committee.

' "A delightful welcome in a delightful town," she said.

'Dressed in a tailored brown tweed coat and a silk dress, patterned in the same colour, with a scarf loosely knotted round her fine throat, a close-fitting henna straw hat, which only allowed a few locks of her light brown hair to play round her cheeks, a brown leather bag on her arm and simple brown shoes of leather over silk stockings of a lighter shade, Sweden's future queen looked every inch the princess she is.

'Princess Louise's eyes are a dark hazel colour and wonderfully expressive. She uses them more than words to communicate her impressions and feelings. She wears her hair in a rather unusual way, a fact which was only discovered when she removed her hat in The Country Club to do her hair and powder her nose. The front in large Marcel waves, was cut short and sat close to her head just like any other bob. But the back of her hair, which is said to be long and heavy, was gathered in a loose knot at the nape of her neck. Her long slim hands are seldom still. She took a lively interest in every point of the programme, and in the organ recital given in the Tabernacle by the organist, Frank W. Asper, she seemed to find a special enjoyment. At the end of each number she nodded her approval and talked happily to those around her. Afterwards she inspected the organ and asked to be allowed to keep as a souvenir the pin which had been used in the customary demonstration of the Tabernacle's acoustics.

' "Just think of being able to hear such a little thing fall two

H

hundred feet away," she said, and stuck the pin in the revere of her coat.

'In the official interview that was granted to the press before the tour of the town, Princess Louise seemed well prepared for the questions, which had evidently been asked her many times since she had first set foot in America. She skilfully avoided, with a trace of smile, the question of divorce and its justification. Sweden has namely the most radical divorce laws in the world.

' "I don't really know very much about divorce, either in my own country or in your America," she said.

'Since she became the Crown Prince's bride in 1923, she has always called Sweden "my country", although she was an English aristocrat, Lady Louise Marie Alexandra Irène Mountbatten, a great-granddaughter of Queen Victoria.

' "Certainly I think that women should take part in business and other professions if they are competent to do so," she said. "And the same goes for politics, although I think a thorough training in this field is necessary. Women are just as intelligent as men and presuming they have had a good education, are able to claim respect and admiration just as much as men, if they devote themselves to it."

' "However, I don't think women should neglect their homes," added Her Highness quite emphatically. "The home, when all is said and done, is more important, isn't it?"

'Women's fashions in Sweden are evidently much the same as those in Utah, and bring with them difficulties of the same kind. The royal skirt was quite wide and when the Princess stood on the steps waiting for her husband, her skirt was suddenly caught by a breeze and flapped threateningly near a pair of royal knees. But with the same gesture that one finds on a windy corner of Main Street, the future Queen of Sweden gripped her skirt with a firm hand and vanished up the steps.

' "Much as I would like to, I can't stay here," she cried and her cry was followed by more than a smile. It was an honest, hearty laugh.

'If in everyday language it has been unanimously said of Gustaf Adolf that "He's a prince!" then it really must be said of his royal consort, Louise, that "She's a real princess!" '

\*     \*     \*

Now, not long after the American tour, there was a great change in Louise's life. On April 4, 1930 Queen Victoria (the Queen of Sweden) died in Rome, and although the Queen had withdrawn almost totally from public life during her last years because of ill health it was only now that the full responsibility of being the country's first lady descended upon Princess Louise. During her first years in Sweden, Queen Victoria had taken a great deal of trouble to make life easy for Princess Louise, especially by warning her of the mistakes she had made when she first came to Sweden herself. Louise was always able to rely on her mother-in-law for help or advice and between them there had developed a great understanding. Yet, although it was well known that Queen Victoria was extremely fond of Louise, they had little in common. Nearly all the past Queens of Sweden had grown up in sheltered environments and their isolation had continued when they came to the throne. They generally had been brought up with the idea that the monarchy existed by the grace of God and that it was a part of their position that an invisible wall should separate them from their subjects. And Queen Victoria had been brought up in the same tradition. In contrast, Louise was a democrat at heart. Since she had royal blood in her veins, naturally she had been schooled always to appear dignified in public, but at the same time she loathed pretentiousness. Lord Mountbatten told me that his sister often used to praise democracy as it was being developed in Sweden and would maintain that, to her way of thinking, no other political system favoured the enlightened development of a country so much as the Swedish version of democracy. 'The foundations of this attitude,' Lord Mountbatten said, 'had been laid during her childhood. For we were brought up in freedom of thought and freedom of opinion, in keeping with our own times. Our mother, who was a remarkable woman, had far sighted ideas in many fields.'

The Margravine of Baden adds that Princess Louise greatly admired Swedish women and especially respected the natural simplicity and lack of affectation of Swedish girls who had grown up in modest circumstances and whose husbands had become successful. 'In no country,' said Princess Louise, 'have I ever met so little vulgarity as in Sweden.'

After Queen Victoria's death Princess Louise became Honorary President of the Sophia Hospital Board and the work she did for nurses and hospitals was, characteristically, one of Louise's most valuable contributions to Sweden. When she took over, Louise took great pains to improve conditions for nurses, for she realized that the regulations governing nurses' lives were extremely severe and old-fashioned. In those days, nurses were forbidden to wear ordinary clothes when off duty (except on leave), were not allowed to wear their hair short or skirts with hemlines more than six inches from the ground, and their wages were based on the theory that nursing was a vocation and not a profession.

Miss Lotten Rignell, who was superintendent of the hospital from 1930 to 1947, told me that Princess Louise was particularly concerned because she realized from her own experience that, if a nurse was to give of her best, it was essential that her working conditions and hours should be good. And, when it came to making the necessary changes, the Crown Princess insisted upon the importance of preserving the special traditions and atmosphere which gave the hospital its distinctiveness; and she wanted modernization to be introduced with subtlety and tact, so that the older nurses did not feel ignored and so that their experience would be regarded as a valuable heritage by the nurses of the new generation. Also, Louise understood the need for consultation. 'It was typical of Princess Louise,' Miss Rignell says, 'That she thought the Sisters should be given the opportunity to have a say in any question which would finally affect them.'

Another organization which received Louise's active support was the Queen's Central Committee, begun by Queen Victoria at the outbreak of World War I and designed to provide equipment for the militia and to act as a supporting organization for the Swedish Red Cross. When Crown Princess Louise took over as head of the Central Committee, both the Militia and the Red Cross had vanished from the picture, so the organization was renamed the Queen's Aid Committee and concentrated on raising rent subsidies for families in need. As there was only a limited amount of money at their disposal, the Crown Princess took the line that it was better to help fewer people and achieve more, although in some cases she used her own resources so as to be able to help more effectively.

\*　　\*　　\*

The next major family event was on October 20, 1932, when Prince Gustaf Adolf (or 'Edmund' as he was called in the family), the Crown Prince's eldest son by his previous marriage, married Princess Sibylla of Saxe-Coburg and Gotha. They went to live at the beautiful little Haga Palace outside Stockholm and there, during the thirties, were born the 'Haga' princesses—Princess Margaretha (who is now the wife of John Ambler), Princess Birgitta (married to Prince Johann Georg of Hohenzollern-Sigmaringen) and Princess Désirée (now married to the Swedish Baron Niclas Silfverschiöld). The youngest of the Haga princesses, Princess Christina, was born in 1943 and became the first Swedish princess to go to University, when she was accepted at Radcliffe College, Harvard.

Then, in 1935, came the first of a chain of tragedies which seemed particularly terrible as it followed soon after an event of great happiness for the Scandinavian royal families. On May 25, 1935, Princess Ingrid (the Crown Prince's daughter) was married to Crown Prince Frederick of Denmark, the heir to the Danish throne, in Stockholm and King Leopold and Queen Astrid of Belgium[1] came to Stockholm for the wedding. All the family remarked how happy Queen Astrid looked as she rode in the procession through the crowded streets and how beautiful she seemed in her sable fur and a light green toque made from the plumes of birds of paradise. She was always spontaneous, and after the procession she is said to have exclaimed to her sister, Crown Princess Märtha of Norway[1]: 'You've no idea what fun it is to be Queen!'

Three months later King Leopold and Queen Astrid were driving along a stretch of road near Küssnacht, in Switzerland, when their car skidded and plunged down a slope. Queen Astrid was killed instantly. She had been greatly loved both in Sweden and Belgium, and on September 18th Louise wrote to Dolla from Sofiero:

'*Dear Dolla,*

'What a ghastly tragedy Astrid's death. We were quite overwhelmed by it and one is haunted by the thought of poor Leopold. It is heartbreaking. Margaretha,[2] poor soul, is still at Stuyvenberg. He asked her to stay on after the funeral to help him go through Astrid's things. He lives at Laeken with his mother and comes to see the children at Stuyvenberg or they go to Laeken every day. He can't bear to live in his old house and the children soon are moving to Laeken. I am sorry for those poor little children not to grow up in the atmosphere of their own house to keep the memory of their mother alive. Uncle Charles and Ingeborg[3] have been quite wonderful, bearing their great sorrow in a splendid way. We motored at once to them to Fridhem, when we heard the news, in Bertie's car. On the way back from Brussels, Ingeborg spent a couple of days with us, as

---

[1] Astrid and Märtha were daughters of Prince Charles of Sweden (the brother of King Gustaf V of Sweden) and Princess Ingeborg of Denmark.

[2] Princess Margaretha of Denmark, sister of Queen Astrid and Crown Princess Märtha of Norway.                [3] Queen Astrid's parents.

Uncle Charles luckily had a lot of Red Cross work to do in Stockholm. Now Märtha and her children are with them at Fridhem. Ingeborg said for Astrid one must not grieve. She had really only known great happiness in her short life and was at her zenith, loved and popular, and who knows what sorrow and troubles she had been spared. I suppose she did not need to live longer in this world. It was quite wonderful to hear in Belgium how she was loved and admired by everyone. They said it was not only a calamity for their King but also for the country. She had done so much in the short time she was there; I admired her very much. She was a splendid personality, who really knew how to cope with her difficult position in a foreign country.

'Don't you think Mussolini must really be not quite sane? I believe he thinks he is an old Roman living in those times. Monstrous that one man can produce the catastrophe he is doing. Let alone for his unfortunate country and Abyssinia, but what will be the result for the rest of Europe and even Africa. I boil internally with indignation and helpless rage.

'With love to Berthold and heaps of love to yourself. I hope you and the family are well.

> *Your very loving*
> *Aunt Louise.*'

Then in January 1936 there occurred the death of King George V of England. Louise was very fond of George V and in a letter to Dolla dated Stockholm, February 11, 1936 she described the funeral.

'*Darling Dolla*,

'Since I last wrote to you we have been in London for five days. I just had to go over to Cousin George's funeral. He was always so kind and friendly to me and so kind to all my family, and as my King, I admired and respected him so much. Few Kings have been respected so much and his goodness of heart and devotion to his duty made him loved by his people.

'The funeral was the most wonderfully impressive ceremony I have ever experienced, a simple dignified grandeur and the crowds were unbelievable. Even when we passed a long way back in the fourth carriage, the crowd was completely silent. A wonderful experience to see that mass of reverently silent people.

'The day before the day we arrived, there was a men's dinner and reception of all the delegates at Buckingham Palace. Dickie had got a pass for us to go to Westminster Hall, so Georgie, Nada, their children, Philip, Dickie, I, Isa and Stina Reuterswürd[1] went there after dinner. We were shown to a door in the middle of the Hall and could stand there just opposite the coffin and see the stream of people pass. The simple dignity of that guarded coffin in that vast old hall was most wonderfully impressive. You can understand that it meant much to me being able to be in England. However Swedish I am, I still feel so completely English.

'Dickie got leave to come from Malta. It was a great joy being together with him again after over two years. Don[2] also stayed with Grandmama,[3] as you know. We all had great talks and discussions, as you can imagine. Don I find has grown up very much. I like him enormously. Of the other relatives that came over for the funeral, I saw practically nobody. Cousin May[4] asked us to tea one day. She looked, of course, very tired and drawn. David[5] joined the tea party, I am sure to help his mother. Elisabeth[6] told me he is quite touching with his mother, just only thinking how he could help her.

'Marina[7] was occupied with the dressmaker when we called.

---

[1] George and Nada are the Marquess and Marchioness of Milford Haven; Philip is the Duke of Edinburgh; Dickie—Earl Mountbatten of Burma; Isa—Baroness Buxhoevden, previously Lady-in-Waiting to Princess Louise's Aunt Alix, who was the last Tsarina of Russia; Stina Reuterswärd was Princess Louise's Maid of Honour.

[2] Don—the Queen's cousin George Donatus, Hereditary Grand Duke of Hesse and the Rhine.

[3] In letters to her niece, the Queen's mother, the Dowager Marchioness of Milford Haven, is always called Grandmama.     [4] Cousin May—Queen Mary of England.

[5] David—Edward VIII, later Duke of Windsor.

[6] The Duchess of York, now the Queen Mother.     [7] Marina, Duchess of Kent.

George[1] was really sad about his father's death and wrote a most touching letter to Grandmama. Cousin George had become so much softer with his sons as he got old.

'This is a worse scrawl than usual as I am writing in bed. I caught a cold or a kind of 'flu in London and have been in bed a week now, with slight bronchitis. Too maddening being laid up, as some American friends, the Blisses, came to stay with us for four days and I was going to have the grandchild here while Edmund and Bylla[2] are away.

'I have got something terribly sad to tell you. I am sure you will be so sorry about Folke and Estelle's eldest little boy[3] who died ten days ago. He got inflammation of the ear from 'flu and had to have a mastoid operation. All went well the first two days and then the inflammation and poison went to the brain. Oh, it is too tragic to think of what the poor parents went through. I have not seen them, as I went to bed the moment I got home. I believe they are wonderful.

'My love to Berthold[4] and fondest love to your dear self.

*Your loving*

*Aunt Louise.'*

On November 16, 1937, occurred the greatest disaster that has ever struck the House of Hesse and which can only be compared to the murder of the whole of the Russian Imperial family at Ekaterinburg in Siberia. In an air crash in the November fog outside Ostend, five members of the House of Hesse died on their way to the wedding of Prince Louis of Hesse and Sir Auckland Campbell Geddes's daughter, Margaret. Their plane collided with a factory chimney 180 feet high which was hidden by the fog, and

[1] George, Duke of Kent.      [2] Prince Gustaf Adolf and Princess Sybilla.
[3] Gustaf—eldest son of the Countess Estelle and the late Count Folke Bernadotte. Estelle Bernadotte is the daughter of the late American industrialist H. Edward Manville and Estelle Romaine. Her husband was a first cousin of King Gustaf Adolf and became President of the Swedish Red Cross in 1946. On September 17, 1948 he was assassinated in Jerusalem while on a mission for the United Nations.
[4] Berthold—the Margrave of Baden.

virtually the whole family was wiped out. The head of the family, Grand Duke Ernest Louis of Hesse (Queen Louise's uncle), had died only a month before the accident. Only two members of the main House of Hesse were now left alive, Prince Louis, who later quietly married Miss Geddes and a small daughter of the Hereditary Grand Duke George Donatus, who was only six months old and who had been left behind at home, as she was too young to attend the wedding. Two years later, she died of meningitis.

Those who died at Ostend were Grand Duchess Eleanore of Hesse, her eldest son Grand Duke George Donatus, his wife Cécile (sister of the Duke of Edinburgh) and both their sons, Louis and Alexander.

November 16th had always been regarded as an especially unlucky day for the House of Hesse. It was on November 16, 1878 that Princess Marie ('dear little Marie', as Queen Victoria used to refer to her in letters) died of diphtheria.[1] And it was also on November 16th (in 1903) that Princess Elisabeth, the eight-year-old daughter of Grand Duke Ernest Louis, died in circumstances which have been compared to 'the last scene of a Jacobean tragedy'. Princess Elisabeth was the Grand Duke's daughter by his marriage to Princess Victoria Melita and in November 1903 she had been sent on a visit to her Aunt Alix (the Tsarina Alexandra Feodorovna of Russia). According to the popular account, a glass of transparent liquid was standing on the Tsar's desk. Elisabeth drank it, became violently ill, and a few days later she was dead. The cause of her death was never completely established, but it was rumoured that the liquid in the glass had contained a toxic bacteria culture and had been intended for the Tsar. This story, however, was strongly denied at the time and both meningitis and paratyphoid were mentioned as possible causes of death.

Only five months after the air crash at Ostend, on April 8, 1938, Princess Louise's elder brother George, the Marquess of

[1] See page 34.

Milford Haven, died of cancer. As has been mentioned in the Introduction, Lord Milford Haven had fallen and broken his hip during February, and in consequence he had to go into hospital where it was discovered that he was suffering from cancer of the bone. George had always been extremely popular in the family and his death at the early age of forty-six was a terrible shock to the Mountbattens. Nor was the next decade without misfortune, for on January 26, 1947 there occurred a tragedy which gave Crown Prince Gustaf Adolf and Princess Louise very great cause for grief. After Christmas the royal family had moved back to the palace in Stockholm, but on January 26th Princess Louise and Dolla had been invited to tea with the King at Drottningholm. Although communications between Sweden and Germany were not yet functioning satisfactorily, Count Folke Bernadotte, head of the Swedish Red Cross, had during the course of the day succeeded in getting through a message that Dolla's younger sister, Princess Sophia of Hanover, had given birth to a son.

Louise and Dolla were discussing the news excitedly, while King Gustaf sat at his embroidery, when suddenly a footman entered and said that the Crown Princess was wanted on the telephone in the next room. She took an unusually long time over the phone call and, in Dolla's words, 'It was a completely different person who returned, walking with heavy steps and despair in her eyes'. She had heard that Prince Gustaf Adolf, the Crown Prince's eldest son by his first marriage and thus second in line to the Swedish throne, had been killed in an air accident at Kastrup. Only a few months before the accident, his wife Princess Sibylla had given birth to a son, Prince Carl Gustaf, the present Crown Prince.

# CHAPTER 5

# World War II

As in the other countries of Europe, so in Sweden too, the war brought the royal family into prominence as a symbol of national hope and courage and it also brought them closer to their people. One of Princess Louise's first wartime activities was a fund called Winter Light to provide carbide lamps and candles. In those days many rural areas of Sweden lacked electricity and so, when petrol and paraffin were requisitioned, large parts of the countryside were left without any source of light. In order to reach as many people as possible, the Crown Princess appeared on the radio and anyone in Sweden during the war will remember not only Winter Light, but also the Crown Princess's Gift Committee for the Defence of Neutrality, which provided warm clothing for the troops. The Gift Committee was, in fact, so successful that the whole of Sweden seems to have been knitting and the forces claimed that they were veritably inundated with stockings and jerseys, scarves and protectors. Encouraged by parcels of knitted clothes, the men were emboldened to ask for other things. One soldier requested an accordian and added at the end of his letter, 'Thanks in advance!' 'Well, as he's already thanked us,' said the Crown Princess to the other Committee members, 'we might as well send him one.'

Another of Princess Louise's wartime activities was 'Sewing at the Palace'. In 1939 the Red Cross were frantically collecting pillows and mattresses for schoolchildren who were being evacuated and they asked the Crown Princess whether the bedding could be stored in the Stockholm Palace. So, an apartment was opened up and at the same time the Crown Princess arranged sewing groups at the Palace. With the help of the Singer Sewing Machine Company a number of machines were quickly installed and soon about forty women were making clothes, which were sent wherever they were needed, especially to children both in Sweden and abroad. The Crown Princess enjoyed sewing and was very good at it, even though she was left-handed. Louise always maintained that this made sewing more difficult and she also used to complain that her handwriting was ugly, because as a child she had been forced to use her right hand against her natural inclination. And it is curious to observe that, according to the Margravine of Baden, in the Battenberg family one member of each generation has always been left-handed.

During the war, the Crown Prince and Princess found them-selves in a particularly difficult position, as they had friends and relatives on both sides. Nevertheless, their feelings about the war were absolutely clear. They were horrified by the behaviour of Hitler and Mussolini—especially since, being in a neutral country, they were able to form a clear picture of international events. They had early news of the concentration camps in Germany, and as a result had a very great sympathy with the Allied cause. At the same time they felt strongly that Sweden should remain neutral. Sweden had not been involved in any war for a hundred and fifty years and they felt that so long as Germany did not threaten to invade, then the Swedes should not compromise their neutrality.

As it turned out Sweden's neutrality proved a boon for Princess Louise's family. Relatives in Germany, in England and also in other countries (including the Greek royal family) who could not write to each other direct while the war was on, were able to use Louise to clear their correspondence. It was not, however, simply a matter of forwarding the letters, for Louise had to copy out every letter and re-address it as if from herself; and, as a mark of their gratitude, on her seventieth birthday Louise was given a gold case in the shape of an envelope on which were engraved all the names of the relatives whom she had helped.

Also, Louise was busy with refugee work. Pressure from the East had forced forty thousand Finnish children to seek refuge in Sweden, and so the Crown Princess set up a home for Finnish children at Rådan, an old building about half an hour's walk from Ulriksdal. The expenses of running the home and the keep of the children were paid for by different members of the royal family, but the heart and soul of the enterprise was Princess Louise. There was accommodation for eighteen children, the home was planned with great care, a superintendent appointed, children's nurses engaged, and in February 1942 they were ready to receive the first eighteen small pale children to arrive from Finland. Rådan really became a labour of love for Princess Louise. She walked over there every day and devoted as much of her time to the children as she could. Naturally, she became extremely fond of them and the affection was mutual. As soon as the children caught sight of her, they used to rush towards her crying '*Kron*prinsessa' ('*Crown* Princess'), their lilting Finnish voices emphasizing the first syllable, and the two smallest children especially, Timo and Tuula, captured Louise's heart. When Rådan closed in 1943, the Crown Princess continued to take an interest in the children, particularly Timo and Tuula, and when she visited Helsinki after the war Louise got the Swedish Embassy to arrange a party for the former refugees.

Another refugee whom Princess Louise took under her wing was 'Malibeth', Princess Marie Elisabeth of Wied. Malibeth and Louise had become friends when her father Prince Victor of Wied,[1] was the German Ambassador in Stockholm. Then with the fall of the Third Reich, Princess Marie Elisabeth's private world was completely shattered and she became seriously ill; but fortunately Louise was able to arrange for her to be brought to Sweden and admitted to a nursing home, where thanks to good attention she soon recovered. For a while, Princess Marie Elisabeth stayed with Princess Louise and Crown Prince Gustaf Adolf, but soon she felt she ought to be independent and decided to train as a beautician. When she asked Princess Louise whether

---

[1] The Wied family were related to the Swedish royal family through Queen Sophia (the consort of Oscar II) who was born Princess Sophia of Hesse-Nassau.

she thought it was proper for a princess to become a beautician, Louise expressed surprise that the question should even have bothered her and later, when Princess Marie Elizabeth started a correspondence course, Louise used to correct proofs for her and once even contributed a rather unusual article. While going through some old papers, Louise had found a prescription of the lotion which Catherine the Great of Russia used to remove freckles. Catherine was famed for her interest in the opposite sex, and was extremely careful of her appearance, so it is quite possible that the lotion may be effective, though Princess Marie Elisabeth considers that the ingredients are too strong. The recipe read:

> *Whites of 6 eggs*
> *6 tablespoons Eau de Cologne*
> *6 tablespoons strained lemon juice*

*Whisk the whites of the eggs until stiff. Add lemon juice and Eau de Cologne gradually as you whisk. Let the lotion stand thus uncovered for two hours, after which the liquid is poured into a bottle. The lotion should be shaken before use; rub over the face and let it remain for about ten minutes. Wash off with warm water and rub a little cream into the face, so that the skin does not become dried from the lemon and white of egg.*

Louise also helped the Princess correct the proofs of her books. Marie Elisabeth had written a series of children's books about a small troll named Trubbnos, which was the result of requests for bedtime stories by Princess Christina and one of which was translated into English under the title *Tiptilt*.[1]

Relatively little of the work Princess Louise did during the war was known to the public, as she always felt that her personal life had nothing to do with the outside world. But, that she seriously strained both her physical and financial resources is

[1] London: Thomas Nelson & Sons, 1964.

clear from the Margravine of Baden's recollections of Louise's wartime activities.

'I wonder,' she says, 'how many lives Aunt Louise really saved during the war, and afterwards too? There were, for instance, two old ladies in Munich with whom she had come into contact quite by chance. One of them was a violinist. I know that they literally managed to keep alive all through the war because of what she sent them. She also contacted the old German teacher of her predecessor, Crown Princess Margaret, and she was one of the many my aunt helped and sent parcels to.'

Of the many others, perhaps the most interesting are a monk and abbess in Israel, who are connected with the story of Princess Louise's Aunt Ella.[1]

Ella had married the Grand Duke Serge of Russia who was assassinated in the streets of Moscow by the Nihilists on February 17, 1905. After her husband's death Ella founded the Order of Martha and Mary (the only sisterhood of nursing nuns in Russia) and became their Abbess in 1910. She was revered almost as a saint in Russia, but nevertheless like the rest of the Russian royal family she was arrested during the spring of 1918, when two men in uniform came to take her away from the convent in an armoured car. She asked if one of the Sisters, Sister Barbara, could go with her and then quickly got a few belongings together and, as there was no time to make the rounds of the hospital and the old people's home, she summoned the sisters together in the Chapel and gave them her last blessing. They were all crying, but Ella remained dry eyed. And then she and Sister Barbara, both of them wearing their ordinary grey habits, stepped inside the armoured car. At first, they were imprisoned in Perm from where she wrote that they had been guarded by Lithuanians who were extremely kind to them, but then the Lithuanian guards had been replaced by Russians who were brutal and whom she 'greatly pitied'. From Perm they were

[1] See Introduction, page 32.

removed to Ekaterinburg and from there to Alapaevsk a small town to the north, where they were kept imprisoned during the first weeks of the summer, and where they were joined by some of Ella's relatives. Then, on the evening of July 18th, a lorry pulled up outside the school building where they were being detained and they were abruptly ordered to get in. Among the prisoners was the Grand-Duke Serge Michailovitch, the son of Grand-Duke Michael of Russia, the Grand Duke's equerry and valet, and four other Russian princes.

'Soon enough they cleared the little town and were in the open country, and the splendours of a high summer evening broke upon them. The Grand-Duchess and Prince John began singing the *Magnificat*, and the others joined them. The guards did not silence them. The last verse sung, Elizabeth, watching the evening sun gild the tops of high firs of a wood ahead of them, began *Sviete Tikhiy* ("Hail, Gentle Light"). They came through a forest fragrant with mushrooms and wild strawberries. They came to a vast open space edged with trees to the east, with distant chimneys of some settlement seen in the distance. There the lorry stopped.

'The guards jumped down and ordered the prisoners to follow them. Less than fifty yards ahead they saw the open mouth of a disused mine-shaft, and the guards began pushing them towards it. Grand-Duke Serge Michailovitch struggled so violently that one of the men shot him but very clumsily. The Grand-Duke was not killed when they threw him down the shaft. There are no details extant about any of the others except the Grand-Duchess. With the guards' hands clutching her shoulders, she knelt at the very edge of the pit and said very clearly and loudly: "Dear God, forgive them, they know not what they do."[1]

'Deep as the shaft was, it was not deep enough to kill them, and the guards flung a couple of hand-grenades in the wake of the last prisoner. One grenade wounded the Grand-Duke's equerry.

[1] This paragraph has been slightly altered.

I

'Presently the lorry drove away. Later, peasants from the nearest hamlet drew as near as their fear permitted them. There were so many soldiers round about the neighbourhood that any effective help was out of the question. The peasants heard chanting coming up all through that night and the next day. It had begun very clear and firm; then it grew blurred, rang more and more faintly until silence fell upon that open space.

'A little later, the White Army, having taken Ekaterinburg reached Alapaevsk and hoped to rescue the prisoners kept at the school-house. Instead, the men were directed to the mouth of the mine-shaft. They had brought equipment with them, and one by one the bodies were brought to the surface. Elizabeth's veil had a large piece torn off. That piece had been used by her to bandage Prince John's right arm probably broken by the fall. He, Elizabeth and Sister Barbara had the three fingers of their right hand folded as though they were about to make the sign of the cross.'[1]

At the time of Ella's death, in the neighbourhood of Alapaevsk there happened to be a monk named Father Seraphim, who was the son of a merchant in Moscow who had greatly admired the Grand Duchess. Father Seraphim remembered Ella's sorrow that she had never been able to make a pilgrimage to the Holy Land and he made a vow that he would take the bodies of Ella and Sister Barbara to Palestine. Accordingly, he left Russia with their two coffins and after two years had succeeded in transporting them as far as Pekin. There, it was necessary to change the travel-worn coffins for new ones, and they were opened in the crypt of the Russian Church in the presence of the clergy and a number of émigrés. According to eye-witnesses, the Grand-Duchess's body was still incorrupt and the three fingers of her right hand were still folded in the sign of the cross. When the Marquess and Marchioness of Milford Haven heard that Ella's body had arrived

[1] E. M. Almedingen, *An Unbroken Unity—A memoir of Grand-Duchess Serge of Russia 1864-1918*. London: Bodley Head, 1964.

in Pekin, they managed to obtain permission to transfer her body to Jerusalem where—with Princess Louise—they were able to attend the final interment in January 1921. The coffins were buried in a little Russian Orthodox Church that had been erected years before by Ella's late husband, Serge, on the slope of the Mount of Olives, near the Garden of Gethsemane. Near the church there is a Russian convent, and the head of the convent was the Abbess Tamara (originally, Princess Tatiana of Russia)[1] who was both Ella's niece and the sister of three of the young Russian princes who died in the mine-shaft.

Three times a year a requiem is sung for the Grand-Duchess and Father Seraphim, today over ninety years old, lives on the slopes of the Mount of Olives. A Swedish bishop who had visited Palestine, told Crown Princess Louise that both the Abbess Tamara and Father Seraphim, despite their modest existence were in need of help and so Louise regularly sent them money.

These, however, are only a few of the people who Princess Louise helped. 'She was not,' says the Margravine of Baden, 'one of those people who gave up, and I know that over the years she sold her private jewelry to be able to fulfil the obligations she had undertaken.'

And finally, there is a delightful story about one of Princess Louise's more unusual pieces of war work. Alicia Pearson tells me that in 1940 her son-in-law, Major Michael Smiley of the Rifle Brigade, was taken prisoner by the Germans at Dieppe. It was extremely difficult to get parcels from England to him in the prisoner-of-war camp and so, as Mrs Pearson knew that Crown Princess Louise was organizing help for prisoners-of-war, she asked Louise whether she could possibly do anything for him. Sure enough, a parcel arrived at the camp for Major Smiley, containing—amongst many other coveted articles—a bundle of

---

[1] Princess Tatiana was the eldest daughter of Grand-Duke Constantine of Russia. She is not to be confused with Grand-Duchess Tatiana, the daughter of Tsar Nicholas II, whose letters appear in the last chapter of this book.

underclothes. 'They must have been some of the King's under-clothes,' Mrs Pearson says, 'for my son-in-law told me that his friends in the camp said to each other, "Have you *seen* Smiley's pyjamas?" So, I assume they must have been marked with the King's monogram with the crown above.'

# CHAPTER 6

## The Sinking of the Kelly

MEANWHILE, in June 1937—just about the time of his thirty-seventh birthday—the Queen's brother Louis had been promoted and so became one of the youngest peacetime captains ever. Not long before the war broke out, Lord Mountbatten was appointed to the command of the Flotilla leader *Kelly* and seven other ships of the K Class, who formed the Fifth Destroyer Flotilla. When Lord Mountbatten received his command, however, all the ships of the Flotilla were still under construction, but the *Kelly* was the first to be finished and she was ready in the nick of time, just before the end of August 1939. Lord Mountbatten took her over from the builders, Hawthorn Leslie, and steamed her down from their yard at Hebburn-on-Tyne, to H.M. Dockyard at Chatham, where he commissioned her with a crew of some seventeen officers and two hundred and forty men. Although it was not of course possible for a captain to select his men, it is known that many men in Chatham who had served with Lord Mountbatten before, did what they could to get themselves drafted to the *Kelly*. In his speech to the ship's company on commissioning day, Mountbatten pointed out that in peacetime the commissioning programme for one of H.M. ships lasted three weeks. During this time, all the ammunition, all the stores, all the fuel and all the fittings of the ship were brought on board, sorted out and stowed away. During this time too, the men were taught their action stations and became familiar with their ship.

'Well, you've read your papers,' he is reported to have said, 'and you know that Ribbentrop signed a non-aggression pact with Stalin yesterday. As I see it, that means war next week, so I will give you not three weeks, but three days to get this ship ready to sail. None of us will take our clothes off or sling our hammocks or turn in for the next three days and nights until this job is finished. Then we'll send Hitler a telegram saying "The *Kelly's* ready—you can start your war".'

When Hitler started his war, the *Kelly* was ready. She played her full part in the war, and although her captain protested that he did nothing out of the ordinary and nothing that every other destroyer was not doing at the same time, yet because the *Kelly* was mined and repaired, torpedoed and repaired and finally sunk by dive bombers, and because Mountbatten and his Flotilla staff were torpedoed in a night action when they were aboard the destroyer *Javelin*, which was leading the Flotilla while the *Kelly* was being repaired, therefore quite a story grew up about the *Kelly*. Noel Coward, a life-long friend of Mountbatten's, used to visit him in the *Kelly* and he wrote the script for the film *In Which We Serve*, without mentioning it to Mountbatten until the script was finished. Mountbatten was worried to find the film based on the story of the *Kelly* and he persuaded Coward to change the circumstances as much as possible so that the captain in the destroyer *Torrin* should not resemble himself. However, the disguise was not very successful and in his book *Last Viceroy*[1] Ray Murphy describes the film as follows:

'It was possibly the only motion picture made during the pre-Pearl Harbour stages of the war which captured the imagination of audiences both sides of the Atlantic, and which was able to produce in Americans the illusion of living through those burning moments of England's lonely months against the Axis. . . . Shown simultaneously in both England and America at a time when, according to the Germans, the British Navy had been obliterated, it did more than any other picture of the war to stir the public, by showing them without the aid of false heroics or sham posturing the heroism of a few. It also did much to restore

[1] Ray Murphy, *Last Viceroy*. London: Jarrolds, 1948.

the morale of the Royal Navy and to make its officers and men doubly proud of their Service. Indeed, that usually callous film magnate, Sir Arthur Jarrett, once told me that he had wept while reading the script. What made the film so incomparably superior to others of the same kind was the simple truth of the story it tried to tell—the story of Lord Louis Mountbatten during this time when, in his ship *Kelly*, he was in command of the 5th Destroyer Flotilla. The story as told, however, was, and only could be, a shadow of the reality.'

Eventually, on May 23, 1940, the *Kelly* was sunk during the Battle of Crete. It was typical of the close bond between them, that Mountbatten wrote a special account of the sinking of the *Kelly* for his sister, and his letter is given below.

'On 23rd May, I understand that the German radio announced that the *Kelly* had been sunk with all hands, which included her Captain. I hope this did not worry you and that you realized it was German propaganda. Edwina was very worried at first but as soon as the news came through that we had been picked up, the Admiralty told her and put her out of her misery. Patricia and Pammy were worst hit because their stupid Governess brought them out of school to tell them I was missing, because she believed the German propaganda, and so they were pretty worried children for 24 hours.

'As a matter of fact it was a bit of a miracle that we were picked up, at least those of us who survived, which in the case of the *Kelly* was less than half the Officers and men.

'The *Kelly* and some of the destroyers of my flotilla had been stationed in Malta and when we were not out on sweeps, we were subjected to a lot of air attack in harbour which was unpleasant and frightening. However, except for the *Jersey*, who was sunk just after passing the breakwaters into Grand Harbour by a magnetic mine, none of the rest of my flotilla were damaged.

'When the news came to Malta of the beginning of the Battle of Crete I, realized that we should be sent for to take part. I went and called on the Admiral, Ford, and I gave him a suitcase which contained a suit of blue uniform, a suit of white uniform, pyjamas, underclothes, a sponge and a toothbrush, and I told him that if the *Kelly* was sunk, as seemed quite probable in the Battle of Crete, and if I were picked up, as I hoped I would be, I would be presumably taken to Alexandria and I would be grateful if the Admiral could put my suitcase into the next R.A.F. plane flying from Malta to Alexandria. He promised he would do so. I got the suitcase ready because as we were the latest and finest destroyers, I was sure we would be used for rearguard action in the most dangerous exposed positions and we would be the most likely to be sunk. In any case, after 21 months of intense activity in war, it was unlikely that the *Kelly* could go on having lucky escapes.

'Shortly after this I got the signal to join the Fleet and we sailed. We joined the Mediterranean Fleet at the same moment as a medium level bombing attack took place and a number of bombs were aimed at us, but luckily we were able to dodge them.

'Later that evening on May 22nd, I was ordered to proceed into Canea Bay to bombard Maleme airstrip which the Germans had just captured and which the New Zealand Brigade were waiting to counter-attack as soon as our bombardment lifted.

'Having lost the *Jersey*, I only had three ships of my own Division instead of four and they were the *Kelly*, *Kashmir* and *Kipling*. We set off around the North-Eastern Cape of Crete and quite early on the *Kipling*'s steering-gear became defective and as I couldn't risk having a ship whose steering wasn't perfect following me on such a hazardous night operation, I told her to rejoin Rear Admiral Rawlings, having first steered to the westwards for at least three hours not to betray the presence of this force. The little cherub who sits up aloft and looks after us poor sailormen must have put the *Kipling*'s steering-gear out of action, for it was due to this incident that we owe our lives. As we entered Canea Bay, a large *caique* was sighted, loaded with German troops steering towards Crete. Both ships opened fire and sank her very quickly, the wretched Germans jumping into the water in full marching order. In any other circumstances, we would have stopped to pick them up, but even at 30 knots it was doubtful if I could get into position to carry out the bombardment in time, so I had to push on.

'We hadn't got the exact position of the aerodrome, but worked out from a contour map where the airstrip must be. After having completed our bombardment we withdrew at high speed and came across another *caique* carrying ammunition. Shortly after we started firing at her, she blew up in a very spectacular way.

'Dawn broke as we rounded the North-Eastern Cape and we steamed at 30 knots down the Kithera Channel to rejoin Rawlings' force. As the sun rose a German DO 215 appeared out of the East and was engaged before she dropped five bombs, which missed *Kelly* astern; forty minutes later three more DO 215s made a high-level bombing attack on *Kelly* and *Kashmir* in the face of good 4.7″ controlled fire. Both ships avoided the bombs. I sent for my breakfast on the bridge and I continued reading C. S. Forester's book about my favourite hero, Hornblower, called *Ship of the Line*.

'Just before 8 a.m. we sighted a mast above the horizon and I hoped it belonged to the *Kipling*, though I couldn't think why she had waited for us.

'By now the sun was well up, the sea was calm and it was a lovely Mediterranean day. Just about 8 a.m. we suddenly saw ominous black objects. Their distinctive shape soon revealed them as the dreaded Stukas, the Ju87s. They had a reputation for diving almost vertically on ships and only releasing their bombs when they were so low that they couldn't miss. They were hard to distinguish against the rising sun but presently we could see that they broke up into two parties of about twelve in each.

'I pressed the alarm rattlers, for this required full action stations and I hoisted the signal to the *Kashmir* to "act independently".

'The first party made for the *Kashmir* and they started diving in waves of three. I could see the bombs dropping round her and all her guns were firing. Then a wave of three peeled off from our lot and started to dive. I put the telegraphs at "full ahead". I gave the order "Hard-a-starboard" to bring the ship under the dive-bomber to force it to dive ever steeper in the hopes it would finally be pushed beyond the vertical and lose control. This happened and the bomber hit the sea close by, sending up an enormous splash. I reversed the wheel "hard-a-port". The next dive-bomber was also forced to dive steeper and steeper and this one we actually shot down into the sea. The next one also missed.

'But now to my horror I saw that the third or fourth wave had hit the *Kashmir* somewhere amidships and she was finished. I remember thinking "Oh, God, even if we are not hit now, we shall have to stay and pick up the survivors and they will get us then!"

'I think it was about the third wave of three where one of the Stukas suddenly came lower than the others and although I had the wheel over to hard-a-starboard and we were turning at over 30 knots under full helm, the bomb was released so close to the ship that it couldn't miss. It hit square on X gun-deck and killed the crew of the twin 4.7″ gun mounting, including that nice young boy Michael Sturdee who was in command.

'The next wave were coming in and I gave the order to the navigator "midships" and then "hard-a-port" but we only listed over more heavily to port. All ships list outwards under full helm at full speed and this list was getting worse. I gave the order "stop engines" and then heard the coxswain shout up the voice pipe "Ship won't answer the helm. No reply to the engine room telegraphs!" Then I realized we were for it.

'The next wave of Stukas had started their dive towards us and I remember shouting out "Keep all guns firing", an unnecessary order for all the guns continued to fire until the gun crews were actually washed away from their guns. I realized the bomb must have torn a gaping hole down near X magazine, as we had lost our stability and were rolling right over. I suddenly saw the water rise on our port side in a raging torrent of over 30 knots and thought "Whatever happens I must stay with the ship as long as I can. I must be the last to leave her alive." We were over beyond 90 degrees now and I climbed up on to the distance-correction indicator of my station-keeping gear which I had invented and was fitted in the flotilla. With my arms, I clung round the gyro-compass pedestal. And then the sea came in a roaring maelstrom. I saw officers and men struggling to get out of the bridge and then I took an enormously deep breath as the water closed over my head. The awful part was that even after we were upside down we continued to race through the water, though of course at a rapidly decreasing rate. Somehow I managed to flounder and work my way across the upside-down bridge until I got to the bullet-proof bridge-screens. Here I had to pull myself under, and up to this moment it was horribly dark. A faint glimmer of daylight appeared on the other side of the bridge-screens but the water was churning round and I could distinguish nothing.

'I suddenly felt my lungs were going to burst and that I would have to open my mouth unless I could somehow keep it shut. With my right hand I gripped my mouth in a vice-like grip and with my left hand I held my nostrils shut. It was a fight of will-power. Would my hands obey me and keep my mouth and nose shut longer than the reflex action which would force me to open them and swallow a lot of sea water?

'I had my Gieve waistcoat on, but had not blown up the rubber ring which is fitted in the waistcoat. This was lucky, because it made it easier for me to get out from under the bridge, but now I had to kick hard to fight my way to the surface. Slowly, infinitely slowly, the water got brighter and brighter and then suddenly, with lungs bursting, I broke surface. I gasped for breath, but the next moment I saw the stern of the ship approaching us with both our great propellors still revolving in the air. They looked as though they were going to come right over us and hit us. I saw the navigator, Lieutenant Maurice Butler-Bowdon, with his back to the ship. I yelled to him to "swim like hell" because I was afraid that the propellors would hit him. We both managed to get clear but only by a matter of six or seven yards!

'At this moment, up bobbed one of our Stoker Petty Officers, a great character and a bit of a humorist. He looked at the "pilot" and then at me and then produced a typically cheery crack. "Extraordinary how the scum always comes to the top, isn't it, Sir?" I looked round. I could see one Carley raft, which someone must have had time to release before the ship turned over. I saw men all round me in the water and yelled out "Everybody swim to the raft."

'I suddenly noticed I still had my steel helmet on, and this seemed ridiculous in the water so I took it off and threw it away. I pulled the mouthpiece and tube out of my waistcoat and blew up the rubber ring. That made it easier to stay afloat. Then at that moment, suddenly and unexpectedly a row of splashes appeared between me and the Carley raft; then with a roar one of the Stukas shot overhead with her machine-guns firing at us. I bitterly regretted throwing away my tin hat; you have no idea how naked one feels in the water without one when one is being machine-gunned.

'By now I had reached the raft, and gave orders that only the wounded were to be allowed inside the raft; those who were not wounded were to hold on outside and those for whom there was no room would hold on to the men who were holding on to the raft.

'The dive-bombers came again, and again a hail of machine-gun bullets swept by, this time hitting some of the men around the raft. As men died or were killed, I had them gently taken out of the raft and men recently wounded put in to take their place. It was a gruesome and unpleasant business, and yet the sea was calm, the sun was shining and it reminded me of so many bathes I had had in the Mediterranean in the days before the war.

'My eyes were stinging and my mouth had a bitter acrid taste and looking round I saw everybody's face smothered in heavy oil fuel, looking like negro minstrels. This added greatly to our discomfort and to the unpleasantness.

'I thought it would be a good thing to start singing to keep up people's courage and so I started that popular song "Roll out the barrel" and the others soon joined in, which seemed to help.

'And then the miracle happened. The *Kipling* appeared from below the horizon at full speed coming to our rescue. She had seen the twenty-four Ju87s diving on us and didn't think we would be able to survive. It was a gallant act of the Captain, for he was obviously going to draw the attacks on himself now.

'The *Kelly* was just afloat. One could see the bottom under the bows afloat. Suddenly she started to go as the *Kipling* approached and I called for "Three cheers for the old ship". It was for me the saddest moment of a sad day.

'As *Kipling* approached, she unfortunately grazed the sharp bow of the *Kelly* under water and was holed. Luckily the hole was in the reserve feed tank which meant no water actually got into the ship.

'*Kipling* lowered scrambling-nets over her side. I told everybody to swim to the scrambling-nets as soon as they could. I towed a very badly wounded man, who was bleeding freely, but by the time I got him as far as the *Kipling* he was obviously very dead and so I let him go.

'As soon as I got on board I went up to the bridge. I was still in command of my flotilla and the *Kipling* was under my orders, but naturally I did not interfere with the Captain, Aubrey St Clair-Ford, who was a brave, brilliant and very competent man. I thanked him for coming to our rescue and asked him to go over and pick up the survivors of the *Kashmir*.

'This was a much more difficult job, for she went down far more slowly than the *Kelly* and there were no less than five Carley rafts and they had more survivors than the *Kelly*. Hardly had we got opposite the first Carley raft and stopped the engines than some Junkers 88s appeared. Although not of the terrifying vertical dive-bomber type, they dived in a shallow dive and the Captain had to go ahead with the wheel hard over to avoid being hit. Every time he came back to a raft the same thing happened. Finally I told him to lower his fast motor-boat who could then go round collecting the survivors from each raft and would be able to come alongside the *Kipling* in whatever position we were, without having to try and manoeuvre the whole ship alongside a Carley raft. Aubrey thought this a good idea and gave the necessary orders.

'Hardly had the boat reached the water than he came to me and said "There's another Junkers 88 diving at us. I'm afraid I shall have to go ahead out of it."

'I shouted to the men in the waist to "cut the falls" of the motor-boat. This was necessary because the fast motor-boat is not a "sea-boat"; it is normally only lowered in harbour. There is no quick-release hook but only a big steel shackle with a screw-pin which takes half a dozen turns to unscrew. There was no time to do this. That is why I told them to cut the actual rope falls which were holding the boat.

'A man with a knife dashed at the foremost falls and cut them. I shouted "Cut the after falls, you bloody fool!" because I knew what was going to happen.

'I had personally supervised a course of all the Engineer Officers of my flotilla at the Experimental Oil Fuel Establishment at Haslar, to ensure that they should be able to increase speed at a far greater rate than had been customary. The *Kipling* was no exception. Her 40,000 horse-powers were applied with such speed that the ship leaped forward and the bows of the motor boat were driven under. My cry to cut the after falls had been heard by my own First Lieutenant, Lord Hugh Beresford and the First Lieutenant of the *Kipling*, John Bushe. Together they leaped to the after falls at the moment when the ship had gathered such speed and the heavy motor boat had sunk so deep in the water that the after davit was pulled right over and seemed to crush them as the falls tore away and the boat sank in the sea together with the two First Lieutenants. Hugh was one of my oldest friends; he was a midshipman with me in 1927 in the *Queen Elizabeth*. He was a great-nephew of Papa's great friend, Lord Charles Beresford. I think this incident hurt me more than any that day.

'The Captain remarked "This is going to take a very long time now. I only hope they don't get us before we pick up all the *Kashmir's*." I replied that that was my responsibility and told him to go ahead. With great skill and great courage he gradually nosed his way from one raft to another in between the persistent attacks of the Ju88s. But it was a long and painful business and after two hours some of my own Staff Officers who had been saved came to me to ask whether I would not consider allowing the *Kipling* to leave the rest of the *Kashmir's* survivors and proceed to Alexandria. They pointed out, with complete justification, that the *Kipling* now had on board all *Kelly's* survivors, more than half of the *Kashmir's* survivors, and it was becoming more and more difficult to pick up the remainder and avoid being hit by the bombers. I decided that we should stay. After three hours, there was only one more raft-load to be picked up and this proved particularly difficult because the attacks were getting worse. After consulting the Captain, my staff came back and urged that the right decision was to let the *Kipling* go before she was sunk with the loss of an additional five or six hundred lives. I decided we would stay to pick up all we could. I felt it would be better for us all to be sunk together than to leave our flotilla-mates struggling helplessly in the water without any prospect of being saved.

'At last we were able to turn for Alexandria. The damage to the *Kipling* prevented her from doing more than about half speed, so we limped home at 16 or 17 knots, the mess decks and upper decks everywhere being crowded with survivors, many of them wounded and in poor shape.

'I went round with a notebook and pencil which I borrowed, to get particulars of the more severely wounded and to find out which of their families they wanted me to send messages to, to say that they had been saved.

'I found that my Leading Steward, Kamenzuli, had been killed and my Petty Officer Steward, Micellef, had been injured and badly burned. I was particularly sad about this, for they were the only two of the original Maltese retinue who had volunteered to stay with the ship when the remainder were released on our not going to the Mediterranean.

'I had a word with the flotilla Engineer Officer, Commander Mike Evans. He had been in the Engine Room when we turned over. In accordance with my strong orders, no one had moved at all until he gave the order to try and get out. By this time the ship was upside-down and they had to jump feet first through the water to the two little circular engine room hatches. Somehow or other several of them managed to escape by this method but their experience must have been a great deal worse than ours on the bridge.

'When I finished going round the men I went back to the bridge. The attack was still going on. I sat in the Captain's chair on the starboard side of the bridge and watched with admiration the way Aubrey managed to dodge the bombs. Of course, these were shallow dive-bombers and not the steep dive-bombers and so it was much easier, but even so there were a horrible lot of near-misses. I counted over eighty near-misses, some of them so close that everybody on the bridge was drenched with the spray. Her guns-crews had been augmented by some of the best gunnery ratings from the *Kelly* and the *Kashmir* which helped to fight off the bombers.

'Finally they gave up the attempt and so we steamed on through the night. At dawn we ran out of fuel but the *Protector* was sent out to meet us and give us some more fuel.

'As we entered Alexandria Harbour, everyone who could still walk crowded out on to the upper decks. There must have been between four and five hundred, crowding every inch.

'The Mediterranean Fleet, which had only got back shortly

before us from the battle, were moored close together in Harbour. All the ship's companies cleared lower deck and gave us a heart-warming cheer as we steamed past.

'I went ashore in the first boat that was sent for us, to report to the Commander-in-Chief. At the landing-stage I was met by the cheery, grinning face of our nephew Philip, who had come to meet me. He roared with laughter on seeing me and when I asked him what was up, he said: "You have no idea how funny you look. You look like a nigger minstrel!" I had forgotten how completely smothered we all were in oil fuel.

'The Commander-in-Chief, Admiral Sir Andrew Cunning-ham, sent a car to collect me and put me up in his own house and lent me some clothes. I enquired about the famous suitcase, which would now be so handy, but it never turned up. Later enquiries showed that the Royal Air Force had been too clever by half. A printed label with my name and the Broadlands address on it was still attached to the suitcase, so disregarding Admiral Ford's orders to take it to Alexandria, they flew it straight back to England, where it arrived but was not of much use. So I had to go, like everybody else, and buy some ready-made clothing.

'That evening, the surviving Officers of the *Kelly* had a dinner party at the Club. We had been a very happy Mess and now nine were missing and only eight of us were present. And yet the evening was a tremendous success. We reminisced about the happy times of the Commission. We talked in turn about each of those who were absent in terms of warm friendship and affection. It was rather as though they were just temporarily away and not gone for good.

'The next day came the painful business of saying goodbye to the survivors of the ship's company. Those who were not wounded were being drafted to other ships to carry on with the Battle. I made them one of my little speeches, but without any jokes, and when the moment came to shake hands with each of them, it was almost more than I could bear. I somehow felt this

K

really was the last of the *Kelly*, for while the ship's company were gathered together, her spirit appeared to survive. Yet I couldn't help feeling her spirit would survive, because we had all loved the ship so much and were such a happy band of brothers. I have never known a ship with such a tremendously high ship's spirit and I don't suppose I ever will again.

'I was sent home by the Commander-in-Chief by air via the Central African route and with delays the trip took me more than a fortnight.

'I reported to the Prime Minister personally on return and gave an account of the Battle.

'To my utter delight, I have been appointed in command of a fine new ship and will soon be back again in the battle at sea. I have something extra to fight for now. I have to pay back an enemy who butchered my men in the water after he had sunk the ship.'

Naturally Louise's reaction to the sinking of the *Kelly* was one of great sympathy. She cabled Lord Mountbatten to say she had received his account of the Battle and then later, sent him the following letter from Ulriksdal.

Ulriksdal,
July 8th, 1941.

'*Darling Dickie*,

'I sent you that laconic cable just to let you know I had had the account of the sinking of the *Kelly*. I could not well say in a cable how thrilled, proud and harrowed I had been. How I had been longing to know how the *Kelly* was lost and what had happened to you and how you were saved. God, what days you went through. So it was on the 23rd of May, that that foul dive bomber, who himself disappeared with his plane into the sea, got the *Kelly*.

'I am glad for you that so many of your crew were saved. How lucky the sea was warm as you had to be so long in it till you were picked up. My blood froze and boiled with horror and rage that the men in the sea and you were machine gunned, like doing it to wounded people. How can one! The only reason I can imagine, a form of mad, beastly revenge because of Germans being drowned when their boats were prevented from landing in Crete. I won't try and think of it anymore.

'Dickie dear, I am so sad for you. You lost your beloved fine *Kelly* you were so proud of. I had hoped she was a charmed ship and I had hoped to see her some day.

'A kind thoughtful member of the British Legation staff has sent me a photo of the *Kelly*, done out on patrol the first time after her refit, a stormy sunset sky and picturesque photo, but some time when we meet again keep a good photo of her for me. I am anyhow now going to have this one framed to go with the photo of your "P.31"[1] in 1918.

'It was lovely getting Mama's wire when you had arrived home. It made me so happy for Mama knowing she had you well and fit at home.

'Poor Nada, I wish there could be some nice, good reason for her David to come home for a while.[2]

'I hope sometime I will hear some news of Philip from Mama to pass on through his sisters to Alice. She wrote to Dolla by air mail a while ago, said she had not felt so well for years and was busy nursing and looking after the poor.[3]

'Also for poor Andrea,[4] I would like to be able to send a little news. He still lives on board the yacht *Davida* at Cannes, and says he is not hungry as he is a small eater! Food conditions are near starving on the Riviera. He was so thankful he heard the news you were saved and hoped it was really true. He is now so

[1] "P.31" was one of the Portsmouth Escort Flotilla with fifty officers and men of which Lord Louis Mountbatten was First Lieutenant and Second-in-Command, when just eighteen years old in World War I.

[2] Nada is her sister-in-law, the Marchioness of Milford Haven. David is the latter's son, the third Marquess of Milford Haven.

[3] Alice is her sister, Princess Alice of Greece. Philip is the Duke of Edinburgh and Dolla, the Margravine of Baden.

[4] Andrea is Princess Alice's husband, Prince Andrew of Greece.

cut off from outside news as the port authorities have confiscated his radio.

'How I wonder what job you will get or have got.

'There is little news to give you about myself. We are having more or less a holiday now and enjoying a quiet time in this lovely place, so improved since you were here. Gustaf plays a lot of golf.

'I am writing to Mama too so this can't be too long. I will end now.

'Ever, ever so much love, Dickie darling,

*Your loving sister,*

*Louise.'*

P.S. What a comfort it is, only few and small air raids lately in England.

# CHAPTER 7

# Queen of Sweden

O<sup>N</sup> October 29, 1950 the old King of Sweden, Gustaf V,[1] died peacefully at Drottningholm in his ninety-third year after a reign which had spanned four decades and Crown Prince Gustaf—now to be known as Gustaf VI Adolf—succeeded to the throne. There was no coronation, since early in this century the Swedish royal family decided that they were not justified in putting their country to the great expense of ceremonial coronations. Today, therefore, although the Swedish sovereign bears all the adornments of royalty for the great ceremonies of state and although the Crown is always placed beside the throne at the opening of Parliament, nevertheless it is never set upon the King's head.

Louise's reaction to the change from Crown Princess to Queen was typical of her democratic leanings. She found the promotion grossly exaggerated and complained to Dolla that people had crowded so closely round the Palace that her car could hardly get out of the gates. As Queen Victoria had died twenty years ago, in 1930, and Sweden had not had a Queen since, it was perhaps not surprising that there was unusual excitement, but Louise did not feel at home as the centre of attention and in one letter she wrote to Dolla: 'People look at me as if I was something remarkable. I don't look any different from what I did yesterday, do I?' And Louise was particularly upset to find herself barricaded in by a crowd outside the couturier's, when she went to try on her mourning clothes. Eventually, she escaped to a neighbouring house and was met by her car some distance away.

Soon after the accession, King Gustaf Adolf and Queen Louise

---

[1] At King Gustaf's funeral, King George VI was represented by the Duke of Gloucester. Lord Mountbatten also attended.

abolished some of the more antiquated formalities at Court, made changes in Court posts, pruned the staff and reorganized the Palace officials. Similarly, they brought Court etiquette up to date and in 1954 published a new edition of the *Regulations, Instructions and Ceremonial to be Observed at the Swedish Court,* which had last been revised in 1911, changing the title to *A Guide to Duties at the Swedish Court.*

Of the two of them, it was natural that the King should stand out more prominently. In some quarters disquiet was expressed at the thought of a 'professor' on the throne, but the forcefulness of Gustaf Adolf's first two speeches as King helped dispel some of these misgivings.

A characteristic that Louise had in common with her husband was her extreme thoroughness. When she became Queen, one of her first actions was to go through every one of the five hundred and fifty rooms in Stockholm Palace and decide which should be modernized. As a result, many of the Palace rooms now bear the impact of the Queen's personality. The White Sea Room, the grandest of the assembly rooms, was previously rather a bleak chamber and the arrangements for celebrations not particularly impressive. But, I remember looking down from the musicians' gallery at the special decorations for King Gustaf Adolf's seventieth birthday, after the Palace had been modernized. There were Savonnerie carpets and oriental rugs, groups of sofas and chairs in matching colours, lilac-coloured satin curtains draped softly beside the tall windows, crackling fires, livery-clad footmen serving, and here and there lilac, azaleas, and delicate laburnum. Everything glittered in the light of the baroque chandeliers. Bejewelled ladies in stately dresses and uniformed gentlemen wearing orders stood chatting together. Then the Master of Ceremonies raised his staff and the King entered, and at his side walked the Queen in beautiful jewellery and a dress of satin brocade.

It has been said that Queen Louise was primarily an ordinary person, but when appearing in public she was the personification of queenliness. She always took great care with her clothes and the combination of jewels she wore with them on State occasions and she enjoyed both entertaining and going out. When it came to preparations for festivities at the Palace, everything had to be done just as she wanted it and nothing was left to chance. The character of parties at the Palace was changed when King Gustaf Adolf and Queen Louise came to the throne. For some time, it had been the custom for the King and Queen to hold 'representation dinners', to which were invited select members of the public. These had tended to be rather uniform affairs, but now the royal couple invited guests from a much wider circle, including representatives from commerce and industry, from the cultural world, the civil service and the diplomatic corps. Both the King and Queen were born with enquiring minds and they were eager to meet as many people as possible from different walks of life. At these dinners, they tried to discourage formality and small talk, and were determined to make good use of the opportunity to really get to know their people.

The Queen's improvements at the Palace, however, were concerned with more than parties. Special care was devoted to the guest apartments, which were redecorated, and Louise tried to make them as comfortable as possible and to give them a personal touch. The staff received the Queen's special attention too. Staff amenities had become rather out of date, so Louise had their rooms fitted with radios and electric heating. Also, she took trouble to acquaint herself with everyone's family circumstances, and showed a keen interest in their children, all of whom received presents from her at Christmas. And, from time to time, she liked to arrange small parties for them.

Once the modernization of Stockholm Palace had been completed, the Queen clung to the reins firmly and I well remember her liveliness and vitality when she received me at the Palace. The Queen's Lady-in-Waiting, Brita Steuch, met me in the Hall of Mirrors to say that Her Majesty would be with me in a minute. As the Queen was detained on the telephone for some time, I was

shown towards a door which opened on to a chain of rooms—
the Green Room, the Blue Room, the Museum Room, and
finally, the Queen's study where with the telephone receiver to
her ear, Queen Louise sat gesturing vividly. Her thin figure
looked small and far away, but nonetheless she radiated vitality
and it flew into my mind that here was the dynamo in the heart
of the Palace, the centre of the great machine. The impression
was strengthened as the Queen came with swift steps towards me
and opened the conversation at a lively tempo. When pressing a
point, she spoke so quickly that the words tripped over one
another. I am told that sometimes when she grew really excited,
she would skip both words and sentences, so that one had to
guess what it was she wanted to say. And always when she spoke,
the lively expression in her face seemed to vary with her words
and gestures.

Queen Louise devoted a great deal of energy not only to the
modernization of Stockholm Palace, but also to Drottningholm,
where the royal family came to live more and more during the
winter.[1] In many ways, Drottningholm is the creation of the
Queens of Sweden, and the word *Drottning* is in fact Swedish for
queen. Queen Hedvig Eleanora, widow of Carl X Gustaf, commissioned Nicodemus Tessin the Elder, the leading architect of
the time in Sweden, to design the present palace. The building
was begun under his direction, and at his death the task was
completed by his son, Nicodemus Tessin the Younger, who was
to become famous throughout Europe. The work on the interior
of the Palace continued during the last four decades of the
seventeenth century and was completed at the beginning of the
1700s, and so the building is in the style of seventeenth-century
French palaces with contributions from Swedish baroque.

The next Queen to be involved with Drottningholm was
Louisa Ulrika, consort of King Adolf Frederick and sister of
Frederick II of Prussia. She had it enlarged after her marriage to

---

[1] It may be mentioned that she had considerable assistance from the Marshal of the
Court, Lieutenant-Colonel Wilhelm Tham.

Adolf Frederick in 1744 and the interior was done largely in the rococco style. She is said to have loved the Palace and once exclaimed, 'All my foolishness has gone into adding to and decorating Drottningholm'.

When Louise became Queen in 1950, she completed the modernization and made it considerably more comfortable. She also succeeded in giving a certain warmth and intimacy to the Palace's most beautiful room, the Large Stone Room, which was —and still is—used for family gatherings and for guests. The brightly coloured tapestries of hunting scenes, which cover the walls, were commissioned in Delft in the 1640s for the coronation of Queen Christina of Sweden. In two corners of the room stand Chinese urns—a relic from the days of Queen Louisa Ulrika— in which lilac trees are always planted. But what sets its stamp on the Stone Room is the magnificent saffron-yellow carpet, which was presented by King Alfonso XIII of Spain when he visited Stockholm in 1929.

Many of the people close to the Queen have told me how she organized the running of the Palace. She wrote 'orders' on small pieces of paper, either at her desk or at the dining-table, and the pieces of paper were then sent to whoever they concerned. Louise took an active, detailed part in absolutely everything and decided the placing of guests, the allocation of rooms and so on, herself. She was extremely particular that everything should be in order, and when Admiral Stig H:son Ericson was appointed Grand Marshal of the Court, the Queen told him without delay all that it was important for him to know about her domain. He had understandably spoken rather vaguely about the different guest rooms—and within an hour he received a sheet of quarto from the Queen, on which she had typed out the names of all the guest rooms and a brief description of each.

The Queen very much enjoyed being consulted over even the smallest detail. And although the King usually did ask her opinion, she was often heard to say that she did not 'want to be a parcel'. And occasionally she could express opposition to a decision on which she had not been consulted in the first place especially as she was sometimes rather hasty to draw conclusions.

In general, however, she was the soul of willingness. The French have an expression for two people who are close to one another—'*On les voit toujours sur le même pas*'. This was certainly the case with King Gustaf Adolf and Queen Louise, and her husband's well-being was always her first consideration. She regarded it as her special mission to see he did not overstrain himself. She constantly worried about the terrifying number of his engagements and urged the Grand Marshal of the Court to reduce them. And it was she who insisted that he should follow his doctor's advice and rest. The relationship between them was tender and gay, solicitous but not without banter. The Queen used to tease her husband about his reluctance to read novels. She claimed that he had only read two novels since their marriage —and that even then he had asked whether he had to read every page. To this, Louise replied that, unlike archaeological treatises, novels are read for pleasure and so one can skip the dull bits. In fact, Louise always had a tremendous sense of humour and when she was awarded the Grand Cross of the Legion of Honour, she protested that she did not want to receive it 'because I myself am growing smaller and smaller, and the sashes bigger and bigger. So finally, there will be a sash and nothing else'.

It was this same naturalness that made her popular during the royal tours of Sweden that followed the accession, and during one of these tours, a woman from Dalarna in central Sweden remarked:

'We found her a personality with style and will and a good person with enough imagination to be able to put herself in other people's situations and therefore to understand them. She did not just show herself and utter the usual conventional phrases, but she really identified herself with each and everyone's daily life.'

An incident from this tour of Dalarna gives an idea of the Queen's visits. In Falun, the largest town in Dalarna Province, the Queen went to the home of Maria Thunstedt, the eighty-two year old widow of a carter in the mountains. She went round the little red mining cottage consisting of one room and a kitchen, built by the slag-heap in Väderkvanbacken, where the old lady had lived since her marriage fifty-seven years before. The Queen sat down in the rocking-chair by the window and after a few moments, they were talking quite happily together. They talked of flowers, of the sweet-peas and bride's veil (*gypsophilia*) in the cottage garden, of the Queen's own gardening, of the children and grandchildren whose photographs lined the chest of drawers, then finally the old lady showed Louise the gold medal her husband had received for long service.

Similarly, the state visits of King Gustaf Adolf and Queen Louise were invariably a success and during their visit to France in May 1963 Louise accomplished the by no means inconsiderable feat of winning the admiration of President de Gaulle. Admittedly, omens for the visit were favourable, since King Gustaf Adolf (as a Bernadotte) was 'a great, great grandchild of France'[1] and there was thus a special bond of affection. The climax of the first day's programme was the banquet in the Elysée Palace and, as dusk began to fall over the park, President de Gaulle—with the kind of gesture of which the French are incomparable masters—presented a grand pageant for his guests. Beneath the trees, knights from *La Grande Armée* rode their whinnying horses; soldiers wearing green dolmans embroidered with gold (the uniform of the 1st and 7th Hussar Regiments—the regiments which, in the time of Napoleon, had fought under Jean Baptiste Bernadotte) marched past in glittering ranks; and the drums and trumpets sounded *A nous la gloire* and the *Marche d'Austerlitz*. Later, at the State banquet, Queen Louise earned de Gaulle's affection by saying: 'I hope you will excuse me not speaking very good French. But, after all, it was the French

---

[1] When Oscar II, the grandson of Jean Baptiste Bernadotte, visited the World Exhibition in Paris in 1900, during his official speech he referred to himself as '*le petit-fils de la France*'.

spoken by your soldiers in 1914.' The President then noticed that the Queen was wearing the French Soldiers' War Medal and, when he asked why it had been awarded, was told that it was for nursing wounded soldiers at Nevers.

'Madame,' he said, 'I salute a former member of our French Army. Surely no Queen has ever won our War Medal before?' De Gaulle and his wife are said to have taken an immediate liking to Queen Louise, and he once told the Swedish Ambassador in Paris that he 'admired her for her intelligence, her humour and her fantastic charm'.

The King and Queen of course paid many visits to England too. During one visit, in May 1955, when they were entertained to dinner by the Board of Admiralty at the Royal Naval College, Greenwich, the royal couple were the subject of two rather unusual toasts.

First, the First Lord of the Admiralty proposed the health of the King and Queen of Sweden.

'While the Board of the Admiralty has been anxious to entertain your Majesties before this date,' he said, 'it does give us particular pleasure now, that the postponement has meant that Her Majesty finds her brother (Lord Mountbatten) in the post of First Sea Lord, which her father held with such outstanding distinction. As the daughter of a great sailor, the sister of two sailors, and the aunt of two sailors, we give Your Majesty a particular welcome here tonight.' Then, after the toast had been drunk, the First Lord rose again to say: 'We have drunk the health of His Majesty the King of Sweden, but as tonight is a purely naval occasion, the Board of Admiralty feel that we must have a second toast to His Majesty as Admiral of the British Navy and, if I may so call her, to *his naval Queen.*'

Later, he explained that Queen Louise's early life could not have been more closely connected with the Royal Navy and that she had been brought up 'following the White Ensign'.

'I am told that she did three commissions[1] in the days before World War I,' he said, 'I feel that she has probably seen more of the famous warships of those days than any naval officer in this room tonight.'

[1] Usually, when Naval families talked about doing a 'commission' in Malta, they referred to the normal two year period between recommissioning a ship and paying off. Thus three commissions would mean a total of six years spent in the mediterranean. Of course, families did not remain the whole time at Malta, but it meant that they spent part of the six years there.

# CHAPTER 8

## Lord Mountbatten's Letters

THROUGHOUT their lives Lord Mountbatten and Queen Louise were frequent correspondents. Out of all their letters, those which Lord Mountbatten wrote to his sister from abroad provide the most fascinating reading, therefore this chapter is devoted to them. In a letter from Ethiopia in 1953, Lord Mountbatten wrote 'I suppose I have flown close on half a million miles in my life' and since then he has been a constant traveller, so the letters come from every corner of the globe. The extracts in this chapter, with one exception, are taken from Lord Mountbatten's correspondence with Queen Louise between 1960 and her death, in 1965. The first letter, Lord Mountbatten wrote during a cruise to the Red Sea in the autumn of 1953.

*The Red Sea, October 31st, 1953*
'On Saturday evening the sailors of the *Surprise* put out a seine net and got a lot of queer fish, amongst them a puffer fish. This was a fish of about 12 lb weight, which had blown out its chest to about twice the size of the biggest pouter pigeon you have ever seen. In fact it was like a miniature balloon and I thought it was dead. It had apparently been landed two hours before and had remained in a blown-up condition. Having been caught in a net, it was quite undamaged and evidently alive. I got a bucket of sea-water and put it in, and it just fitted into the top of the bucket. It floated with its inflated tummy up and lay there for perhaps two or three minutes. Then presently it began the deflating process with two or three belches of air and then it started its little fins moving; fins that were rather like Japanese fans coming out of holes in the side, and with a tremendous effort it turned itself the right way up and belched out the rest of the air. It then

tried to swim round, but was too big for the bucket and merely pushed the water round.

'It turned out to have the most attractive face I have ever seen in a fish. It looks like a mixture between a pretty girl, a lapdog and a baby seal. It had large gentle eyes and a little round mouth with large teeth, rather like a rabbit's. It was grey and speckled brown and was obviously very friendly and appealing. Edwina,[1] Marjorie and I would have liked to have kept it as a pet but couldn't see how we could do it and so released it. On getting back into the sea, it elongated itself into quite a long fish and swam away with a happy little wiggle of its tail.'

*Treetops, September 27th, 1960*
The next extract is an account of Mountbatten's visit to Treetops near Nyeri in Kenya, the place where Queen Elizabeth II acceded to the throne.

'Just before lunch, we all drove to the Outspan Hotel at Nyeri, which is only half an hour's drive away. Here we were greeted by Mr Sherbrooke Walker, the owner of the hotel and the creator of the famous Treetops. He had invited our entire party to be his guests (except Hughes, the District Commissioner attached to me, who had gone home to his house in Nyeri). General and Mrs Tapp and his A.D.C. are also in the party.

'Sherbrooke Walker enquired after Pammy and gave us a vivid account of the night she spent with Lilibet and Philip at Treetops, and pointed out that Lilibet actually acceded to the throne while on the top of a huge Mgumu tree.

'The Mau-Mau afterwards burned this tree down but fresh branches and leaves are beginning to sprout from the old stump, so they have not killed it.

'The new Treetops is a much more elaborate affair than the

[1] The members of Lord Mountbatten's family appear in various letters throughout this chapter. Edwina is Lord Mountbatten's late wife. Patricia—his elder daughter. John—her husband, Lord Brabourne. Pamela (Pammy)—Lord Mountbatten's younger daughter. And David—her husband, David Hicks. For fuller details of Lord Mountbatten's family, see Introduction, page 43–4.

old one, and is built on tops of trees on the opposite side of the water-hole to enable visitors to get a favourable sunset light for taking photographs of the animals.

'There was hardly a moment when there was not an animal or interesting bird of some sort or another in view. The greatest fun was at tea-time on the roof where the baboons came and pinched the food we were eating if we did not feed them enough. In the evening I signed my letters and memorandums to the Chiefs of Staff surrounded by wild animals.

'Mr Sherbrooke Walker, the Game Warden, and indeed all the experts, agreed that this was the worst time of year to see animals from Treetops, because it is the driest, and this year was the worst year because there had been an uninterrupted drought for four months. No elephant had been seen for eight days, and generally the show of animals had been poor.

'With these depressing forecasts for the night, we sat down for dinner. Halfway through, we were informed that elephant had arrived. We tiptoed out, making no sound and found a dozen elephant licking the salt right under us. Hardly had we got over our first intense excitement, when one of the elephants made a soft trumpeting sound and we looked round and saw another small herd approaching through the trees. Every ten minutes or so, another small group of elephants came in, until we had counted a total of sixty, all cows, and including over a dozen calves, some of them barely two or three weeks old and busily suckling from their mothers.

'Although the approaching elephants trod so softly that we had no warning before they suddenly appeared through the little clump of trees on which Treetops is built, once they had joined up with the main herd, there were gruntings and blowings and gurglings. Several elephants shook trunks with each other and they generally monopolised the salt-lick and the water-hole, to the exclusion of all other game. They went off in turns to drink from the only secure part of the bank.

'It was only after well over an hour that our hosts could persuade us to come back and finish our dinner, and then we sat out watching the elephants until midnight when the last one moved on.

'I then turned in, but most of the others, led by that super-enthusiast, Patricia, decided to remain up.

'At 12.30 a.m., Patricia called me to say that two rhinoceros were drinking on the opposite side of the water-hole. After drinking, they disappeared. She told me that they had reappeared right under Treetops but were so very suspicious and shy that the noise of my coming out made them run off.

'Half-an-hour later, I got a message that the rhinos had appeared again. This time I got a wonderful view of them from very close quarters, until I decided to go and see if Patricia was watching them from the upper floor, but the slight movement I made frightened the rhinos away again. These were not the pair I first saw drinking at the far side of the water-hole, which were of equal size, whereas this pair consisted of one very big and one medium rhino.

'The floodlighting of the salt-lick, and indeed practically the whole water-hole, is magnificent and much better than from the old Treetops. I have not been called so often while turned in at night since I was in command of a ship. Indeed the whole atmosphere was rather like the operations room of a ship, with people brewing hot drinks and writing up their notes.'

*Georgetown, March 7, 1962*
The following extract describes Mountbatten's journey to the Kaieteur Falls in Guyana.

'The Governor and some of his staff accompanied me and some of my staff on a most exciting expedition. We all embarked in a Grumman Goose amphibian aircraft, taxied down the Demerara River and flew off for the Kaieteur Falls. I cannot describe how much I was looking forward to this visit.

'When I was in Georgetown in 1920, I heard exciting tales of the almost mythical Kaieteur Falls. At that time, they were very

L

inaccessible, as it was estimated it would require at least five days to a week to make one's way on foot or on a horse through the thick tropical jungle. I was unable to locate anybody in George-town who had ever seen the Falls, but accounts of explorers and people who had been in contact with the local aborigines, the Amerindians, had fantastic tales to tell. I was always determined that I would go back one day when air travel had opened up the route, to visit the famous falls.

'They are on the Potaro River, at a distance of 160 miles from the coast. In fact they are only some 310 miles north of the equator.

'Flying up the valley of the Potaro, one suddenly sees the mist rising across the hills, and then the Falls themselves burst into view with breath-taking majesty.

'The river at the point of the Falls is some 300 feet wide, which of course is a small width when compared with the Niagara or Zambesi, but there is a great volume of water and it falls in a single drop of 741 feet. This is almost five times as high as Niagara and a little over twice as high as the Victoria Falls.

'We landed on the Potaro River, just above the Falls. The whole place is the type of virgin rain jungle for which Central America is so famous. A couple of Amerindians are employed by the Bauxite Company on river measurements, and a trail has been cut through the jungle to enable one to get various views of the falls. To get there overland still involves a round trip of ten to fourteen days on foot or horseback, and there is only this one Grumman Goose, piloted by that wonderfully experienced pilot, Harry Wendt, which does the trip occasionally, mostly for V.I.P.'s or rich tourists.

'Luckily the Governor had been there before and was able to act as guide. He told me he doubted whether more than 2,000 non-local people, including British Guianians of all shades, had ever seen the falls, because of the great difficulty in getting there This made it all the more exciting.

'I was just recounting the tale of the poisonous snake which we nearly stepped on in the rain forests of the Victoria Falls,when the co-pilot of the aircraft pulled me aside as I almost stepped on to a labaria, a thin black snake and a very deadly one. Next, we came across an immense column of ants on the march.

'I cannot say how beautiful and exciting the walks through the jungle were, but the moment of great excitement was when we started to hear the thunder of the Falls, and then suddenly we were upon them and everything else faded into insignificance beside the grandeur of the Kaieteur.

'We spent almost three hours scrambling up and down the various jungle tracks to get new views and new photographs.

'Finally, we got back to the plane very late and had a hurried picnic lunch. A tame Naracabra, or Trumpet Bird, insisted on sharing our lunch, and pecked our shins if we didn't feed it.

'The most exciting moment of all was still to come. There is only a fairly short stretch of the Potaro River which is straight and clear between some small rapids and the edge of the Falls. I got into the co-pilot's seat and set my ciné-camera going as we shot along the river. Then suddenly we took off, but had not got to a height of more than three or four feet before we were over the edge. I hope the film comes out, for no words of mine can describe the thrill, which greatly exceeds that of taking off from an aircraft-carrier for the first time.

'I forgot to say that the rivers of British Guiana are inhabited by a little fish called a *pirai* or *pirana*. It only grows to eight or nine inches in length but is a voracious man-eater. Its teeth are so sharp that bathers often don't realize they have been bitten until they come out of the river streaming with blood. Given the opportunity, they would very easily kill a man.

'I changed back into uniform in the amphibian and warned the soldiers that we were going to land late.'

*Trinidad, March 8, 1962*
'This has been a non-stop fifteen hour day with scarcely time to blow my nose. After dinner I had a meeting with the Governor,

the Premier and the Minister of Defence of Trinidad. I got back to the Governor-General's house at 11 p.m. He told me that, when he understood that Patricia and John were coming with me, he had proposed for us to arrive on Monday night or Tuesday morning, to see the last day of Carnival. He said to me "Carnival here is something really out of this world."

'He then told me there were 142 steel bands in the Carnival competition. All the bands had followers of at least 100 and some had 800 to 1,000, and I believe the record number of followers was 2,000 to a single band. They spend the whole year saving up for the costumes they are going to wear.

'As Lord Hailes said, the quality of the Carnival could hardly be bettered if the population had been eighty million and rich, instead of eight hundred thousand and poor.

'I was about to complain that he might have let me come and see the Carnival by myself, when he took the wind out of my sails by saying "Of course, I knew that you had only come to work and didn't have any time for the Carnival. So I dropped the idea as soon as your daughter dropped out." What a lamentable reputation to have. Nearly as bad as Edwina.

'Incidentally, everyone spoke in the same euologistic way about her in Trinidad, as in British Guiana.'

*Mexico City, February 27, 1963*
Another letter from the same South American tour describes a *charreada* specially arranged in Lord Mountbatten's honour.

'The charros had laid on a special charreada in my honour. They had invited all the members of the Corps Diplomatique, the officers and men of H.M.S. *Ulster*, the crew of my *Comet*, and had a large Army band in attendance.

'The charros gave a magnificent exhibition of horsemanship, including throwing steers, buckjumping on steers and jumping from one horse bareback on to another. But what interested me most were the charras, about a dozen girls wearing enormous hats and flower print dresses of almost crinoline size but quite short. They rode side-saddle on a man's Mexican saddle with the right stirrup hanging empty. They wore high boots with a huge rowel spur on the left heel, which they used very freely. They rode as well as the men, coming in at a terrific speed and pulling up their horses right on their hocks with their very long curb bits.

'Incidentally, the wife of the President of the charros, who appears to be the President of the charras, sat next to me. She was wearing the traditional old charra clothes, a long tight black habit with silver buckles all the way down the side, a beige leather bolero and an enormous hat.

'She spoke quite good English and I discovered afterwards that she had been having English lessons in the last month in anticipation of this event. At the end, the band played "God Save the Queen" and we drove to have lunch with the Indian Ambassador at his residence. His name is Bhandari and he was on the staff of India House when I was working there in July 1948. He made a very charming speech in proposing my health, in which he stressed how much all the people of India had loved Edwina and me, so much so that they had invited me to stay on as the first Governor-General of independent India. The Mexican Foreign Secretary, Tello, could not get over his astonishment at hearing this statement from an Indian and told Mary Garran, the Ambassador's wife, that if he had not heard it with his own ears he would never have believed it possible that the Indians could entertain such friendly feelings towards their former rulers, for he said the Mexicans to this day hated their former masters.'

*Cuzco, March 5, 1963*
During a trip to South America in February-March 1963, Lord Mountbatten took the opportunity to visit the famous 'lost' city of the Incas, Machu Picchu. In 1522 the Incas were crushed by the Spanish Conquistador, Francisco Pizarro, who was lured there by tales of their immense wealth. He landed at Tumbes, near the northern border of Peru, then advanced as far south as

Cajamarca, where he succeeded in ambushing the Inca King, Atahualpa. As ransom, he demanded one room to be filled with solid gold and two rooms to be filled with solid silver to the height he could reach on the wall. After Atahualpa had forced his subjects to provide the ransom, Pizarro killed him.

Among Inca legends there had persisted through the centuries the tradition that there was a hidden city somewhere in the Peruvian jungle. On July 24, 1911, it was discovered by Hiram Bingham, Professor of Latin-American history at Yale University, built on a saddle between two peaks 8,800 feet above sea level.

Lord Mountbatten and his party reached Machu Picchu via a special light railway, in places a veritable switchback.

'Finally, at 3 o'clock, we reached a siding at which a car and a bus were awaiting us. The Peruvian General drove me up quite quickly in the car. We got to the little hotel which has been built at the top of a 2,000 foot high precipitous slope, hidden from the actual town of Machu Picchu itself. The rest of the party came on in the bus.

'I immediately pushed on in the rain into the city. As we got there, the rain stopped, the clouds lifted and the sun began to shine. It was an altogether sensational and unforgettable sight. I have seen most of the great sights of the world and I can think of none that excited me more than this first glimpse of the lost city of the Incas.

'There are in all some two hundred houses, most of the walls of which are standing, but they are now all roofless. It is considered that the population was normally between 2,000 and 2,500. When the cemetery caves were examined, of 175 skeletons unearthed, some 150 were female. It is thought that a remnant of the shattered Inca Empire, known as the "Chosen Women", was sent to this ancient retreat to escape the Spanish Conquistadors, and lived there in state until they gradually died out and a forest covered their secret.

'This is the first time that I had seen an example of the famous Inca walls. They built these of huge blocks of stone, all of different shapes and sizes, but so beautifully cut to fit each other that one cannot get a blade of a pen-knife in any of the cracks, although no mortar was used. This is all the more marvellous, considering the Incas had no hard metals, but probably only gold, silver and copper, none of which would make a cutting knife. They probably used obsidian in the same way as the Aztecs. But considering how very brittle obsidian is, and how beautifully these stones were worked, the result still remains a near miracle.

'Below the town there are nearly one hundred beautifully constructed stone-faced terraces, hundreds of feet long—and great hillside farms stretching to the sky. Untold centuries ago, armies of stonemasons had built these walls, cutting the rocks and moving them with manpower, without wheels. More armies of workers must have carried tons of top soil, perhaps from the valley below, to make arable land that is still fertile today.

'The main streets of this curious city are stairways; there are over one hundred of them, large and small.

'The Machu Picchu water supply system is an ingenious procession of small gushing fountains, roughly bisecting the city from top to bottom, which once brought water within an easy distance of the inhabitants. Led by stone aqueducts from springs about a mile up the mountain, the water was piped to the fountains through an intricate network of holes bored through thick granite walls. A stream flowed through a hole bored in the top of each little fountain so that women could fill their earthenware jars, then fell to a basin carved in the rock beneath and passed through a duct to the next fountain in a long cascade.

'Machu Picchu is an impregnable fortress, which a handful of men could defend. The natural bulwarks were fortified by an outer wall, an inner wall and a dry moat, plus an intricate locking device carved in the massive city gate.

'At 4.20 p.m., the rain clouds started to build up again and the pilot of the helicopter which had been sent to fetch me was anxious to be off. I had taken a tremendous lot of photographs, and although I could easily have spent another couple of hours there, I felt the opportunity of a flight over this extraordinary city was not to be missed. I was told that this was the first helicopter ever to land at Machu Picchu.'

### *Teheran, April 23, 1963*

'After tea we all went to visit the Crown Jewels. David and Pamela had strongly recommended this. It took quite a bit of arranging, as it was one of the closed days. This made it all the pleasanter, since we were the only party going round the Crown Jewels, except for Mrs Dean Rusk, who had just arrived with her husband, who used to be one of my planners in Delhi in 1943.

'I must say the way the jewels are now displayed by Boucheron is most impressive. The most valuable item in the exhibition is a large globe of the world encrusted with 51,000 precious stones. Oceans are entirely in emeralds, Europe is in diamonds, America in rubies etc.

'The most lovely and attractive exhibit was a snuff box, looted by the Shah in India in 1739, which consists of 75 flat and square-cut emeralds mounted with the minimum of gold and almost flawless. It is said to be valued at close on two million pounds.

'We were shown the rival diamond to the Koh-i-noor, the Drary-i-noor, 188 carats. The Kiani Crown must have given the Shah quite a headache as it weighs 10 lb.'

### *Kumasi (the Ashanti capital), October 11, 1964*

'Pammy, David and I next drove to the residence of the Regional Commissioner which was a fine house built for the Prince of Wales' visit in 1924, and in which the Queen spent the night in 1961.

'Lunch was supposed to be at 12.30, but our principal guest, the Asantehene (King of the Ashantis) had not turned up by one o'clock, so I urged that we should start luncheon, and when he finally turned up quarter of an hour later, the Regional Commissioner and I went out and met him and conducted him to the lunch table.

'He sat next to me and we had a fascinating conversation about his regalia, and particularly the famous Golden Stool of Ashanti. He told me that it was made of solid gold by God, some 300 years ago, and came down from the skies through the incantation of the Chief Priest of the then King of Ashanti, Nana Osei Tutu. It is now regarded as a sacred object, and kept locked away and only produced once a year at the Assembly of Chiefs. I was told by the curator of the Museum that in Ghana among the Chiefs, the Chief's stool usually has precedence over the Chief, being the more important of the two!

'You will remember that our Uncle Liko[1] contracted malaria when he fought in the Ashanti War of 1896 and died on board H.M.S. *Blonde*, so Ashanti has a sad memory for our family.

'An unexpected further connection with our family is that the flagship of the new Ghana Navy is called *Ejura* after a town in Ashanti, and she was launched by Patricia. At that time she was H.M.S. *Aldington*, but had her name changed when she was given to the Ghana Navy. I was invited to pay an official visit to her later on and persuaded the King to meet me on board.'

*Hongkong, February 23, 1965*

'I spent yesterday morning with the three services. I first went to the excellent new Naval Base, H.M.S. *Tamar*, which I had seen under construction in 1961 and which is now complete.

'It is the most modern and one of the finest Naval Bases we have, and I had a good look at it. The Commodore, Symonds, told me that 138,000 British and 420,000 American naval liberty-men landed from warships during 1964. He told me that he had entertained 86 different American Admirals in his house and,

[1] Prince Henry of Battenberg. See page 30-31.

with repeat visits, the numbers were well up into three figures.

'I then went in the Admiral's barge to the R.A.F. station at Kai Tak. They have four Hunters (of 28 Squadron) and four Austers (of the Army Air Corps) and they service all other visiting R.A.F. and R.N. Aircraft.

'At 11 a.m. Lieut.-Gen. Sir Dennis O'Connor fetched me and we drove up the centre road to the north of the New Territories through Kowloon. Curiously enough, he was my Vice-Chief of the Defence Staff, as his predecessor, McLeod, had also been. I have never seen such fabulous development as is going on here. Mountain tops are being pushed into the sea and sky-scrapers are being built on reclaimed land and flattened hills. The average number of new apartments or homes being built in this one small Colony is four-hundred a day.

'A complete new town of half a million inhabitants is growing up at Tsuen Wan, which was a rustic village when I saw it four years ago.

'We stopped on the slopes of Tai Mo Shan mountain to look across the Sek Kong valley.

'We then drove down to the Headquarters of 48 Gurkha Infantry Brigade Group for a briefing by their Brigadier. Much of it was a complaint about the modern family system in peace-time where the movement of his own Headquarters and other troops had been governed by what family movements could be made. He advocated a conscript army with no wives, and even officers and N.C.O's, whom he admitted could be married, could only see their wives occasionally. This, he said, would produce a far better fighting army.

'My own comment at the end was "I suppose you're a bachelor" and his reply "Yes" was greeted with laughter.

'I lunched with the officers in the Brigade Headquarters Mess, which they share with a squadron of the Inniskillings. After lunch, Rory O'Connor presented me with the most charming gilt badge of the Hong Kong Army, on behalf of all ranks.

'Patricia and our old friend, Peter Murphy, arrived by car after lunch and I changed into plain clothes to join them.

'I had previously driven to have a look at the polo ground and now a typical China polo pony, a twelve and a half hand Tat, was produced. I had forgotten how small they were when I played on them during my first visit.

'I recounted my favourite tale of polo in Hong Kong. I was playing No. 1 for the *Renown* team against Hong Kong in 1922, when our Number 3 hit a long ball up, which hit my pony fair and square under the tail. It clipped its tail down, I galloped between the goal posts, and when I pulled up, the pony put its tail up and the ball dropped out. Was it a goal?

'The Assistant Commissioner for Police for the new territories drove me, Patricia and Peter to Lok Ma Chau Police Station, which looked directly over the frontier into China, a couple of hundred yards away. We spent a long time studying the Chinese landscape and watching movements of soldiers and peasants through binoculars.

'Then the Assistant Commissioner left us, but we still had three motor-cycle outriders to take us on a tour of the western road back through Sha Tin. We stopped at the Sha Tin Heights Hotel for a drink and then drove on into Kowloon to the Peninsular Hotel, which we reached just before four o'clock!

'Here we were met by Sir Solly Zuckerman, my scientific colleague at the Ministry of Defence, who was going as far as Australia in my R.A.F. Comet. He had spent the morning visiting the Hong Kong Oceanograph Research Ship and had talked with their enthusiastic young scientists.

'We then went on a fascinating shopping expedition. Patricia bought a really "smashing" cheong san, the "Suzy Wong" model.

'Patricia, Solly and I went back by one of the remarkable Hong Kong ferries. There are so many car and passenger ferries that one never has more than a couple of minutes to wait. We counted nine ferries actually doing the passage across the harbour and another fourteen boats moving at the same time.

'We got back to Government House just before six, to find Mr Rony Lee had arrived with my suit, shirts and pyjamas, which I tried on finally. They all fitted perfectly. The whole lot had been made in under forty-eight hours over a weekend. If they could work like this at home we should not be in the economic difficulties we find ourselves in.

'I dealt with reports and correspondence and then we three drove to the house of Run Run Shaw, where we met up with Peter, the Lomans, the Hartley Shawcrosses, some of Run Run Shaw's family and a very rich Frenchwoman from Aden, called Madame Christiane Besse. Her husband gave St Donats Castle in Wales for the Atlantic College and is a Governor. In Singapore I had visited the fantastic house of Run Me Shaw, the brother of Run Run Shaw of Hong Kong. The story goes that the elder brother used to hang about the offices of the Shaw Company for messages, saying "Run, run?" and when he had been sent on a message, the younger brother would say "Run me?" At all events, they are both multi-millionaire film magnates now.

'Dinner was on board one of the famous floating restaurants in Aberdeen Harbour, called the "Tai Pak". We were sculled out in three or four sampans to the gaudily-painted and brilliantly-lit vast houseboat, which formed the restaurant.

'We were first taken to select our fish, Solly and I handled a truly colossal crayfish, and subsequently various exotic fish of the Wrasse family were pulled out of the fish tanks in nets for us to select what we wanted cooked.

'We had a twelve-course Chinese dinner which was the most delicious I have ever eaten. Although the surroundings were garish, the party was gay and the evening very romantic. In fact we did not leave until midnight.'

*Nondugl, February 26, 1965*

In the following letter, Lord Mountbatten describes the Bird of Paradise sanctuary at Nondugl in the interior of New Guinea.

'We flew down the Bayerr River Valley and then through the 9,000 foot high Treamairne Gap. We then turned back along the Wahgi Valley and landed at the village of Banz.

'Here I transferred to a Bell helicopter with the District Commissioner, and the others went in a twin-engined Cessna C.336 aircraft and we flew to Nondugl, where we were received by Sir Edward Halstrom, the famous wealthy Australian zoologist, who had at his own expense created the Bird of Paradise sanctuary at Nondugl, set in the midst of the most beautiful gardens.

'This area, he told us, had been particularly rich in Birds of Paradise but he reckoned that the natives had shot over 100,000 of these glorious birds in the last twenty years for their head-dresses, even though the export of Bird-of-Paradise plumes was now prohibited for ladies' hats and dresses.

'However, as the natives are probably going to give up native costume in the next five or six years, there is some hope that the birds will multiply again.

'I took some ciné films of a most glorious variety of incredibly beautiful birds and of some tree-climbing kangaroos.

'The local District Officer and his wife had organized a very pleasant buffet lunch under an awning in what might well have been the Garden of Eden, it was so lovely and the climate so glorious. No wonder they are called "Birds of Paradise".

'After lunch we drove along the famous Skyline Drive, along the spine of a small mountain range, which gave us a wonderful view of the glorious countryside.

'When we got to Nondugl Village, we found a vast gathering of native warriors and Chiefs drawn up in front of a roughly constructed dais, which we climbed upon. On our side were all the villagers and on the other side about 1,000 warriors.

'Unlike those we had seen before, these almost without exception had the tremendously long black tail-feathers of the Princess Stephanie Bird of Paradise and one had an extremely rare head-dress of yard-long white feathers from the Ribbontail Bird of Paradise.

'After we were in position, they started chanting and dancing. It was rather like a very crowded Highland Ball with the eightsomes crushed close together, and there is no doubt that they were in fact dancing in teams in a set pattern.

'I was presented with the plumes of a Marquis of Mariga Bird of Paradise which I fixed to the top of my cap, to the great enthusiasm of the natives.'

## Letters from Lord Mountbatten's World Tour in 1961

During February and March 1961, Lord Mountbatten as Chief of Defence Staff of Great Britain toured the world visiting British overseas commands and attending meetings of the Australian and New Zealand Chiefs of Staff and as British delegate to the ANZAM[1] meeting in Canberra. The R.A.F Comet *Sagittarius* took him to the Middle East and the Far East. He then continued via Australia and New Zealand to the Fiji Islands, Hawaii and California, before returning to England. Throughout the tour, he wrote as regularly as usual to Queen Louise and his first letter was from Aden.

### Aden, February 9, 1961

'We landed at Khormaksar twenty minutes late on account of the head winds, at 2.10 p.m. local time, on February 9, 1961. This must have been the sixth time I have been to Aden since 1921, and the dramatic situation of the town, so reminiscent of Gibraltar, always thrills me. . . .

'At 4.0 p.m. I flew by helicopter to Lahej, some twenty miles in the hinterland. After passing over the desert, one suddenly comes to a large oasis, irrigated from a wadi, in which stands the capital of the State of Lahej, a town of some 10,000 inhabitants. It is, of course, of Arabic architecture, with some very find buildings. Inside the Palace, the Sultan of Lahej, who is the Minister of Defence in the new federation government, had collected his

---

[1] ANZAM stands for Australia, New Zealand and Malaysia.

brother Cabinet Ministers, all of them Sultans themselves of different States in the Federation.'

*Singapore, February 12, 1961*
The journey went on to Kuala Lumpur, then Singapore—where they arrived on February 12th. Lord Mountbatten and his staff drove into Singapore on a road which had been named after himself Mountbatten Road and which ran through the old city airport at Kallang.

'We drove to Eden Hall, the residence in Singapore, to which the Commissioner General moved when he lost Bukit Serene in Johore Bahru. It is a very pleasant house, but not so big and sumptuous as the old place.

'My host is the Commissioner General for South East Asia, the Earl of Selkirk. He has been away in the Cameron Highlands and only got back just before me.

'I attended a full meeting of the British Defence Co-ordinating Committee for the Far East (which consists of the Commissioner General, the three Commanders-in-Chief and the Australian and New Zealand Commissioners) for a couple of hours.

'Geordie (the Earl of Selkirk) then drove me on to the Prime Minister's offices, which are in the old Town Hall. The Prime Minister, Lee Kuan Yew, was away in the Cameron Highlands, so I was received by Mr Byrne, the Minister of Labour and Law. He showed me the Council Hall in which I took the surrender of the Japanese in August 1945, and said he would erect a brass plaque to commemorate the event.'

*Bangkok, February 15, 1961*
'We took off at 10 a.m. from Singapore and we arrived at Don Muang Airport, Bangkok, at 12 noon local time. There was the usual large reception committee headed by our Ambassador, Sir Richard Whittington, and the Chiefs of the Armed Forces. There was a particularly smart guard of honour, with band and

colours of the Royal Thai Air Force, and as we had been warned it was an official arrival, I wore white full dress and the Grand Cross of the Order of the White Elephant. The King had sent his Assistant Private Secretary to meet me and look after me during the visit, as I was to be His Majesty's guest.

'A Rolls-Royce, driven by one of the royal chauffeurs, was placed at my disposal. The Private Secretary drove me in this to Pitsamuloke Palace, which is one of the main guest houses used by the King for his guests.

'My own suite is enormous and sumptuous. There are fourteen full-length stained glass windows in my bedroom and a T.V. set on which we got American films dubbed into Thai.

'A magnificent luncheon was already laid on for us, at which I sat at the head of the table as host. The servants here are from the Palace, wearing the traditional royal liveries, and there is a large guard of soldiers and police at the gates and front door.

'After lunch, the Ambassador arrived for a talk and later I left with some of my staff and drove first to the really magnificent new tourist shop which had first-class Thai souvenirs of all sorts, including the famous Niello silverware. The girl in charge of the shop was the daughter of my old friend, Prince Subha Svasti, who under the code name ARUN, was my liaison officer in Kandy with my force 136 Unit operating in Thailand.

'Shortly before 8 o'clock I drove with some of my staff to the Chitlada Palace where the King now lives. On entering the park, I noticed we drove along a fairly narrow footpath, which the Rolls-Royce could hardly pass along. I enquired if all the guests used this path and was told "No, only the King".

'We drove past the Palace and on to a very dashing modern building a couple of hundred yards away, known as the *Pagabiron* or "recreation centre".

'There were over a hundred guests already assembled, but I was led straight through to where the King and Queen were sitting by the most luxurious, enormous swimming pool I have seen for a long time.

Princess Louise at five years of age
(*Reproduced by permission of Pressens Bild, Stockholm*)

*b* Princess Louise aged fourteen at Sopwell, St Albans

Princess Louise in 1904. The caption was written by Nona Kerr and inspired by Princess Louise's expression

*d* Princess Louise. Photograph from Mrs Margaret Heywood's collection
(*Reproduced by permission of Mrs John Preston*)

*Lady who gave up all for lost.*

2

*a* Prince Louis of Battenberg wi[th] his sons Georgie and Dickie

*b* Meeting of cousins at the tu[rn] of the century. Princess Alice on the left beneath the bust w[ith] Prince Louis on her la[p]. Next to her are Princess Lou[ise] and Prince George; and to [the] right of them, their cousin Prin[ce] Waldemar of Prussia, who h[as] his brother Sigismund on [his] knee. On the extreme right [is] Princess Elisabeth, only daugh[ter] of Grand Duke Ernest Louis

Prince and Princess Louis of Battenberg with their family in Malta, 1897. Louise is standing between George and Alice

4

*a* Louise and Alice at Osborne on the Isle of Wight, 1898

*b* On holiday with Aunt Irène in th North Frisian Islands. Waldemar i holding the bridle of Princess Louise' pony

*c* Louise sitting between Alice (*right*) and Waldemar (*left*)
(*From H.M. King Gustaf Adolf's collection. Photograph by Court photographer, Carl Berg, in Darmstadt*)

*d* Louise and George at Windsor Cast in 1900

5

*a* Heiligenberg Castle in Hesse. The family's favourite summer home
   (*Reproduced by permission of Mrs John Preston*)

*b* Mustering of the family on H.M.S. *Implacable* in Malta, 1902
   *Back row:* Princess Alice, Prince Louis, Princess Victoria (with Dickie on her knee),
   Princess Louise, and (*far right*) Nona Kerr
   *Front row:* Georgie sitting in front of Prince Louis

6

*a* Family gathering at Schloss Kiel, 1904

*Back row:* Grand Duke Ernest Louis, his daughter Elisabeth, the Tsarina of Russia (Aunt Alix), and Prince Henry of Prussia

*Middle row:* George, Prince Louis of Battenberg, and the Grand Duke Serge of Russia with his hand on Prince Waldemar's shoulder

*Front row:* Princess Victoria with Dickie on her knee, Louise, Alice, and Princess Irène with her youngest son Prince Henry on her knee

*b* Louise and her brother George tobogganing

7

*a* The Tsar's children, 1910
  *From left to right:* Tatiana, Anastasia, Alexei, Marie and Olga

*b* The Short Biplane in which Princess Louise flew at Eastchurch near Sheerness in 1911

8

a Tsar Nicholas II and two of his daughters, Marie (*left*) and Olga (*right*), on a visit to Bad Nauheim in 1910

b Princess Louise with her brother-in-law Prince Andrew of Greece, at Heiligenberg Castle in 1905

c Louise with her Aunt Anna, the wife of Prince Franz Joseph of Battenberg, at Schönberg in 1904

d Princess Victoria (*right*) with her sister Ella (*left*) at Wolfsgarten in 1910

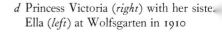

9

*a* Louise aged 18 with her niece Dolla on her knee and Dickie and Margarita (Dolla's sister) beside her, in 1907

*b* Bathing before World War I. Princess Victoria is holding Dickie; Louise is on the right

*a* Louise scrubbing an oil cloth table top at the V.A.D. hospital during World War I
(*Reproduced by permission of Paul Popper Ltd*)

*b* With Ida Wheatley during a pause from work

*c* As a nurse in 1915:
(*Reproduced by permission of I.M.S., Stockholm*)

*d* At the hospital in Palaves

Family group outside Lord Louis Mountbatten's London home in November, 1923
*Back row:* Crown Prince Gustaf Adolf, Lord Louis Mountbatten, the Marquess of Milford Haven and Prince Andrew of Greece
*Middle row:* Louise, Lady Louis Mountbatten, the Marchioness of Milford Haven and Princess Andrew of Greece
*In front:* The Dowager Marchioness of Milford Haven
(*Reproduced by permission of I.M.S., Stockholm*)

Photograph taken at the wedding reception in Kensington Palace. The best man was Prince William. The older bridesmaids are (*from left to right*) Louise's nieces, Sophia, Cécile, Dolla and Margarita. The page and small bridesmaid are the Earl of Medina and his sister Tatiana

(*Reproduced by permission of I.M.S., Stockholm*)

'After a friendly talk, they introduced the guests at their table one by one and then joined in the circle for drinks. At dinner I sat on the right of King Phumipol and opposite Queen Sirikit.

'The King explained to me that the large hall next to the colossal swimming pool was the gymnasium and badminton court for his children and their school friends.

'At the end of dinner, about fifteen of the male guests got up and moved on to the stage, on which there were music stands and instruments. They immediately started playing jazz. His Majesty explained that these were all his personal friends, who had learned to play in his band with him, and that they rehearsed twice a week and came to play for big parties on the fairly rare occasions when he gave them.

'The King also organized a party of high grade crooners, among whom I recognized Seni Pramoj, who was the Prime Minister when I was here in 1946.

'After dinner we moved to small tables set in the gymnasium, facing the stage.

'I sat between the King and Queen at a table on a square of red carpet. The King announced that he had arranged special old Thai dances for me, and sixteen of the most lovely girls I have ever seen then came on in traditional costume and did a beautiful dance in the tradition of North Siam.

'The Queen explained that they were either cousins, ladies-in-waiting, or daughters of high Court officials, as they preferred to have amateurs at their more intimate parties. After the exhibition of dancing finished, the King went up to lead his band, playing a saxophone, and left me alone with the beautiful Sirikit.

'No one danced, and I wasn't sure what the form was, but presently one of the older Princes came up with his wife and introduced her and said "You will remember opening the Flower with her in 1946." I smiled affably, as I hardly knew what to say. Then the Prince in a loud whisper said "I am sure Her Majesty would like you to open the Flower with her".

'Evidently the Queen had overheard, for she smiled encourag-

M

ingly and still not knowing what was meant, I said "Would you like to open the Flower with me?" She replied "I would love to" and got up and walked towards the floor, and it was only then I realized that I was expected to open "the floor" with her.

'The band was playing a dead-slow English waltz. The floor was very sticky and no one else danced. The Queen said "Do you like waltzes?" and I replied "I would prefer a foxtrot". So she walked over to the King and asked him to play a foxtrot. She said "Is that better?" I suggested it was still a bit slow. So she walked over to the King again and this time the band struck up a really good tempo.

'An awkward thing about court etiquette is that practically nobody asks the Queen to dance, except elderly members of the royal family. However, it suited me, as I was able to have plenty of dances with her during the course of the evening and she became more and more friendly and amusing.

'From time to time, Queen Sirikit would call up one of the young ladies, who, on approaching the Presence, fell on their knees, in accordance with Thai protocol, at the edge of the red carpet and advanced the last three or four paces on their knees in full evening dress. The Queen would then say "Would you like to dance with Lady Ruda? (or whatever the name was) and I found myself in the curious position of asking a beautiful girl to dance while she was on her knees before me.

'I stayed on until after 1 a.m. and never missed a dance.

'I cannot remember when I have enjoyed an evening so much as this. There wasn't a single unattractive woman in the room and at least sixty of them would each have won a beauty prize anywhere. After the floor had been powdered and the band pepped up, the party hotted up more and more. Sirikit is the best company and the gayest companion I have met in years and she and the King have invited me to come back to Bangkok.

'Next morning, some of my staff and I drove to the Grand Palace. We looked through the Palace and went round the Temples and Pagodas, and in to see the Emerald Buddha, who was still in his winter clothing (his clothes are changed three times a year by the King).

'We went round the cloisters with their great paintings of the Ramayanas, and then back to the Phra Chitubhom, the compound of which adjoins the compound of the Grand Palace. Here, I again took movies and stereophotos of the fantastic and exciting profusion of Pagodas and Temples and figures of the Nio, the Temple guardians, and the demon kings of the Ramayanas. It was light enough to try to take a photograph of the reclining Buddha in his big temple. This Buddha has always fascinated me. His nose is certainly bigger than me, and my A.D.C. pointed out that one of his ears would make a very nice double bed. His body is covered in thick, solid gold leaf and he is a most imposing figure.'

## *Hongkong, February 16, 1961*

'It was cold, overcast and drizzly this morning. At 8.40 a.m. General McLeod, Commander of the British Forces, who used to be my deputy Chief of the Defence Staff, collected me and drove me to his Headquarters, where a very smart guard of honour with colours and band of the Royal Northumberland Fusiliers was drawn up.

'After this, I went to the conference room, where I had a briefing and discussion with the heads of the services.

'At 10.10 a.m. I drove to the Naval Base, where my party took off in helicopters for five hours with the Army. I was accompanied by two of my Army staff. During the course of this visit, we covered by helicopter almost the whole area of the leased territories and must have seen most of the 400 square miles they occupy. We visited in turn the 14th Field Regiment, R.A., the 2/10th Gurkha Rifles, the 81st Company of the R.A.S.C. and after lunch the 1st Royal Warwicks.

'Brigadier Kent, who served under me in Sumatra, and who commands the 48th Gurkha Infantry, took me round his command.

'The R.A.S.C. Company is one of the few left in the British

Army of mounted troops and they have 100 Chinese soldiers with pack mules and 6 horses.

'The 1st Warwicks paraded their regimental mascot with their Quarter Guard, an enchanting little gazelle from Arabia.

'The sun did come out in the afternoon and we had a lovely view of the harbour. It is quite staggering the way in which Hong Kong has grown, even since 1946, and I am told that they have now over three million people, mostly concentrated in Victoria and Kowloon, more people than in the whole of New Zealand.'

### *Jesselton, February 21, 1961*

The next letter was sent from Jesselton in North Borneo. It was in Jesselton that Lord Mountbatten's wife, Edwina, had died exactly a year before on the night of February 21, 1960 during a tour of the Far East for the St John Ambulance Brigade, of which she was Superintendent-in-Chief. In the extract below, Lord Mountbatten describes his conversation with Dr Clapham who was called to certify Lady Edwina's death and with other people who were present during her last days.

'He said Edwina looked very beautiful and at peace with the world. He reckoned her heart had quietly stopped beating from exhaustion, probably about 2 a.m., on the morning of the 21st February, just a year ago.

'He showed me the room in Government House where they put her, dressed in her white St John uniform. Sentries from the armed forces were mounted outside the room.

'I next spoke to Dr Blauw, a German Jewish refugee from Nazi persecution, who had been in the Colony since the 1930s and who has a great reputation as a brilliant doctor. He was at that time the Commissioner of St John, but resigned immediately after Edwina's death.

'Both the acting Governor and he persuaded Edwina with great difficulty to be properly medically examined. He came to the conclusion that there was nothing organically wrong with her, but that she was completely and utterly exhausted.

'He told her that she ought to go to bed and rest. This, of course, she refused. He then said that she really must cut everything possible out of her programme and rest as much as she could, as he did not see how she could carry on. All she said was that she was determined to carry on with her full programme.

'After further pressure from the acting Governor that night not to leave in the morning, but to take an extra day in Jesselton as a holiday, she said "We will see in the morning". And when the morning came she was dead.

'What struck me most about my conversations with all the people, was that she had somehow cast a stronger spell over them than ever before, for they one and all developed a feeling of admiration, one might almost say adoration, which was quite uncanny.

'I think myself there was something very special about her, in the last few weeks of her life, for I heard similar expressions in Singapore and Malaya.

'One year ago tonight Edwina died, and although this visit has been in some ways harrowing I would not have missed it for anything in the world, for now I know exactly how her last two days were spent and how happy she evidently was although so tired and ill.'

*Canberra, February 23, 1961*

After Hongkong, Lord Mountbatten stopped for three days in Canberra. He mentions a call on the Prime Minister, Sir Robert Menzies, a meeting with the Australian Cabinet and Service Ministers, and a meeting with the Australian Chiefs of Staff Committee, which he attended with the High Commissioner, Sir William Oliver. On the third day, Tuesday, February 23rd, he wrote:

'This has been a non-stop day, after an extremely exhausting visit, although I have attended some very worthwhile and important meetings. Australia has tired me out a great deal, more than the whole of the rest of the trip put together so far, and I can hardly wait to get among the fish.'

### New Zealand, February 25–26, 1961

In New Zealand, after his meeting with the New Zealand Cabinet and Chiefs of Staff, Lord Mountbatten did at last get a chance to relax and also to fish. The fishing ground was situated in the Bay of Islands, 'which of course being nearest the Equator, is the hottest part of New Zealand and delightful at this late summer time'.

'An unbelievably lovely morning, with blue sky and hot sun. We boarded the very latest and smartest fishing launch, the *Leilani*, 46 feet long, 14 feet beam, displacing over 20 tons. She was the latest word in fishing luxury. We went straight out into the open Pacific without a ripple on the long lazy swell and passed through a school of Black Fish, which is a very large variety of dolphin. They came and played all round the boat and I hope I got some good movies of them.

'We suddenly sighted the tail of a marlin, and the skipper with great skill manœuvred his boat ahead of the fish, and the moment it saw the bait it shot across so fast that it actually missed the bait at its first attack and had to swing round with a boil of water to get it at its second attack, and then the line ran shrieking out for a good hundred yards and the fight was on. I felt all the old thrill at seeing the lovely great fish jumping and fighting on the surface, but I had forgotten how exhausting big-game fishing can be. It took one hour and eleven minutes to land him.'

### Fiji, March 2, 1961

However, the New Zealand visit was not confined to big-game fishing. There was a long string of conferences, followed by the flight to Fiji.

'We landed at the big International Airport at Nandi on the west coast of Viti Levu, the biggest of the three hundred and sixty islands in the Fiji group.

'At 3.15 p.m., there was a conference with the Governor, the New Zealand Colonel and Group Captain, the Commissioner of Police and Colonial Secretary.

'In the evening, I met the Committee of the Returned Soldiers and Sailors Association and was very glad to note that among the ten members, no less than five were Fijians, one with the D.S.O. and two with the M.C. After doing business with them as Grand President of the British Commonwealth Ex-Services League, I met the representatives of the Royal Overseas League, and then the President and Secretary of the local Royal Life Saving Society, as I am also the grand president of these two.

'There was a dinner party of thirty. Opposite me was seated Lieutenant Colonel The Hon. Ratu Edward Cakobau, who has just been appointed a district commissioner. When the bandmaster came in for his glass of port, Ratu Edward leaned across and said to me, "The bandmaster comes from the worst cannibal district in the island".

'I asked Ratu Edward if he were a great-grandson of King Thakimbau (though I believe the local spelling is Cakobau), and he replied "Yes". I then asked him whether he knew that his great-grandfather had been to lunch with Queen Victoria, in the late 1870s. He replied "Yes". I then told him that the King had sat next to our mother, who being a very cheeky young girl, had asked him if he regretted having given up cannibalism, and that she had always said that he had replied that all he missed was babies' toes.

'Ratu Edward was highly amused and said, "I don't think that can be right, for I always heard my great-grandfather particularly liked ladies' fingers".

'Another amusing story I heard about Edward Cakobau is now quite well known. When he was shown the menu on board the ship bringing him back to Fiji recently, he said to the Head Waiter, "This menu is horrible, bring me the passenger list".

'After dinner the Governor had arranged for native dancing and singing in the garden. It was a lovely, warm, clear tropical night with a full moon, and the whole scene was one of indescribable beauty.

'Some eighty girls aged about fifteen or sixteen, from the Adi Cakobau school came and performed. There were three teams of a dozen girls and a leader to each who danced separately. Two lots had palm-leaf bows tied to their ankles. The third lot sat on the ground and did a graceful dance with their hands and had the palm-leaf bows tied to their wrists.

'Their part-singing was really extraordinary, and reminiscent of the Lushai girls in Shillong. Mostly they sang Fijian songs, but they also sang Offenbach's *Baccarolle*.'

*Honolulu, March 3, 1961*

'Yesterday we landed at Hickham Field, Honolulu at 9.35 p.m., having flown over 3,000 miles the same day. The U.S. Commander-in-Chief of the Pacific, Admiral Don Felt, was there to meet me, together with the various other senior officers, including Major-General John Carey, U.S.A.F., who used to be on my staff in S.E.A.C.

'Don Felt drove me straight to the lovely guest house alongside his own house and stayed with me for an hour's *tete-a-tete* and gossip. After that I worked late on the briefs for our meetings.

'I arrived in whites at CINC PAC HQ at 9 a.m., to be received with full honours; a very smart U.S. Marine honour guard with their full colours and a band and a 19-gun salute.

'I was very touched that during my inspection of the guard, the band played the slow march of the Preobrajensky Guards, which had been played for me the last time by a band of the King's African Rifles at Lusaka in Africa, who turned out to have an ex-Royal Marine bandmaster. I asked the U.S. Marine bandmaster how he came to play this tune, and he said he had obtained it from the Royal Marines at the Edinburgh Tattoo, and had been told it was my special march, which Marine Bands always played in my honour. I told him how touched I was. You

may remember Uncle Serge[1] was the Colonel of the Preobrajensky Guards and gave the music to Alfonso[2] who used it for
his Halberdier Guards, and who gave me the music for Royal
Marine Bands in my ships.[3]

'After this we adjourned to Felt's house where we had an off-
the-record meeting with the component commanders and senior
staff officers and Sir Harold Caccia, our Ambassador in Washing-
ton, who had come to attend these meetings. Of the twelve people
in the room, nobody had less than two stars.[4]

'At 10.15 a.m. we moved down to the regular morning briefing
meeting, showing the situation throughout the Pacific and the
latest situation in Laos.

'At 11.15 Rear-Admiral Ramsay took our party out in a barge
and showed us exactly where all the American ships were sunk
by the Japanese on 7th December, 1951, and I took films of the
only two wrecks still remaining. . . .

'In the evening I went on to a dinner party of thirty-six, given
by Walter and Louise Dillingham, the uncrowned social and
industrial King and Queen of Honolulu. They have a fabulous
house near Diamond Point as well as a 3,000 acre estate in the
north of Oahu. They told me they had entertained you and
Gustaf on your visit to Honolulu.

'The tablecloth was of spun gold and so were the napkins.
On the sideboard, there was a complete team of four women
polo players of the Tang Dynasty.

'At the end of dinner, old Walter Dillingham, a remarkably
alert 85, made a speech, claiming that our friendship started in
1920, when I was here with David[5] and that he had first interested
me in taking up polo. I made a very short reply.

'After dinner there was some really delightful native music,
singing and dancing. In one dance, three girls balanced glasses

[1] Grand Duke Sergius of Russia.                    [2] King Alfonso XIII of Spain.
[3] In 1964 at the Tercentenary Celebrations of the Royal Marines, Lord Mountbatten
presented to them the music of this march which they have adopted as their Regimental
slow march.              [4] i.e. all were at least Rear-Admirals or Major-Generals.
[5] Prince of Wales.

half-full of red wine on their heads and hands, and ended rolling over on the floor without spilling any.

'All this took place in the patio of the Dillingham's Spanish villa, with Diamond Head towering above us, and the full moon just below the rim, throwing a light on the whisps of cloud being driven over the ridge by the trade winds. This made it look like a fanciful volcano and was incredibly beautiful.'

*San Francisco, March 6, 1961*

'Admiral Felt joined me at breakfast at 8.20 a.m. and drove me to Hickham Field, where I threw my lei of frangipanies on to the tarmac, which I am told is the new custom in pressurised aircraft, when you cannot open any window to throw it into the sea. This should ensure my return to Honolulu.[1]

'We lunched on board and landed at 4.40 p.m. at the Naval Air Station, Alameda, in San Francisco.

'Next day I attended a luncheon of the famous Bohemian Club in their vast club premises. You may remember Gustaf attended one of their meetings in one of the giant sequoia groves.

'The luncheon room holds about 600 people. Nearly 700 turned up and 100 had snacks in the bar and stood round the walls for my speech. I was assured by the President that this was by far the greatest gathering they had ever had to luncheon in their 85 years' history.

'In the chair was no less a person than one of the three great surviving U.S. national war heroes, Fleet Admiral Nimitz, who is regarded with the same sort of veneration as we regard Winston.

'After lunch, Nimitz drove me to the University of California, which has 41,000 students of which 22,000 attend the campus in Berkeley, which is one of the three gigantic townships on the other side of the Bay from San Francisco—Oakland, Richmond and Berkeley.

'Here he showed me and my staff the original brass plate which

---

[1] It did. Lord Mountbatten returned with his elder daughter, Patricia, Lady Brabourne, in 1965.

Sir Francis Drake nailed up at Drake's Bay, some 30 miles north of San Francisco, in 1579. By this he took possession of the country for Queen Elizabeth I. Although he careened the *Golden Hind* in what is now Drake's Bay, thick fog for a whole fortnight prevented him from seeing the narrow entrance to the Golden Gate, and thus sailing into San Francisco Bay.

'The Admiral had given me a replica of the brass plate previous to this visit.

'In the evening, I met half a dozen British sailors and Royal Marines who had served with me at different times and settled in San Francisco.'

*Nebraska, March 7, 1961*

The last letter from the tour is dated Omaha, March 7th and Lord Mountbatten writes:

'We landed at Offutt Air Force Base near Omaha, Nebraska, after a three-and-a-half-hour flight.

'General Power, the Commander-in-Chief of the Strategic Air Command, is away in the Pacific, but his deputy Lieutenant-General Griswold met me and the other senior officers gave me a fascinating briefing, explaining how the Joint Strategic Target Planning Staff works. The very confused reports in the news-papers had only given me a very vague idea and so this briefing was very valuable.

'I then got up to go, as it was time for take off, but Griswold remarked that he had another presentation prepared for me on the future of space exploration and defence. This seemed such a fascinating subject that I delayed the take-off by half an hour, as I knew this would not interfere with our programme in Canada.

'This presentation was quite fabulous and showed the im-mense scope of space travel which lies within our scientific grasp during the next ten years. If there is general disarmament, this will be a wonderful age, but if our ability to control space is solely to be used to increase destructive capabilities, then I see little chance of the world surviving.

'Being right at the end of my great tour now, I can give you a summing up: this has been an exhausting and rewarding trip in which I feel I have been able to get a more or less simultaneous view of the problems of British Defence in the Middle East and the Far East, and the problems of the Chiefs of Staff and Ministers in Australia, New Zealand and Canada.'

### *Mountbatten's Memories of the Second World War*

The letters contained in this section include recollections of the period during World War II when Mountbatten was Supreme Allied Commander in South East Asia.

### *Fort Benning, Georgia, June 15, 1960*

'We arrived at 1.30 p.m. at Lawson Airfield, which is the U.S. Air Force Station attached to Fort Benning in Georgia.

'I had been here with General Marshal in 1942 and found it had grown enormously. This is the Army Infantry Centre. Major-General Harris, who is in command here, drove me off to their parade ground for the honours. Here there was a fine guard of honour, band and saluting battery. They played "God Save the Queen" and fired 19 guns and then the whole parade marched past in line. It was a magnificent performance, but I was surprised to find several hundred spectators in the stands watching the whole show, including a number of retired Generals and their wives.

'From here we went to Victory Pond, which is an artificial lake used to demonstrate river-crossings. The equipment they had made my mouth water. I had not seen the crossing of a river since I saw the 14th Army crossing the Irrawady with virtually no equipment and in the face of Japanese opposition.

'We then moved to another corner of Victory Pond, where we were given a demonstration of Ranger training. We were treated to a long history of the Rangers and were told that the U.S. Ranger Battalions more or less owed their inception to Davy

Crockett. They were surprised when I told them I had been responsible for the raising of the first Ranger Battalion by suggesting it to General Marshal and putting it through proper Commando training in the Combined Operations Command. However, they have certainly kept up the spirit of Commando training.'

*Paimpol, July 13, 1961*

'We arrived punctually at 5 o'clock at Paimpol. This is the town that is twinned with Romsey[1] of which I am the High Steward, and which invited me to come to receive Honorary Citizenship in recognition of this fact.

'A large band of about seventy from one of the regiments was drawn up and then we set off, following the band through the streets of Paimpol, beginning with the newly-christened "Rue de Romsey".

'The town was festive and decked out with flags and bunting and there were a lot of people in the streets who waved and cheered and followed us to the Mairie, where speeches were made by the Mayor and by myself.

'The next item on the programme was the ceremony of planting the red horse-chestnut tree which I had brought with me from Broadlands to commemorate the occasion. There was a large hole in the grass plot in front of the Mairie and I filled in about six shovelfuls of earth. However, when I had finished, everyone joined in—the Mayor, the Deputy Mayor, the Prefect, the Admiral, and finally the Beauty Queen herself; all threw spadefuls of earth on to the roots of the tree.

'The next item was a *Vin d'Honneur* in the Mairie to which all the local notables came. Here, I was presented with a model of one of the Iceland fishing schooners, immortalized by Pierre Loti in books such as *Les Pêcheurs d'Islande*, and christened *La Paimpolaise* after the well-known French song. This I said I would give to the Town Hall in Romsey on my return.

[1] The town nearest Broadlands, Lord Mountbatten's home.

'At 6.15 I went off with my old friend the Comte de Mauduit to visit his home, the Château du Bourblanc, on the outskirts of Paimpol. It might amuse you to know what I said about de Mauduit in my speech: "Although this is the first time I have had the pleasure of visiting Paimpol, it is not the first time that I have met your people".

'It was in January 1941, that I was on board the *Kelly* in command of the 5th Flotilla of Destroyers on patrol in the Channel, when we got an echo on our very early form of radar set. I had already been involved in an action with German Destroyers in the Channel, so I pressed the alarm rattlers, and the guns and searchlights were all trained on the echo. I then gave the order to illuminate and the searchlight's shutters were opened. In the beam of our searchlights we caught sight of a small open fishing-boat. Unfortunately, the Pompom gun of the *Kelly* opened fire without orders, but instantly obeyed the cease fire gong, fortunately without having hit the boat—though the occupants afterwards said that the projectiles whistled close over their heads!

'We brought the party on board, which consisted of the Comte de Mauduit and some half-a-dozen gallant men from Paimpol who were setting out for England to join the Free French Movement. We then completed the patrol; and on returning to Plymouth we landed them.

'On 13th May this year we had the Annual Reunion Dinner of the survivors of the Ship's Company of the *Kelly*. The Comte de Mauduit was invited, and he paid us the honour of coming over for it. At the dinner I was able to point out to him the man who had been the trainer, and the man who had been Captain of the Pompom which had opened fire on him; and I invited them to make restitution by giving him a drink after dinner.'

*Quebec, September 17, 1963*

'During the drive to Rockcliffe and Uplands, and the flight to Quebec, I was once more enchanted by the beauty of the woods in this part of North America at this time of year. Edwina and I had first seen this phenomenon on our honeymoon, driving in the Adirondacks. The startlingly beautiful effect is due mainly to the maple tree, whose leaves go from normal green to all shades of yellow, orange and vivid red, before they drop off. I have never seen anything like it in any other part of the world.

'We took off at 3 p.m. and arrived at Ancienne Lorette, the airport for Quebec, just before 4.15. I was met by representatives from the Governor-General and the High Commissioner and accompanied by my staff we drove to the Citadel in Quebec, which we reached at 4.40.

'I was immediately taken up to meet the Governor-General, General Vanier, an old friend, who gave me a very friendly reception, talking indiscriminately in fluent English or French, to which I replied in the language he chose.

'I asked him if I could go out on the battlements, as it was here in August 1943 that the Prime Minister, Winston Churchill, walked me up and down for a serious heart-to-heart talk. Seeing the battlements brought back the memory of this extraordinary morning very vividly.

'He began by enquiring after my health, for I had been very ill from overwork. I told him I was O.K. again. He asked me what I thought of the situation in South East Asia. I replied that it was the worst muddle of the war, that we had nothing but defeats at sea, on land and in the air and the situation looked pretty hopeless.

'He then asked me if I would go out and put it right. Thinking he wanted one of those quick fact-finding tours, I replied that I was too busy preparing for the invasion and suggested he should send Pug Ismay.

'The P.M. stopped in his tracks and to the best of my memory said, "You don't seem to understand what I'm asking you to do. I want you to go out and set up the Supreme Allied Command yourself and put matters right".

'I replied that I wanted 24 hours to think it over. He asked me

"Why? Don't you think you can do the job?" To this I am afraid I replied rather cheekily something like this: "I've got a congenital weakness for thinking I can do anything. But I know I cannot do this job unless the President and all the British and American Chiefs-of-Staff genuinely support your choice. I want to see them each separately to test their feelings and if even one of them is doubtful, I am afraid I cannot take the job".

'He gave me permission to go ahead and said that I should find that they would all support me. Indeed this turned out to be the case, and that is how I accepted the job to go to South East Asia.'

*Kandy, Ceylon, February 3, 1964*

'Patricia and I were staying for the night in the King's Pavilion. It was rather late when we drove to Katugastota to see the elephants have their evening bath. We got some rather amusing films of them lying in the waters of the Nahaweli Ganga. We drove back to Kandy in a small car, passing the stables along the old ride, where I used to go for a ride most mornings before breakfast.

'We drove as far as the little lake, where we spotted two or three trees on which hundreds of flying foxes were hanging. It was beginning to get dark. I clapped my hands and shouted and presently the flying foxes started taking off and flying round. The air was almost black with them and there must have been hundreds, if not thousands of them. They are most fascinating creatures with a wing-span of at least a foot-and-a-half and have always been one of the features of the King's Pavilion.

'Patricia and I got out at the old stables and then from there we walked down to Snake Villa, where my Flag Lieutenant and his wife, who was one of the W.R.A.F. Signal Officers, lived. Later on, Peter Murphy moved down there from the main house himself. We wandered back in the gloaming through the garden to the King's Pavilion, where I occupied my old bedroom, which is a colossal room. Patricia slept in what was my little sitting room next door.

'These rooms hold particularly nostalgic memories. For instance, I was lying in my bed suffering from amoebic dysentery
with my Commanders-in-Chief around me when we kept touch
with the assault and capture of Rangoon.

'We had a small dinner-party of about twelve in the old dining-
room. The Lay Custodian of the Tooth told me that the Temple
Authorities had agreed to allow Patricia and me to see the famous
Buddha's Tooth, but the time just did not permit. This is a rare
honour and I myself have only seen the Tooth once, when I
accompanied the Prince of Wales in 1922.

'The Tooth is kept inside seven successive caskets and the Lay
Custodian has one key and the two High Priests in the two
Temples have each a key and it required all three to be present
to open it.

'I remember the Tooth was very large, and when I asked a
Dutch Officer of my staff, who was a Buddhist, how he
accounted for the tooth being so enormous, he replied that
Gautama Buddha was a man of gigantic stature, as witnessed by
his footprints on Adams Peak.'

*Freetown, Sierra Leone, October 6, 1964*

'Next, we drove to the Myohaung Officers' Mess at the Wilber-
force Barracks, about four or five miles out of Freetown up in
the hills.

'Myohaung is a fine new Officers' Mess which the Officers of
the 1st Battalion of the Royal Sierra Leone Regiment and the
Headquarters Staff use together. The Governor-General, the High
Commissioner and my own staff were guests. There were some
eighteen British Seconded Officers and all the rest were Sierra
Leone Officers. They clearly get on extremely well together, and
the atmosphere was delightful. I sat between Brigadier Blackie,
the Force Commander, and Lieutenant-Colonel John Bangura,
the delightful Commander of the 1st Battalion. There were many
arguments as to whether there should be speeches or not, but I
finally agreed to make a fairly short one. Colonel David Lansana

N

had wanted me to give a half-hour's lecture on the Defence situation in the world, but I really couldn't face that at a social occasion. However, I made them a stirring speech about the Battle of Myohaung after which their mess is called, and which is the principal Battle Honour on their Colours. I told them how in January 1944, when the Japanese had cut off a large part of the 7th Indian Division on the Arakan front, that the 81st West African Division was ordered to advance down the Kaladan Valley in order to relieve the pressure and force the Japanese to fall back.

'I told them that this was the first victory against the Japanese in Burma and they were right to celebrate "Myohaung Day" on January 24th each year, and I hoped they would always continue to do so. I told them how proud I was that this Battle should have been fought under my command. I then presented them with one of my CDS badges for their mess.'

### Nehru's Funeral

On May 27, 1964, there occurred the death of Jawaharlal Nehru, the Prime Minister of India since 1947. Nehru was undoubtedly one of the world's great leaders and as the Swedish Prime Minister, Tage Erlander, said, it was difficult 'to calculate the consequences of Nehru's death. Despite his gentle and peaceful spirit, he was a power factor of unimaginable strength and a unifying force for the millions of India's people, who in him saw a guarantee of peace and progress'.

During his official visit to Sweden, in June 1957, Nehru had been the guest of King Gustaf Adolf and Queen Louise at their summer residence, Sofiero. For Queen Louise therefore it was of particular interest to read Lord Mountbatten's letter about Nehru's funeral in Delhi and the ceremonial cremation on the banks of the sacred river Jumna. As India's last Viceroy and Queen Elizabeth's personal representative at the funeral, Earl

Mountbatten was one of the central figures at what must be regarded as a great moment of destiny in Indian history. Lord Mountbatten's letter to his sister is reproduced here almost complete.

*Delhi, May 29, 1964*

'Patricia rang me up the day before yesterday, just after the news broadcast which announced that Jawaharlal Nehru was seriously ill. She reminded me of her conviction that when he said goodbye to us in Delhi after our lunch with him on January 29th that he knew that he would never see us again. She was convinced then he hadn't got much longer to live and now she prophesied that he was dying.

'I had my hair cut and at 9.30 Ronnie Brockman rang through to the barber's to say that Jawaharlal had died, and he had already made preliminary arrangements for me to go out for the funeral which he assumed would be the following day.

'I dashed back to the office. Duncan Sandys rang me up to ask whether I would be prepared to go out and represent H.M. Government and I said of course I would. I got in touch with Michael Adeane, who told me that the Queen wished me to represent her personally at the funeral.

'Meanwhile the Prime Minister (Sir Alec Douglas-Home) had decided that he would go himself to represent the British Government and wanted me to arrange an aircraft. An R.A.F. Comet 4 with an extra slip crew was immediately laid on but, because of its short endurance, it would have to refuel at least twice on the way out and we could not have got there in time. I then rang up Sir Timothy Bligh, the Prime Minister's Private Secretary, and he arranged for a Rolls-Royce Boeing 707 to be laid on by B.O.A.C.

'I rang up Pammy to ask if she would like to accompany me to the funeral and she immediately accepted.

'We had been told the aircraft was going to leave at 2.0 p.m. but it was then delayed, because Sir Paul Gore-Booth, the

British High Commissioner in India, was on leave in a remote part of Cornwall and we were to wait for him. Besides Pammy, my party consisted of my A.D.C., Squadron Leader Peter Lithgow and Military Assistant, Major Tony Aylmer, of the Irish Guards, and of course Chief Petty Officer Evans. The Prime Minister had with him Tim Bligh and three stenographers, and there were four or five pressmen coming out for the funeral. Otherwise, the vast aircraft was entirely empty. We landed at Palam, New Delhi, at 6.10 a.m. local time the next day, which was I believe a record, as the non-stop trip lasted under ten hours.

'The acting Prime Minister, Nanda, and Sirdar Swaran Singh, another of the Cabinet Ministers, were there to meet us. A complete turn-out of British Advisers were there in uniform, with their wives, and of course the Acting High Commissioner, Belcher.

'We drove straight to the High Commissioner's residence, 2 King George's Avenue. The house had of course been shut up for spring-cleaning during the absence of the Gore-Booths and had had to be opened up at a moment's notice. Belcher said to the assembled company: "I would like to make a speech about today's arrangements". Alec Douglas-Home chipped in with, "It had better be a good speech or I shall fall asleep, I am so tired".

'A message then came to say that they hoped that I would come and lay my wreath at 8 o'clock at the Indian Prime Minister's residence, and that our Prime Minister should lay his wreath at 9 o'clock.

'We were then informed that all of us were being put up in the High Commission except our staff, who had been put up some distance away, and God knows where Evans was going to be put up. I said that I was sure that I was expected by the President to stay at Rashtrapati Bhavan (the old Viceroy's house) and one of the High Commission staff then said that they had taken it upon themselves to ring up the President's staff and say I would be staying at the High Commissioner's residence.

'I then asked our Military Adviser to ring up the President's

Military Secretary to confirm where we were expected to stay. Back came the reply immediately that the President hoped that I and my party would stay at Rashtrapati Bhavan.

'I therefore sent off Peter and Evans with the luggage to get settled in whilst the rest of us had breakfast, and then Pammy, Tony and I drove off with a Union Jack on the car to the Prime Minister's residence. We entered by the tradesmen's entrance to the compound and came into the house from the east end door. Pammy and I were immediately greeted by Nehru's two sisters, Betty Huthi Singh and Nan Pandit. They conducted us through to the main front hall where Jawaharlal was lying in state. His daughter, Indira, was keeping close watch by the body, which was being guarded by two Major-Generals.

'I first of all placed the wreath of Lilibet and Philip in the position of honour over the feet and Pammy then placed our family wreath beside it. Seeing Jawaharlal lying there, so peaceful and serene, was very harrowing, and altogether too much for poor Pammy. On the way out, we saw Krishna Menon sitting huddled up over his stick near the body and greeted him warmly. Nan asked if we would like to stay in the house, but as it was full of hundreds of people sitting about in every corner, I said I thought I would sooner go up to Rashtrapati Bhavan right away and come back again when the body was transferred to the gun-carriage. She agreed, and so we drove to Rashtrapati Bhavan, where we were greeted by the staff of all grades with warmth, enthusiasm and affection.

'I had a bath and then my dear old barber, Nasir Baig, came and shaved me and massaged me and made me feel more comfortable. There was a distinct earth tremour that morning, one of the first I remember noticing in India. At 10.30 the President received Pammy and myself, and I had an hour's fascinating conversation with him. He told me that Jawaharlal had told him quite recently about my invitation to him to go to Broadlands during the Prime Minister's Conference, and how he would go for the weekend, for he had been on every occasion of visiting

England, even though there was an eighty mile motor-drive there from London.

'He said how delighted he and all of India were that the Queen should have sent me to represent her and that our Prime Minister should have come in person. He told me that Dean Rusk, the American Secretary of State was doing his best to get there in time for the cremation, but he, of course, had much farther to fly.

'I asked him whether he would allow my car to form part of his procession both to the Prime Minister's house and to Rajghat, instead of having a procession of our own as had been suggested, and he kindly agreed to this.

'The timings were all delightfully vague. The Prime Minister and other National Delegations were told to be at the house before 12 o'clock. We were first of all told to be ready to leave from the President's entrance at 12.30, then a message came would we be ready to leave at 12 o'clock. Then we got a message to be ready to leave our rooms at 12.19. We did so and arrived at the President's entrance at 12.25 and then had to wait five minutes in my old study for him. With an adequate police escort, we were able to go in through the front entrance of the Prime Minister's house this time, but had to get out well before we reached the door on account of the crowds and troops. We went straight into the front hall, where there were scenes of great activity going on. Fourteen of the most senior officers of the three Indian services were in there, eight to carry the body personally and six to march by the side as pall-bearers.

'We stood between the President and Padmaja Naidu, the Governor of West Bengal and a very old friend. I saw a number of the Ministers and in the distance my old friend, Sheikh Abdullah from Kashmir, quite overcome with emotion. He had been weeping most of the day, prophesying that this would be the break-up of Jawaharlal's ideal of a secular State. For a man who had been kept all those years in prison by Jawaharlal, this was a truly remarkable demonstration of affection.

'Madden, Jawaharlal's faithful factotum, went and put a rose into his usual centre buttonhole, where he had always kept one. It was a moving gesture.

'It is most disturbing to see an old friend being manhandled, even though it is by Generals and Admirals in being moved from the lying-in-state position to the traditional Indian litter of bamboos and string on which the officers carried him shoulder-high to the gun-carriage.

'Before it was moved, the President and I each laid yet another wreath which was transferred to the gun-carriage to go with him on his last journey. I had originally organized Gandhi's funeral in January 1948, and it had been my idea that the Navy should draw the funeral float. This time there was a new spirit of integration between the services, for the three drag-ropes were manned respectively by the Army, the Navy and the Air Force. While all those movements were going on, a concealed choir sang "Lead Kindly Light" and "Abide With Me".

'A large band led off with an appropriate funeral march, then came the gun-carriage, then came the escort with arms reversed from the Army, the Navy and the Air Force, and I suggested to the President that instead of getting into our cars it would be nice if we at least walked behind the coffin as far as the main gates. He agreed, and so the President, the Prime Minister, Pammy and I walked in the procession.

'At the gates we transferred back into the cars and after great difficulty in breaking through the crowd, got back to Rashtrapati Bhavan at about 1.30 p.m. I changed out of white full dress and we four had lunch together in our dining-room.

'After lunch, one of the Prime Minister's stenographers came to take down the record of my meeting with the President.'

'We were told that we would be leaving at 6.0 p.m. for Rajghat. Then we were told that it would be between 5.30 and 4.30. A little later on a message came to leave between 4.30 and 3.30, but finally at 2.35 the message came that we were leaving in ten minutes. I stopped dictating, dashed back and put on my full dress and we almost ran to the President's door, where we arrived at 2.46, to find that he was already sitting in the car waiting for us.

'We drove off with police at high speed by a detour, only to run into a vast crowd which was returning from lining the funeral route; this brought us to a complete halt. We had to crawl with much difficulty and after about a quarter-of-an-hour, managed to take a turning away from whence the crowds were coming and again we moved at high speed until we ran into the final great crowd on the outskirts of Rajghat. This crowd really was dense and we moved at a snail's pace.

'I must say the crowd was quite astonishing, for in the closed Cadillac they all seemed to recognize me at once with cries of "Lord Mountbatten" or "Lord Mountbatten *ki jai*" and some-times "Lord Mountbatten *zindabad*".[1] I am glad to say Pammy had her own reception. It began with cries of "*Larki* Lord Mount-batten", which means "Lord Mountbatten's daughter". But on two or three occasions, men put their head in at the window and grinning with pleasure, shouted "Pamela". I had warned our car to keep as close behind the next car as possible so as to avoid the risk of being cut off by the crowds getting in between. Unfortu-nately our driver interpreted these instructions so literally that he ran into the police car ahead, damaged our radiator, which gave off clouds of steam and we were brought to a full stop.

'However, the crowd just gathered round and pushed our car along, so we then managed to keep up without much difficulty. Then suddenly the two cars ahead did a spurt and got about 200 or 300 yards ahead of us.

'Obviously the crowd couldn't push us at that speed, so I decided that we would get out and walk. Pammy and I then pro-cessed down a very crowded route, and it was a sort of triumphal procession, because of course there was no difficulty about the

---

[1] 'Lord Mountbatten *ki jai* . . . Lord Mountbatten *zindabad*' are cries of salutation from the crowds and might freely be translated 'Long live Lord Mountbatten'.

crowds recognizing us from far ahead here. As we were walking through the crowd, a man cried out, "Don't go, Lord Mountbatten, don't go."

'Finally we caught up with the President's police car, which was completely stopped in a new jam, and Pammy, Tony and I managed to pile into this. The Cadillac had been hot, but the police car was an inferno and we absolutely dripped. The temperature was over 100°F.

'We reached the entrance to Rajghat at 3.30. Here we dismounted and walked down an open lane where the crowds were held back by prepared barriers and many police with *lathis*.[1]

'We arrived at the funeral pyre simultaneously with the body. In fact, as we came to a standstill, the body was hoisted up and we all saluted. We slowly moved round the pyre, which was built on a structure of brick 6 foot high, so that all could see. Finally, we reached the seats allotted to us and Pammy was enchanted to find that the card on my seat just read "The Ex-Governor General". It was placed next to the President's.

'Meanwhile Alec Douglas-Home and George Brown, Paul Gore-Booth and others were near us, but hemmed in by the crowd and standing up.

'I had heard that Dean Rusk, the American Secretary of State, was making a gallant effort to get over to the funeral. I enquired whether he had arrived and was told he had got there about ten minutes before and was among the crowd of diplomats. I plunged into the crowd and pulled him out and brought him over to meet the President and we managed to get an extra chair put in alongside Pamela. I felt that if the most powerful nation on earth could send their representative at breakneck speed halfway round the world, he certainly deserved a seat near the President.

'Dean told me that it took them fifteen-and-a-half hours' flying time and that they had to refuel twice on the way. We

[1] *Lathis* are the bamboo sticks, usually about 4 feet long and bound with string, used by the police in India. They are rather like the truncheons supplied to the British Mounted Police.

reminisced about the old days when he was a Lieutenant-Colonel on my American Planning Staff in Delhi, in 1943–44.

'The funeral pyre was less gruesome than in the case of Gandhi, for they did at least cover poor Jawaharlal up completely with sandalwood sticks, so one was spared the agony of seeing his body and face actually being consumed by the flames.

'His youngest grandson, in accordance with custom, lighted the pyre and then the troops fired three volleys and the *Last Post* was sounded.

'The President wisely decided to move before the fire had completely done its work, for he realized that once it had, the whole crowd would disperse simultaneously; thus we were able to get out well ahead of the crowds and got back in fairly good time to Rashtrapati Bhavan, much sooner than we expected.

'We arranged to go down and call on poor Indira, Jawaharlal's daughter, at 7 o'clock. She was extraordinarily brave and very sweet.

'When we got back to Rashtrapati Bhavan, Pammy and I went for a stroll in the evening twilight through the lovely Moghul Garden. The heat of the day had gone and, although there are few flowers at this time of the year, the whole setting was as beautiful as ever and brought back exquisite memories of our days in Delhi.

'I had arranged to have dinner served in the garden as usual during summer—this proved to be even more nostalgic.'

CHAPTER 9

*Personality*

WHENEVER possible the King and Queen would spend a few weeks in Italy during the autumn and and afterwards Louise would always come over to visit her family and friends in England. As the years went by she became more and more attached to Sweden, yet she adored England, would never miss her annual visit, and always found time to visit her English friends. It is from her friends and relatives that one gains the most vivid portrait of Queen Louise and King Gustaf Adolf, and so in this chapter the reader will find some of their favourite stories and memories about the King and Queen and I shall also attempt to give a sketch of their characters.

All those who knew her well say that Queen Louise was 'the nicest person you could ever hope to meet'. She undoubtedly had a strong and warm character, and possessed tremendous kindness and a great sense of loyalty and affection. Her nieces say she was a 'great family person' and according to Lady Pamela Hicks, 'there was no one like her for taking such interest in everything that went on in the family. Engagements, weddings. When you were expecting your first child. When the second one came'. She liked children so much and she had a wonderful way with them, and Lady Brabourne says 'there is always one person in every generation round whom everyone gathers. In our family, it was Aunt Louise'.

Louise's most outstanding quality was her unselfishness. She was always prepared to help anyone. She thought extremely little about herself and a great deal about others. Lady Zia Wernher told me that 'Queen Louise was the most unselfish person I have ever met in my whole life—and I've met a great number of people. She was the kind of person who would give her last crust to help someone in need,' and even when Louise was young, her Aunt Alix (the Tsarina of Russia) talked about 'her self-sacrificing nature'. But, although she was open-handed to the needy, Louise was wary of spending money on herself. She frowned on unnecessary expense, especially in running the royal palaces, and could often be heard complaining about high prices in the shops. Perhaps it was a matter of personality, but undoubtedly the thin years between 1917 and 1923 had made a lasting impression on her.

Again, one of Louise's finest qualities was her gaiety. Despite her poor physique she always seemed vivacious—obviously a Mountbatten characteristic—and was always full of laughter. Also, she is said to have had a fairly lively temper and her friends tell me that 'she could sometimes be a little hasty', while Prince Bertil readily admits that sometimes Louise could get really angry. But, everyone agrees that the Queen's bursts of fury passed as quickly as they arose and the late Nils Rudebeck, the Marshal of the Court, once compared her jokingly to her ancestor St Elisabeth of Hungary and described her as 'a saint with a temperament'.

When occasion demanded Louise was not afraid to be critical and could be quite sharp spoken. She was well aware of this herself, however, and once even confessed in public that she was 'a sharp person'. Similarly, she had strong likes and dislikes, and often showed them. This could, of course, have been a troublesome quality in a queen; but, when it really mattered, she always put duty first. When, for example, Kruschev paid a visit to Sweden, Queen Louise received him with great friendliness, despite the role his party had played in the murder of her relatives in Russia. In fact, Louise appears to have been quite without malice and if anyone came to her with gossip that was in the least way spiteful, she would abruptly clip off the conversation with a gesture of disapproval. Also, she was extremely honest. I can still hear her saying in that slightly impatient voice of hers, the words seeming to tumble out one on top of the other, 'I don't like things written about royalty while they are still alive. Wait until I'm dead. Then you may with pleasure write about me. Not until then can you tell the truth.'

Lady Brabourne told me that one of the great things about Queen Louise was her unpretentiousness. At King George VI's funeral, she remembers how there was a long line of cars waiting to come up. Quite early on a sumptious Daimler appeared for Queen Louise. 'For me!' exclaimed Queen Louise, drawing back a little, 'No, it must have come for a Queen.' The funeral was only eighteen months after Louise had become Queen, and it still had not registered that she really *was* a queen herself. Lady Brabourne says that Louise did not suffer fools lightly and found it difficult to be patient with people she thought stupid or who behaved clumsily, and yet at the same time she was the very essence of consideration and helpfulness. Once when Lady Brabourne was riding in Ireland her horse shied against a sharp iron gate-fastening, tearing her leg badly, and Queen Louise immediately wrote her the following letter:

August 19, 1962
Sofiero

'*Darling Patricia,*

'It has struck me that perhaps nobody has told you one must be very careful not to expose a new scar to the sun because the skin gets too sunburnt and the scar stays red ever so much longer, in fact several years. With heaps of love to you all. It was lovely hearing your voice the other day on the telephone. Very much love.

*Your affectionate*
*Aunt Louise.*'

Lady Pamela Hicks describes Louise's nostalgia for England. Queen Louise always found it difficult to leave England after her visits and at the moment of parting, usually towards the end of November, she would stand on the steps of Lord Mountbatten's house Broadlands, near Romsey in Hampshire, and look wistfully across the English landscape. Lady Pamela remembers how her aunt stood there sniffing the slightly pungent autumn air, gazing through the mist at the rain-soaked soil. She knew that in England the autumn would remain for some time to come, but in her other country the long winter was already starting and she would feel homesick for the milder climate she had known in her youth.

At the same time, Louise undoubtedly leant more and more towards Sweden. Each year her family in England noticed how she became more Swedish in her ways; the phrasing of her letters gradually became less English and for the first two or three days after her arrival in England she would speak English with a sing-song Swedish intonation, and was much teased by her English relatives and friends. Also, Louise's attitude towards being Queen was changing. Before her marriage she had instinctively shied away from the thought of becoming a Queen and her reaction to the first taste of sovereignty was shock at the crowd's unreserved homage. Gradually, however, she became more and more proud of being the Queen of Sweden and felt she belonged to Sweden from the very depths of her soul.

There was a demonstration of her change of attitude when David and Lady Pamela Hicks stayed in Stockholm for a few weeks in the winter of 1961. Their visit happened to coincide with a 'representation dinner' at the Palace and so, as David Hicks was new to the family, before the other guests had begun to assemble in the Victoria Room, Queen Louise took him into the Carl XI Gallery. There, the long dinner table was laid with shining damask. On it were delicate crystal and silver side-plates, and down the middle there were the splendid pieces from the silver dinner service, which Queen Josephine of Sweden had inherited from her sister, the Empress of Brazil. With great pride she pointed out that Stockholm Palace was larger than Buckingham Palace. As they walked through the banqueting apartments, she told him the history of the paintings, tapestries and ornaments,

and dallied longest before Queen Christina's coronation tapestries with their motifs from the myth of Dido and Aeneas,
commissioned in Delft during the 1640s at the same time as those
in Drottningholm, and also before the sixteenth-century
Florentine canopy with its rich gold embroidery, partly taken
from drawings by Botticelli.

There was much evidence of Queen Louise's pride in Sweden
and a delightful story is told by Mrs Kerstin Laurin, the wife of
Thorsten Laurin, the publisher and art collector. The King and
Queen were visiting the royal palace at Tullgarn, in Central
Sweden, together with Thorsten and Kerstin Laurin, during the
spring. They walked through the birch groves and oak woods
by the smooth water and carpets of wood anemones. The King
and Thorsten Laurin were walking ahead, the Queen and
Kerstin Laurin behind. The path turned uphill and when they
reached the top of the rise, the Queen stood silent for a moment,
looked at her husband and then back across the landscape. Then,
she turned to Kerstin Laurin and said, 'Can one be anything but
grateful for being able to live in a country like Sweden and to
have a husband like mine?' She was not in general sentimental,
however, as is confirmed by an episode which occurred soon
after the death of her mother, the Dowager Marchioness of
Milford Haven. Queen Louise had gone to England to clear up
her mother's home in Kensington Palace and go through her
effects. One afternoon, Lady Pamela had gone to Kensington
Palace to see if she could be of assistance. She found Queen
Louise with books scattered around her and just in front of her
there lay a pile of torn-out fly-leaves. When Pamela arrived,
Louise was still ripping out the fly-leaves with sharp, energetic
jerks and the last pages were fluttering on to the floor. They were
from books which had been given to Louise's mother by Queen
Victoria and which contained inscriptions such as 'To dearest
Victoria from her affectionate Grandmother V.R.I. (*Victoria
Regina Imperatrix*).' The Queen had now weeded out the books
she wanted to give away but she had decided that it would be

undesirable to leave Queen Victoria's monogram inside. Her niece told her that practically anyone in the world would have been thrilled to possess a book inscribed by Queen Victoria. But, Louise was as hard-headed and as democratic as ever. 'Do you think,' she said, 'I'd want to have a book in my personal library just because it had Queen Victoria's signature on the fly-leaf? That wouldn't make it any more interesting to read, would it?'

Queen Louise's sense of humour will doubtless be a legend in the Mountbatten family for generations. In her first passport, under 'Special Peculiarities' she put 'walks like a parrot'. Even in her very last telegram to Lord Mountbatten, on his appointment as Colonel of the Life Guards, she was still joking: 'CON-GRATULATIONS ON YOUR NEW APPOINTMENT,' she wrote, 'NOTHING SURPRISES ME ANY MORE.'

And once, at the Nobel Prize dinner at the Palace in Stockholm, when the wife of one of the prize-winners asked an attendant to let the Queen know that she would like nothing so much as to take back to her own country a lock of the King's hair, Louise quickly replied, 'Tell her that ever since my husband has been King, his hair has become so thin that he hasn't a lock to spare.' But perhaps the most charming reminiscence of all is told by Alicia Pearson. Often, when Queen Louise was in London, she used to stay at the Hyde Park Hotel and once when Alicia was shown into the Queen's sitting-room, Louise was in the act of transferring the contents from one handbag to another and among the odds and ends was a card on which were written six words in large capital letters: I AM THE QUEEN OF SWEDEN. Alicia could not help laughing, but Louise replied perfectly seriously: 'I like going out shopping by myself and it would be so inconvenient if I got run over and they couldn't find out who I was!'

Many of the observations and memories included in this book were provided by Louise's niece Dolla, the Margravine of Baden.

Dolla was very much in the foreground of Louise's life, as was Salem, the vast castle which belonged to her husband Berthold, Margrave of Baden, who died in 1963. Queen Louise loved Salem —after one visit she wrote to Dolla, 'I did hate leaving Salem. I had such a lovely time there and the time went all too fast. . . . I do feel so at home with you and Berthold,' and so it would perhaps not be out of place to say a word about Salem here.

Originally, Salem was a monastery and for two centuries it belonged to the Cistercian Order. The name is simply a poetical variation for Jerusalem which appears in the Book of Kings, and amongst those who played a part in its foundation in 1134 was Bernard of Clairvaux. Salem contains a wealth of art treasures including some beautiful work by the sculptor Franz Joseph Feichtmayr, who entered the Cistercian Order in about 1706 and by his son Joseph-Anton, the famous sculptor and stucco artist, who died in 1770. Along the corridors of the castle stand statues of wood and stone, interspersed with medieval madonnas, painted in crimson, blue and gold. And on the walls hang hunting trophies, each one with a plaque giving the place of the kill and the huntsman's name, including—among an abundance of monarchs—the poet Schiller.

At the beginning of the nineteenth century, after the dissolution of the Cistercian Order, the monastery was added to the estates of the Grand Duke of Baden[1] and in due course was inherited by Dolla's father-in-law Prince Maximilian of Baden. Prince Maximilian, who was known as 'Red Max' because of his progressive ideas, was the last Chancellor of Imperial Germany and, taking literally Patlo's saying 'He who wishes to help his people must combine the power to think with the will to act', he founded Salem School in part of the castle and entrusted its running to Dr Kurt Hahn; though eventually, because of his Jewish origin, Dr Hahn had to flee from Germany to Britain

---

[1] It was only after the 1918 revolution deposed the last reigning Grand Duke, that the head of the house resumed the earlier title of Margrave.

O

where he founded a similar school at Gordonstoun, as has been mentioned in the Introduction.

One of the anecdotes the Margravine of Baden told me about Queen Louise was the history of the portrait which appears on the jacket of this book. The portrait was painted by the Hungarian Philip Laszlo de Lombos, who from the 1890s until his death in 1937 was one of the most popular portrait painters among the royalty and aristocracy of Europe; and the Margravine told me that it was done in 1907, when Louise was eighteen, the sittings taking place in Darmstadt. When the artist arrived to start work, she said, Louise was wearing her best dress, which she thought suited her especially well and in which she very much wanted to be painted. But Laszlo did not like it. He made Louise rearrange her clothes, then swept a yellow shawl round her shoulders.

'My aunt still sounded slightly indignant,' the Margravine recalls, 'when she told me what happened next. 'Just imagine, Dolla,' she said, 'he caught sight of an old gardening hat which was hanging on the wall, turned it inside out and put it on my head. And not only that, he went on to get a couple of plumes and pinned them on to one side of the hat. Not until then was he satisfied.'

It was Dolla who told me that Louise was, in fact, genuinely shy. Before each appearance in public, she suffered from stage fright—though no one would ever have guessed. At the formal Opening of Parliament, for example, she seemed the embodiment of queenliness as she stepped on to the dais prepared for the royal ladies in the Hall of State and as with dignity she curtsied three times—once to the Diplomatic Corps, once to the Upper Chamber and once to the Lower Chamber. But before the ceremony she was extremely nervous.

Shyness in queens is a strange phenomenon. Queen Maud of Norway, for instance, was so shy that she would stand fumbling with her long white gloves for minutes before she could bring herself to enter the box at a gala performance or a banqueting hall where hundreds of people were waiting. Queen Mary of

England sometimes appeared to be unapproachable purely because she was hiding behind a mask of shyness. And I once had occasion myself to observe the quite exceptional shyness from which Queen Astrid of Belgium suffered, when I was at the same school in Saltsjöbaden, just outside Stockholm. Ten of us were boarding at the time, but Princess Astrid, who was learning French, only attended daily. On the first day, Princess Ingeborg (her mother) came with her and I do not think that I have ever seen such tears. She turned her face away and, shaken with weeping, pressed against Princess Ingeborg, as she was introduced to her future companions. But strangely, after she married Crown Prince Leopold of Belgium, Astrid's shyness completely disappeared.

Yet another case was the Grand Duchess Hilda of Baden, the sister-in-law of Queen Victoria of Sweden. Before public functions she used to stand beside her husband, Grand Duke Frederick, trying to collect enough courage to make an entry. She knew that she was expected to say something special to each of the guests, and this so unnerved her that she often fainted, and—according to Dolla's father-in-law, Prince Maximillian— the ladies of the Court would frantically attempt to revive her with burnt feathers!

The Margravine believes shyness is inherent in royalty. 'I think I have only once in my life met a royal lady without a trace of shyness,' she says, 'and that was Queen Marie of Rumania.[1] But she was also the most beautiful woman I have ever met!'

To return from Baden to Sweden, the King and Queen's domestic life was one of complete harmony. The King and Queen seemed a perfect foil for each other and their mutual devotion and their delight in each others' company was apparent to everyone who knew them. The King loved to spend his evenings quietly at home and whenever they were able to go away on trips to-

[1] The daughter of Queen Victoria's second son Alfred, Duke of Edinburgh, who later succeeded as the Duke of Saxe-Coburg and Gotha.

gether it was a great joy to them. They certainly spread happiness around them, were always thinking of each other and, if ever they were apart, they would always telephone each other and exchange frequent letters.

Regarding Louise's attitude to clothes, her friends do not seem to be in complete agreement. Her family in England say that 'as a woman, Queen Louise was completely lacking in vanity, particularly as regards her personal appearance; and beyond wishing to look neat and nicely turned out, she had no interest in clothes and fashions or in jewelry'. However, as a Queen she was anxious to look her best on great occasions and particularly on state visits abroad when she felt that she was representing the women of Sweden, and so took great pains with her wardrobe although it still gave her no real personal pleasure or interest. Her lack of interest in wearing jewelry was gradually modified by pride in the Swedish Royal Jewels which are extremely beautiful and also of historical interest, since many of them belonged to Napoleon's Empress Josephine, who bequeathed them to her grand-daughter Queen Josephine of Sweden.[1] The Margravine of Baden, however, thinks otherwise. 'My Aunt certainly *was* interested in clothes', she says. 'She was sufficiently feminine to want to have lovely clothes which suited her. But at the same time she did not want to spend too much time on fittings and obtaining them. She often thought the question of clothes "troublesome". And then she found it difficult to find hats which suited her. She did not have what one might call a head for hats'.

The Queen had inherited from her mother an interest in archaeology, but it was undoubtedly due to her husband that she took a far greater interest in archaeology after her marriage and also in Chinese Art, which is King Gustaf Adolf's special hobby.

---

[1] Queen Josephine was the consort of Oscar I of Sweden and was Napoleon's goddaughter. Her father was Eugène de Beauharnais, created Viceroy of Italy by Napoleon and later Duke of Leuchtenberg. Beauharnais was the son of the Empress Josephine of France by her first marriage to the French General, Viscount Alexandre de Beauharnais, guillotined at the age of thirty-four in 1794. Josephine married Napoleon two years later and he adopted her two sons Eugène and Hortense.

The King has a passionate interest in the past and a tremendous knowledge of history. He spends his spare time and money on digs in Italy and Greece, is widely recognized as an authority on Chinese antiquities, and collectors often go to him for a final opinion on the date and origin of pieces which are difficult to place. The King has what is reputed to be one of the finest collections in private hands and he was very pleased when an international organization asked if they could put some of his finest pieces on exhibition.

King Gustaf Adolf is also fond of music, and the Queen and he often went to opera, ballet or theatre. He is an enthusiastic gardener, does his own landscape gardening, designs the layout of the flower beds, crosses his own flowers, and he always loved to take the Queen to the Chelsea Flower Show where he used to buy a great many plants. It was, in fact, the King who personally directed the restoration of the great gardens and grounds of the Palace of Drottningholm, which are now greatly enjoyed by the public.

The King was a fine tennis player and golfer, although the Queen always described herself as 'hopeless'. But, although she was not a natural games player, she was a gifted and courageous horsewoman, always rode side-saddle and used to go for long expeditions, often with her brother Louis, in the Odenwald, the great forests which cover the hills round about Heiligenberg. Her love of horses she shared with the British Royal Family, whom she was of course particularly close to, seeing that Prince Philip was her nephew; and once, when Queen Elizabeth and Prince Philip were staying with them in Stockholm during the Equestrian Olympic Games, their enthusiasm for horses nearly caused a royal incident. Prince Bertil, King Gustaf Adolf's son who is a great connoisseur of food and a *cordon bleu*, had personally supervized lunch in a great tent on the first day of the Olympics. It so happened that on that day there were the cross country events and Queen Elizabeth and Prince Philip naturally did not want to come in until the event was over. When they came in, all Prince

Bertil's finest culinary effects had been deflated, but they came back in such tremendous form that he took it in good part and the feast went ahead with great gaiety, perhaps all the gayer for the fact that the food was no longer *au point*.

Louise was also fond of dogs and always had some beloved and faithful pet with her. Perhaps her greatest favourite was a liver and white cocker spaniel given to her by the officers of the first naval Air Squadron, who had taken her up in 1911. Had it been a dog she would have called it 'Aero', but being a bitch she named it 'Aera'. Her last dog, a Pekinese called Eisei, has now firmly attached herself to the King.

When alone together, the King and Queen usually spoke English—the King's is completely fluent. But they could as easily slide into Swedish or, if they had French or German guests, would talk the appropriate language. The Queen always read the English newspapers, including the *New Statesman*, to which she was a regular subscriber and once when other papers were un-obtainable complained that 'I feel now that I know so little being reduced to *The Times*'! She was progressive in outlook, took an interest in what was going on in the world, and her views were generally shared by the King. 'Look at Sweden,' Louise used to say. 'No slums, no unemployment'.[1]

It has been said that King Gustaf Adolf is 'perhaps the most civilized, cultured and fully politically educated King, within historical memory'. He was, of course, trained from childhood to be a king. He did a period of military service and then went on to Staff College, where he had to take command during Army manœuvres to show he had the necessary qualifications to be a general.

But the King's interests were far from being military and, besides his interest in archaeology, he has a real knowledge of constitutional history and knows world history horizontally, not just vertically. His friends will tell you that he always

---

[1] Today the situation on the labour-market has changed, due to the international business cycle.

remains unruffled in time of crisis and that he can always be relied upon for a clear judgement in any situation. Again, the King has always been a strong supporter of democracy and, during one of his frequent visits to Italy when he was developing his views on democracy to some friends, he laid special stress on 'the value of consultation and the strength of the common will of the people'. Similarly he claimed that today a constitutional monarch can 'make a particularly valuable contribution to stimulate and further matters which he considers are essential, right or specially worth while'.

King Gustaf Adolf's manners are always perfect, since they spring from his basic kindness and thoughtfulness for other people. Nothing is too much trouble for him. He will always pay endless personal attention to his guests, however burdened he is with affairs of state, and he is an extremely gentle person.

Like her husband, the Queen was by nature modest. She never stood on protocol. She loved shopping accompanied by only a lady-in-waiting in Sweden, in England sometimes entirely by herself, and she always insisted on waiting her turn to be served. In England, this was easy because she was seldom recognized. But in Sweden, where she was obviously always recognized, the people would politely make way for her but, with innate good manners, never crowded round and stared.

After the new underground was opened in Stockholm, when her brother and sister-in-law and their younger daughter came to stay, she proudly took them for a ride accompanied only by her lady-in-waiting. They queued for their tickets with everyone else. People in the carriage politely rose from their seats and made little bows to the Queen as she entered, but then they quietly resumed their seats and, realizing that she was on a private family outing, they were at pains not to stare.

Of her close friends in England, many such as her nieces and such as Lady Zia Wernher and Alicia Pearson have already been mentioned. There was also, of course, the late Mrs Margaret (Peggy) Heywood, who was a niece of Princess Victoria's Lady-in-waiting Nona Kerr and who had been a close friend of Louise's since their schooldays with Fraulein Textor in Darmstadt. And there were also Miss Ida Wheatley and Miss Eardley Wilmot, whom Louise met while she was nursing during World War I. They had remained friends ever since and Louise invariably stayed with them or saw them whenever she came to England.

Another friend was Christopher Jenkins. He was a Naval Signal Boy who at the age of seventeen had his leg blown off by a shell in the battleship *Albion* in the bombardment of the Dardanelles. In those days very little was done for limbless men but Prince Louis and Princess Victoria offered to take in a limbless man and so Christopher Jenkins came to live with them at Kent House, since he could not be fitted with an artificial leg immediately and was confined to a wheelchair and crutches. He of course saw a great deal of Louise while he was living with the family at Kent House, but she never lost touch with him and he invariably saw her whenever she came to England. He has never known a day free of pain in the last fifty years, but he never complains, is always cheerful and has always had the greatest veneration and affection for Queen Louise. Although these two people came from completely opposite walks of life, they were really sincere friends, and when Louise died, Christopher Jenkins said that he felt he had lost his greatest friend.

Finally, it should be said that among Louise's greatest friends were her two sisters-in-law, Edwina Mountbatten and Nada Milford Haven. Up to Nada's death, Louise never failed to go and visit her in the South of France, where she had a villa, and she was perhaps an even greater friend of Edwina's, who often went to Sweden or met her at Broadlands or in Malta.

When talking to her nearest relatives and friends, the impression which one gets of Queen Louise and King Gustaf Adolf is of a couple utterly devoted to one another. Indeed, their affection for each other was so strong, that it is sad to think of the unbearable loneliness and solitude of the King who has lost a wife for the second time.

# CHAPTER 10

## The Queen's Death

THE people of Sweden heard the news of Queen Louise's death at 12.30 p.m. on Sunday, March 7, 1965, the announcement being made in a radio message from the royal physician, Ulf Nordwall, which stated simply that the Queen had 'quietly and peacefully passed away'. The news did not come as a surprise, since for three days the Swedish people had anxiously been awaiting the outcome of the battle for the Queen's life. The bulletins had become less and less hopeful, and after a special bulletin on the Sunday, when it was stated that the Queen's condition had worsened and that she was unconscious, it was generally realized that all hope was gone.

Queen Louise's health was never good, and, after a heart attack in May 1951, her strength had gradually diminished. That she managed to remain so lively was largely due to her immense will power, but only those nearest to her knew what the effort cost. After her death one of Louise's close friends, Astrid Rudebeck, the Mistress of the Queen's Robes, said that, 'in the latter days of her life, the Queen was very tired. As usual, though, she did not think of herself, but of him whose welfare for more than forty years had always come before anything else'. And once to Baron Carl-Fredrik Palmstierna, the Private Secretary to the King, Louise remarked, 'royalty should be either healthy or dead'.

Then, in the middle of December 1964, her condition suddently grew worse and at the time of the Nobel Prize celebrations in December (her last public appearance), the Queen suffered a severe heart attack and had to enter Sophia Hospital, the privately run hospital of which she herself was the Honorary President.

January went by and the Queen was still in hospital. On

February 6th she was still weak but had sufficiently recovered for King Gustaf Adolf to take her back to Drottningholm. The weeks that followed were quiet ones, a time which those at Drottningholm felt to be a period of grace. Queen Louise was not, however, the only person afflicted with severe illness in the household, as Prince William (the King's brother), who died the following June, was recovering from pneumonia. Also staying with the royal family was Princess Alice of Greece, who had previously promised to spend her eightieth birthday with her sister and brother-in-law in Stockholm.

Although outwardly life at Drottningholm seemed quite normal, both the royal family and the staff were aware of the shadow of death. Everyone noticed how day by day the Queen was losing weight and strength, and Astrid Rudebeck told me: 'It was pathetic to see how the Queen struggled to force herself to eat. I had the impression that she would have preferred to have given up out of sheer exhaustion, but for the King's sake she mustered all her strength to live'.

The night of March 3rd saw the end of the period of grace. In severe pain the Queen was taken by ambulance to St Goran's Hospital and the King, accompanied by his aide, Baron Sigvard Beck-Friis, stayed at the hospital the whole of the next day. The doctors quickly diagnosed that the Queen had a blood clot in the lower part of the main artery leading to her heart. An operation was necessary immediately, and so one of the most eminent heart specialists in the country, Professor Clarence Crafoord, and his team were called in; but, although the Queen was in the operating theatre for six hours and survived the operation successfully, she lived on only three days.

There are two remarks of the Queen's last days which should be remembered, as they reveal a great deal about her character. Louise was familiar with death and suffering from those years during the First World War when she served as a nurse behind the French lines and, as she was taken out of the ambulance at St Göran's, she said to the doctors: 'Do what you like to me. I put my trust entirely in science'. Then, after she had been carried into the hospital, she said: 'I was in such pain, but first and foremost I had to think about consoling Gustaf'. Indeed, so long as she was conscious, her husband was uppermost in her thoughts. Unfortunately, King Gustaf Adolf himself had been put to bed with a high temperature so was not allowed to share the full vigil by his wife's bedside, and the last words Louise was heard to utter were: 'Give my love to the King'.

The Queen died on Sunday, March 7th. On the following Saturday, March 13th, the funeral took place in Stockholm's most ancient and perhaps most beautiful church, the Great Church situated in the Old City, on an island in the North Channel. It was a full state funeral, a scene of white and grey. On the mirror of the Channel, hundreds of swans swam slowly in grave hierarchy. Heavy snow clouds lingered over the grey March waters and above the grey palace walls, while troops from the Svea Life Guards and the King's own Grenadiers paraded along Slottsbacken and the Grenadiers, with the Swedish banner guarded the entrance of the Church. Outside, the stone-paved streets were strewn with scattered pine twigs.

Inside the Church, guests from many countries had taken their places in the chancel. Members of all the royal houses of Europe were present, also representatives of the Queen's family, of President de Gaulle, Lyndon Johnson, and other heads of state. Solemnly four kings—King Gustaf Adolf, the Kings of Denmark and Norway, and King Constantine of Greece—sat near the head of the catafalque in the chancel of the Great Church. On top of the coffin, which was draped with the Swedish flag and the Union Jack, lay Queen Louisa Ulrika's burial crown and, beside it, her coronation crown, that was made for her by the master craftsman, Jean Eric Rehn.

Undoubtedly the stern, matter of fact beauty of the ceremony was exactly as the Queen would have desired. For, unsentimental as she was, Louise had drawn up the programme for her own funeral. She asked that no personal words should be uttered and chose readings from the Bible, mostly concerned with thanks-giving, as well as the *Andante* from Sibelius's *Symphony No. 2* and 'O God, our help in ages past', her favourite hymn.

From the organ loft, the last chords of the *St John Passion* changed to Bach's *Fantasy and Fugue in C Minor*, then eight sailors lifted the coffin from the catafalque, from where it was taken amid the splendour of wreaths to the royal tomb at Haga. Wreath after wreath was borne by the chamberlains. First those of relatives and sovereigns, and among them a large wreath carried between two sailors and made of irises and red amaryllis The ribbons were in the English colours, and on one of them stood the single word 'Dickie', while on the other there was written in gold lettering, 'In ever loving memory of my darling sister Louise'.

After Queen Louise's death Countess Estelle Bernadotte said that, 'perhaps her work can only be fully appreciated by those who have seen her and the King together in their everyday life. . . . Swedish women allied themselves to Queen Louise and I think I can tell you why. Instinctively, they realized that she was absorbed in the care of her husband, and that was something they understood and approved of'. Finally, it may be thought fitting that the last tribute to Queen Louise should come from her husband. Mindful of what she stood for to others as well as to himself, on the evening of the funeral in conversation with the Margravine of Baden, King Gustaf Adolf said: 'Remember that she would have wished us to carry on as usual. Perhaps a little better *because of her*'.

The demonstration of public affection for Queen Louise at the funeral was quite overwhelming. Some of the oldest citizens of Stockholm said they could not remember any scenes as moving as these. People stood in their tens of thousands in the snow, many of them weeping, a fitting tribute to a life devoted to the King and country of her adoption.

Later, a memorial service was held in Westminster Abbey. The Swedish Flag was borne by a detachment of officers and men from the Royal Swedish Navy; at the end of the deeply moving service, the pipe major of the Cameronians, of which King Gustaf Adolf is Colonel-in-Chief, played a lament; and the great nave and transepts of Westminster Abbey were thronged with the many relations, friends and admirers who had come to pay tribute to Queen Louise.

# Letters from the Russian Imperial Family

URING her childhood Louise was always very close to the Russian imperial family. Family visits were frequently exchanged and Louise herself kept up a running correspondence with her Russian cousins. Altogether the Tsarina Alix had five children—the Grand Duchesses Olga, Tatiana, Maria, Anastasia and the Grand Duke Tsarevitch Alexei, the heir to the Russian throne. The letters from Olga and Tatiana to Louise are so charming that a selection of them are given here as a kind of postscript to the book. Olga (who the Margravine of Baden describes as 'always a little delicate') and Tatiana (who she says was 'the loveliest and most lively of the Tsar's children') were born in 1895 and 1897, and so would have only been fifteen and thirteen years old respectively when they wrote the first of the letters reproduced in this chapter. The earlier letters are full of visits to the theatre, chicken-pox and tobogganing. The spelling and English are at times rather quaint—for, as Olga wrote to Louise in one of her letters, 'my english writing and spelling is not splendid'. By the time of the last letter, a joint one written in 1914, they have obviously become quite grown up. In it Tatiana mentions the death of Prince Maurice of Battenberg, and also that she is acting as head of a committee for refugees. This letter seems particularly sad, as Louise cannot have received many more letters from Olga and Tatiana before their father's abdication on March 17, 1917, which was, of course, followed by the murder of the entire family on July 16th of the following year.

Tsarkoe Selo. 1910
17/30[1] Jan. Monday.

'*My darling Louise,*
'I thank you many times for the letter. I was very pleased to get it. Tell your Mama and Papa that my Papa for my namesday gave me the regiment which before commanded your Grandfather Uncle Alexander,[2] the 8 Lancer Wosnecenski. I do not know how to write the name as it is difficult from the Russian. I am so delighted I have got my own regiment. Olga also got when she was as old as I the hussar regiment, so now we both have one.

'How are you, dear? You said that you hoped that none of us would get chicken pox, but of course *I* got it from Anastasia which is a great bore.

'From the 2nd Jan. Alexei and I went to bed and lay till the 12th. I got up just for my namesday. Then in between Anastasia lay and also had influenza but the whole time we were all together. Baby is lying till now. Marie is also in bed, only Olga, Mama and Papa were not lying till now.

'On the 6th Jan. just before our lessons began Olga went to Petersburg in the evening to the theatre, and came back very late and had to lie in the stupid bed. Better in any case do not show to anyone this letter, *perhaps* it is dangerous as I have got still chicken pox. Mama is now a little better but it makes her tired running every day three times a day upstairs to us whilst we were all in bed. How is your Mama, Papa and all?

'Tell Nona I am awfully sorry I did not thank her for the letter which she sent me with the socks but each time I began I tore it up as I did not like it. I want to see you awfully, Louise darling.

---

[1] Where two dates are given for the letters contained in this chapter, the first date is according to the old Julian Calendar and the second according to the Gregorian Calendar introduced by Pope Gregory in 1582 and adopted by Italy, France, Spain, and Portugal in that year. Great Britain and her Dominions changed to it in 1752, but Russia did not change until May 1923.
[2] Prince Alexander of Hesse, father of Prince Louis of Battenberg.

'Now good bye, my dearest Louisechen. Much love and kisses to you all from your ever loving cousin,

*Tatiana.*

P.S. Love to Clayden.'[1]

Tsarkoe Selo
5/18 November 1910

*'My darling Louise,*

'I kiss and thank you thousand times for the nice long letter.

'We were in the theater "Bonifacius", it was delightfully pretty. Even Mama, Anastasia[2] and Marie[2] were there. Papa, Uncle Ernie,[3] Marie and I sat in your box.[4] It was so lovely, pretty. Mama, Aunt Irène,[5] Olga and Anastasia sat in the big box, and in the little one next to them, Aunt Onor[6] and Uncle Harry. Sunday after church we went to the theater and in the saloon next to your box they showed us the cinimatograph only not like always but like in the theater on the screen and they dance. It is most amusing but difficult to write how it was. After that we four went to the middle box in which the ladies sit and looked how they were praktising a piece. It was such fun to look on.

'It is such a pity you had to go so early away. How is Nona,[7] your Mama, Georgie, Dickie[8] and your Papa?

'The first day we could go in the sledges but on the second day (yesterday) we had to go in the carriages, it was too dirty and little snow.

'I must go soon to luncheon. Alexei lunches also with us, with Papa and Mama. In Friedberg and Wolfsgarten he did not

---

[1] Princess Louise's maid.        [2] Tatiana's sisters.

[3] The Grand Duke Ernest Louis of Hesse and the Rhine.

[4] Queen Louise has added in her own handwriting that this letter describes what they did in Darmstadt, and the box referred to is her Grandfather Alexander's box in the Grand Duke's Theatre in Darmstadt.

[5] Tatiana's mother's sister, Princess Irène, who was the wife of Prince Henry of Prussia.        [6] The Grand Duchess Eleonore.

[7] Nona Kerr, grand-daughter of the Marquess of Lothian, Lady-in-Waiting to Princess Louis of Battenberg.

[8] Louise's brothers, Prince George and young Prince Louis of Battenberg, later the second Marquess of Milford Haven and the Earl Mountbatten of Burma respectively.

because Mama wanted him to speak with the little ones English. The masseuse came with us to Russia and she continues with Mama and us both.

'It would be such fun it you would be here we would be always together. We play Ilaffneau's stories nearly every day, and in the Russian train we have a piano and there we played also, we would not stop.

'We four girls were at the bazar in Offenbach. Olga, Marie, Anastasia went after luncheon to Offenbach. Uncle and Aunty went at eleven. Auntie Irène went at five. At 8 Auntie Irène, Uncle and Aunt[1] and I had to come back to dinner. I telephoned to ask if I may stay longer but the answer never came, then we sat in the motor and just wanted to go home when I see the Hofmarschal[2] running. He came and said that I may stay. I was delighted, flew out and ran upstairs where everybody was walking and looking at us. After I went myself to buy things. We came home at half past eleven in the night. I got up for breakfast and had no headache.

'No good bye, dearest Louise. Love to everybody. Many kisses from your loving devoted cousin,

*Tatiana.*'


Tsarkoe Selo
2/12 December 1910

'*My dear Louise,*

'Did you get my last letter? I am quite lazy to write letters as I have not much time. We are working on Christmas presents and they must soon be ready for Germany. Shall I send you a box with our bonbons?[3]

'The weather is disgusting. It thaws and is very foggy and very wet.

---

[1] Uncle and Aunt refer to the hosts on this visit, Uncle Ernie and Aunt Onor.
[2] The Lord Chamberlain at the Hessian court.
[3] A special sweet made by the Tsar's chef and liked by everybody.

'We are doing nothing particular to interest you. I generally get up early to prepare my lessons for the next day. To-day I did it too.

'We have got a beautiful hill in the garden on which we fly down in little sledges which is awful fun. Sophie Ivanovina[1] is very afraid when we go down in them.

'Forgive me please for writing so badly. I hurry very much but want to write more and can not as I have not a moment free. Please give my love to your Mama, Dickie and Nona. Where is Georgie? and where will he be for Xmas, and your Papa? I should say with you.

'I must stop, sending you tender kisses, dear Louise, I remain your very loving cousin

*Olga*'

Tsarkoe Selo  1911
February 8th
Tuesday

'*Darling Louise,*

'At last I am allowed to write. The chicken pox was too horrid. Three days I lay in bed as I had fever. Yesterday we all went out for the first time. The weather is divine, sunny but cold. The whole January was very cold.

'How is Dickie? Poor boy, Mama said he was so ill.[2]

'We all had chicken pox except Marie[3] who had only influenza. Now the poor little girl, Xenia, of Auntie Minnie's,[4] is so very ill. She had the chicken pox too and now has got peretonis; don't know how to spell this word, and something with the heart. She is very bad poor child, and the doctors have little hope as also she is very delicate and nervous.[5]

---

[1] Probably their maid.
[2] Dickie's illness was inflammation of the lungs, which he contracted whilst at his preparatory school, Locker's Park.
[3] Marie is Olga's younger sister.
[4] Minnie is Princess Marie of Greece, sister of Prince Andrew of Greece who married Queen Louise's sister, Alice.          [5] Xenia did, in fact, recover.

'Mama has gone for the first time to town to Amama[1] and specially she goes to see poor Auntie Minnie who is in an awful state.

'Everybody is ill this winter and there is a lot of chicken pox in town.

'Papa goes often to town to the theatre, to the opera and French theatre.

'Did you get my last letter in the beginning of January? I think after the sixth when I was in the Opera.

'Now good-bye, dear Louise. Many kisses to you all, from your very loving cousin,

*Olga.'*

Standart
12 o'clock in the night
16 July 1911

'*My dearest Louise,*

'So many thanks for dear letter. How sad to leave soon our beloved *Standart*[2] but we will see her soon if all is right in the Crimea which we are looking forward to since I don't know how long.

'My english spelling and writing is not splendid but as it is very late and I am terribly sleepy I can't help it.

'Thousands of fishes are near the yacht. The weather is divine at last, so warm and nice and sunny.

'I got two little letters from Margarita and Dolla who are very pleased with their new little baby sister.[3]

'How nice if Arthur[4] will come to us. When are you going to Jugenheim[5] and Wolfsgarten this year?

'My little cabin is so sweet. Tatiana's one is next door though between our cabins is the bathroom and w.c.

---

[1] Their grandmother, the Dowager Tsarina Marie, widow of Tsar Alexander III.

[2] The name of the Russian Imperial Yacht.

[3] Princess Cécile who married the Hereditary Grand Duke of Hesse and the Rhine, who were both killed in an air crash, with their family, in 1937.

[4] Prince Arthur of Connaught, who was twenty-eight at this time.

[5] The name of the nearest village to the Schloss Heiligenberg.

'I must stop now. Give my love to your parents. Georgie and Dickie and Nona, and with a big hug and kiss to yourself, dear Louise,

'I am your own very sleepy cousin

*Olga*'

Tsarkoe Selo

22 October/4 November 1914

'*Darling Louise,*

'How are you? The whole morning we are occupied in the hospital. I like it very much and when we are free we knit stockings for our wounded who leave for the war again.

'It was so awfully sad to hear of poor Maurice's[1] death. Did he die there or one brought him to England? How is poor Aunt Beatrice?[2] I am at the head of a committee for the refugees and have presided two sittings. I felt very grand but wanted to dive under the table from fright as I have got a very stiff and pompous gentleman who is under me (I hope you understand what she means) and makes me very shy always. Do write to me dear if you can once. I would like to know so much what you do. I have a stomachache . . .

'. . . and could not finish her letter. We just got good news from our army. Where is Minny[3] living and what is she doing? I hope Dickie is all right at Osborne.[4] Many kisses, Louise dear,

*Your loving*

*Olga and Tatiana*'[5]

[1] Prince Maurice of Battenberg, who was killed in the 60th King's Royal Rifle Corps, fighting a gallant rearguard action at Ypres during the retreat from Mons on October 28, 1914.

[2] Prince Maurice's mother, Princess Beatrice of Great Britain and Ireland, the youngest daughter of Queen Victoria; she married Prince Henry (Liko) of Battenberg.

[3] Miss Cochrane, one of Princess Beatrice's ladies-in-waiting.

[4] In 1914 Dickie was a Naval Cadet at the Royal Naval College, Osborne.

[5] This letter was written jointly by the two Grand Duchesses. Olga started and ended it, and the middle part was written by Tatiana except for the remark in parenthesis, which was written by Olga.

# Index